Growing Child®

D1712475

Contributors:

Phil Bach, O.D., Ph.D.

Miriam Bender, Ph.D.

Joseph Braga, Ed.D.

Laurie Braga, Ph.D.

George Early, Ph.D.

Liam Grimley, Ph.D.

Robert Hannemann, M.D., F.A.A.P.

Sylvia Kottler, M.S.

Bill Peterson, Ph.D.

© 2005 Growing Child, Inc.
P.O. Box 620
Lafayette, IN 47902
ISBN: 0-9729649-1- 6
800-927-7289
www.growingchild.com

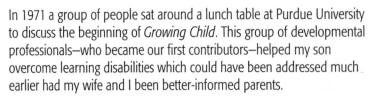

Preface

In 1971 a group of people sat around a lunch table at Purdue University to discuss the beginning of *Growing Child*. This group of developmental professionals—who became our first contributors—helped my son overcome learning disabilities which could have been addressed much earlier had my wife and I been better-informed parents.

The purpose of *Growing Child* was then and still is to provide parents with a child development newsletter that is timed to the age of their child. We wanted to help parents provide the right kind of stimulation at the right time in the child's development; to alert parents to the typical pattern of development; and to encourage parents to consult with their physician when they had questions about their child's development.

As parents, we hope that each of our children will grow up to be a good citizen, a loving spouse, a cherished friend, a friendly neighbor. Most importantly, when the time comes, we hope our children will be ready for school. But parents don't always know what they can do to help achieve these goals, and many times, no one tells them.

Having a child is one of life's most special events, and this occurs with greater ease, comfort and joy when parents assume their roles with knowledge. No one is at their best when they are living in a state of fear or uncertainty, when they are apprehensive about the well being of their child. When parents know what to expect and have reasonable expectations about their child's development, they can enjoy being a parent.

The chapters of this book are the same as the monthly newsletter issues that our subscribers receive. The best way to use this book is to mark your calendar to read the issue that is appropriate for your child's age each month.

Not every child will follow the same development exactly, but they will be close. While it will be tempting to read ahead and to try and accelerate a child's rate of development, this is not always in the best interests of the child and can lead to frustration for both child and parent.

As grandparents, one of our bits of advice to parents is to enjoy being a parent. Don't be in a hurry to make your children into adults and rob them of the joy of mud and dandelions. The time to put away teddy bears and dolls will come all too soon.

There are many ways to raise a child but the key ingredient is your unconditional love. Children need to feel that they are safe and loved. Hannah Kahn said, "Child, give me your hand that I may walk in the light of your faith in me."

We hope you will learn from *Growing Child* articles the importance of unstoppable curiosity, enthusiasm for learning, and realistic goals for your child. Enjoy the light.

Dennis Dunn, Publisher
Nancy Kleckner, Editor

To receive your free bonus from Growing Child, complete this form on line at www.GrowingChild.com/bonus or fill out the information below, and mail to, PO Box 620, Lafayette, IN 47902

Free Bonus For Duration Of This Book

- A free e-mail subscription to Growing Child for each child in the family under 6 years of age

- Growing Parent, a monthly e-mail newsletter to help parents better understand themselves and cope with the reality of living, sent via e-mail at the beginning of each month.

- A monthly activity calendar to enjoy with there children.

- "Grandma Says," a series of special messages via e-mail that include parenting tips, words of encouragement or helpful comments, plus recall notices and health alert messages.

Guarantee

- Book and e-mails are free of commercial bias with our no-advertisement policy.

- E-mail and surface mail addresses are used only to administer subscription accounts and are not disclosed to other individual or organizations.

E-mail address _____

Second e-mail if parents are not living in same household _____

Parent name _____

Mailing address _____

City _____ State _____ Zip _____

Telephone number _____

Birth date of each child under 6 years of age: _____

_____

_____

Hospital that gave you a Growing Child book as a gift _____

This bonus may be transferred to a friend or relative if you do not have access to e-mail.

service@growingchild.com
800-927-7289
PO Box 620
Lafayette IN 47902-0620

Growing Child®

The Challenges of a 2-Year-Old

You may have heard some people refer to this period in a child's life as the "terrible twos." Actually, with a little understanding of the important development taking place, you may come to view the "terrible twos" as the "terrific twos!"

Right now, Toddler is striving for a sense of autonomy, a feeling of being his own person. He is fascinated with expressions of his own will (for example, his frequent use of the word "No!").

He is also striving to be less dependent on his caregivers.

Here are some ways to encourage independence and at the same time avoid negative parent-child interactions:

(1) The 2-year-old constantly wants to help you, a sure signal of extra mess and more clean-up. We urge you to accept his offer and exploit it. Assign him simple tasks that he can do with you. If he wants to dust, for example, give him his own dusting mitt.

This practice is training for the future when he will enjoy bigger responsibilities such as setting the table and putting objects away.

Many parents of older children wonder why their children don't pick up after themselves. The lack of early experience in helping around the home is probably part

Special Note: *Now that your child is 2 years old, the sections titled "Youngster Likes To" and "Give Your Youngster" are being omitted. At this age the comments in the body of each monthly issue more appropriately describe your child's development.*∎

of the answer.

As you and your child work together, talk about what you are doing. Even in an ordinary household situation you can casually teach valuable concepts, new vocabulary and good grammar.

Consider the task of "picking up and putting away." Don't wait until late afternoon or evening when Youngster is tired and fretful. You'll both enjoy more success if you shelve toys immediately after he's through playing with them.

At this age he needs specific instructions rather than general statements. He most likely will be unable to respond to the broad command "put all your toys away." But he will happily participate in a playful duet: "First we'll pick up the big cars. Let's put them down here. Now we'll find the little cars. We'll reach up high to put them on this shelf." As you complete these simple tasks together, a lot of learning is taking place about the concept of space: spatial organization, position of himself and objects in space, and their relationship to each other.

• He is stretching both his mind and his body. He must squat and stretch in order to pick up and deposit the cars. Meanwhile you are interpreting his movements to him and he is matching words to actions: for example, "up" and "down"—very important direction words.

• He is developing his understanding of relative size, "big" and "little," for example.

• He is listening to your use

of language from which he will increase his word supply and later construct his own sentences.

(2) Two-year-old dawdles, and when you press him to hurry, he resists more. How can such situations be handled? There are several approaches you can try:

(a) Make it a habit to talk about the next thing that will happen: "Pretty soon we'll be going to Granny's. We'll leave in five minutes."

(b) Allow him some time to say goodbye to whomever is present or to whatever he is doing.

(c) Offer him a choice. "Do you want to walk or do you want me to carry you?" Abide by his decision once you have offered him a choice you can live with.

(d) If all else fails, entice him away. "I'm going to show you some magic when we get to the kitchen." Then reward him with the demonstration of something simple.

In addition to avoiding a confrontation, some important learning is taking place. Each time you alert Youngster to anticipate an event, his ability to understand and organize the concept of time will increase. And the vocabulary associated with time (e.g. "pretty soon," "five minutes") will become understandable. Also, he will appreciate the fact that you respect him and honor his choice.

Finally, Youngster will get practice in making an important language transformation when he indicates his choice. He will transform the information you pose in a question, "Do you want to walk or be carried?" to the answer he gives, "me walk."∎

Young Stutterers

Stuttering—an involuntary repeating or prolonging of sounds, syllables, words, or phrases—is often first noticed when a child is between 2 and 5 years of age. The child at this age is developing many complex motor and linguistic skills at a rapid rate. He is learning, for example, to handle longer sequences of speech muscle movements, developing a larger vocabulary, and trying to put words together in longer sentences. So, it is not surprising that many children go through a "stuttering" stage.

For many years speech-language pathologists thought that stuttering was caused by paying too much attention to the child's speech and was made worse by attempts to correct it. Some speech-language pathologists still believe this to be the case. They recommend ignoring the stuttering and letting it run its course.

We now know, however, that there are a variety of causes for stuttering. Many contemporary experts have demonstrated excellent results through early intervention and treatment approaches that provide direct feedback to the child to encourage easy speech.

Parents are often alarmed by their child's stuttering. The best way to reduce concerns about stuttering is to learn more about it and to know what things will help the child.

Here are some indicators suggesting a further consultation would be appropriate:

1. A history of stuttering in the family.

2. The child repeats or prolongs some sounds at the beginning or middle of words.

3. The child typically repeats the same sound three or more times.

4. The child prolongs a sound for more than 2 seconds.

5. The child makes faces or uses exaggerated movements of his head, arm, or body whenever repeating or holding speech sounds.

6. There is too much vocal or throat tension each time the child repeats or holds onto a sound.

7. The child demonstrates frustration in trying to communicate.

If some of these characteristics are present, it is a good idea to consult with your child's physician. After examining your child, he or she may decide to refer you to a speech-language specialist. This individual can provide additional information and, if needed, develop a program for prevention or treatment of stuttering.

Some things a parent can do to help a child develop more natural speech are listed below. Remember, it is always easier and wiser to do something ahead of time than try to stop something later. These recommendations will reduce the possibility that stuttering will occur.

1. Make family life less hectic by scheduling events carefully and allowing more time to prepare for them. (*All* children tend to repeat words more frequently when they are excited or hurried.)

2. Plan more communication time that includes individual, undivided attention with the child. Help the child feel good about sharing ideas with others. Talking and listening should be fun.

3. Model good speech by using slower, smoother speech with the child and encourage such use by the child. Talk in terms of "easy" speech.

4. Encourage members of the family to allow time for the child to talk and to complete all sentences without interruption.

5. Help the child with vocabulary and use of language, and provide opportunities to reinforce success.

6. Consult the child's physician if there are any questions about the child's speech.■

Hearing Impairment

The child who is hearing-impaired has trouble understanding the meaning of the sounds she does hear, no matter how alert or intelligent she may be. She also has trouble learning to talk.

In order to detect hearing loss early, three-fourths of the States require hearing tests on all infants born in hospitals. These tests are helpful but are not a substitute for regular hearing evaluations done by a physician.

The prevalence of defective hearing in school age children is estimated to be 5 percent. But this figure usually represents only those children who are placed in programs for the hard of hearing. It does not represent children with mild hearing loss which frequently goes undetected.

Absence of speech, delayed speech development, and speech that is impossible to understand are all symptoms of a possible hearing impairment.

Parents are a most important source of information in helping a physician or other professional detect any hearing problem. The physician will observe Youngster in order to answer questions such as: "How well and what does she learn?" "What sounds are absent from her speech?" "How many words or phrases does she have?"

Your physician will want to check Youngster for possible infection which may contribute to the problem. He may also suggest that you see another professional, an audiologist. Early detection and remedial treatment are very important.■

'She Bit Me First!'

As a parent, it may be embarrassing to be told that your child is guilty of biting another child. A parent's first reaction is sometimes disbelief, "No, my sweet child wouldn't do such a thing!"

This can be followed by shock and horror, "What kind of savage has my child become, biting another human being?"

The reaction of the parent whose child has been bitten is usually no less dramatic, "I can still see the marks of that monster's teeth."

If you question your own child about the matter, you may be told, "She bit me first."

It's generally not helpful to take sides or try to determine who really "started it" or who first said what to whom. It's better to make it perfectly clear—in a no-nonsense tone of voice—that biting another child is never acceptable under any circumstances.

Contrary to what some people may think, occasional biting by a 2-year-old child who is angry or frustrated, is not a sign of deep emotional disturbance. It is behavior, however, that must be changed. Every child who bites another must learn that the biting has got to stop.

Biting behavior usually peaks between 2 and 3 years of age and then starts to decline as verbal abilities improve.

In their efforts to stop this behavior, some parents have tried washing out their child's mouth with soap and water. Others have tried biting the child back "to let her know what it feels like." We definitely do not recommend such drastic and undesirable measures. Besides, they have been found to be ineffective ways of dealing with the problem.

To stop biting behavior, it's not enough to treat the symptoms without dealing with the underlying causes. At 2 years of age, a child does not yet know how to control her feelings when she gets over-excited, angry, or frustrated. So, she may hit, kick, or bite the child who upsets her.

In reality, biting is usually no more aggressive or harmful than hitting or kicking. But biting is often perceived as much more malicious. It usually evokes a greater howl from the victim—and from the victim's parent. That's because (a) biting appears so animalistic and uncivilized, and (b) the bite not only hurts but usually leaves a visible mark.

All normal children experience feelings of anger, frustration, and aggression at some time. They must learn to control these impulses in order to avoid aggressive behavior. Although boys are generally more aggressive than girls, girls are just as likely to bite as boys.

How then do you stop your child from biting? Here are some recommendations:

1. **Provide closer supervision.** The child who bites other children needs more structure and supervision. The person who supervises (usually the parent or teacher) must watch for signs of anger, frustration, or tiredness which often precede biting behavior.

2. **Intervene early.** Many children's problems can be better controlled or prevented by early intervention. For example, if you see the child who bites being teased or provoked, don't wait for trouble to occur. Separate the children from one another as soon as possible.

3. **Reprimand calmly but firmly.** Whenever one child bites another, it is important to reprimand as calmly and firmly as possible: "You must never bite another child."

Then quietly take the child to a room by herself. Give her time alone to settle down and get herself under control. If she continues to yell or scream, it is best to ignore these behaviors as much as possible, unless, of course, you think she will do some damage. Left alone in a room, a 2-year-old will usually calm down in about ten to fifteen minutes.

4. **Teach her alternative behaviors.** In dealing with her feelings of anger or frustration, she must ultimately learn to express her feelings verbally rather than physically. That is a skill that will need much practice. It is also one which will usually improve as children get older and can better express themselves verbally.

In general, thoughtful management of the problem, rather than severe punishment, will improve the likelihood of changing the child's biting behavior.

In summary, among normal 2-year-olds, most cases of biting are due to the child's lack of self-control. The child who bites can usually be helped by closer supervision, early intervention, calm but firm reprimands, and by learning alternative ways to deal with feelings of anger and frustration.

What should a parent do if these techniques don't work and the biting becomes more frequent? This may indicate the child has a more severe problem. If the biting behaviors continue for more than a few weeks, it would be wise to consult a pediatrician or child psychologist.∎

Poisoning Prevention

Sad to relate, most poisonings in young children are caused by substances commonly found in the home, such as medicines and household products.

Accidents in the home are most likely to occur when a parent is preoccupied in some activity, such as preparing dinner or talking on the telephone.

Young children are, by nature, curious about the world around them. They are fascinated by little bottles with colored pills and by containers and sprays of all kinds.

They also like to imitate whatever they have seen an adult do. Parents of a young child, therefore, need to be aware of the possible dangers of poisoning in the home and how they can prevent such accidents from happening.

Here are some recommendations to prevent possible poisonings:

1. **Keep all medicines and household products in a cabinet that is locked or out of reach of children.** Don't underestimate a young child's curiosity and ingenuity in reaching a desired object.

2. **Don't leave a young child alone for a moment—even to answer the telephone—if there is any poisonous substance within reach.** Young children can act fast, and most poisons, unfortunately, also act equally fast.

3. **Avoid taking medicine while a young child is watching.** Children are great imitators but are usually unaware of possible dangers of poisoning.

4. **Buy medications and other potential poisons in containers which have child-proof caps.** The U.S. Consumer Product Safety Commission estimates that hundreds of children's lives have been saved by the use of child-proof caps.

5. **Keep all products in their original containers with their original labels.** Accidental poisonings have occurred when someone was not aware what product was in a container.

6. **Check the label every time that medication is taken to be sure you are using the correct medicine and the correct dosage.** A mistake can easily be made because medicine containers often look alike.

7. **Medication should never be taken in the dark.** Always be sure to turn on a light when giving or taking medicine.

8. **Read the label on all household products to become aware of any potential dangers**. Be aware also of what steps need to be taken if a particular harmful substance is swallowed or inhaled.

9. **Prescription medication should be taken only by the person for whom it was prescribed.** The doctor knows an individual patient's medical history and uses this information in writing a prescription. It is highly dangerous for parents to give a child—even in a small dosage—medication that was originally prescribed for someone else.

10. **Periodically clean out the cabinets of all old medications and old household products no longer in use.** After the products have been disposed of, the containers should be cleaned out and then

Accidents in the home are most likely to occur when a parent is preoccupied in some activity, such as preparing dinner or talking on the telephone.

discarded or recycled in a safe manner.

11. **Be truthful with a child when talking about medication.** Tell the child the name of the medicine being used and for what purpose it is being taken. Don't ever refer to medicine as "candy." This would give the child the wrong impression that medicine, like candy, is safe for children to eat at any time.

12. **Talk to your child, in a calm manner, about the danger of poisoning.** Include possible harmful effects of improper use of medication or household products. They should eat and drink only those substances they are absolutely certain are safe. When in doubt, they should always check with an adult.

What to do if your child takes poison:

If your child swallows or inhales a substance which you believe is poisonous, call your local Poison Control Center immediately. There are more than 100 such centers nationwide.

It is wise to keep the number of your local Poison Control Center near every telephone in your home. In case you cannot find the number of your local poison center, contact your doctor or the nearest hospital or call your local emergency number (usually 911). Prompt action is important. Most children who receive immediate treatment are not permanently harmed.

Parent awareness of the dangers of poisoning is the most effective way to prevent such accidents from happening.∎

A Reasoning Game

We have at times in the past suggested activities that we called sleight of hand or magic. The unseen hand does something to an object while Youngster is asked to figure out what happened. Such games show us the level of her reasoning ability. She must be able to reason, for example, about cause and effect in order to explain a particular result that she observes.

There are many activities that a parent and child can do together that will help to prepare her for later problem-solving. A child of this age will generally be too young to solve these problems by herself. But she will enjoy the parent-child interaction in working together on these projects that will stretch Youngster's thinking about the world around her.

Here is a trick that will challenge her present reasoning ability. Show Youngster a penny and a small ball of play dough. Then place both objects in a paper sack. While they are hidden, press the penny inside the ball. After smoothing over all signs of the penny's entrance, uncover the ball. See if Youngster can figure out what happened to the penny. Will she first look for it in the paper sack?

It is not likely that Youngster will solve the mystery without help. Her sense of how the clay can be molded to engulf another object is hazy, even if she has had some experience in squeezing and reforming play dough.

In providing her with hints, there are a number of ways to proceed. One way is to repeat the problem using a container for the penny, such as a small box. Show Youngster how the box can be opened to reveal something inside. Once the idea of containment is planted in her mind, Youngster has a better chance of solving the clay problem, if it is repeated soon

thereafter.

Another possibility is to manipulate the clay in ways that may provide hints. Twisting the ball apart into two halves may show her that something might have been hidden inside.

Another approach is to select some other small object. Let her see you press it into the ball of play dough. After such a demonstration she will readily dig into the ball for the second object. With this concept of the ball containing something, she should then go looking for the penny as well.

Now test her understanding further. Do the trick with a playing card that is slipped inside the cover of a book. As Youngster's understanding of the principle deepens with additional examples, she will be able to apply the solution to new situations that are different from the original one.

She may even be able to see through a deliberate distortion of reality, as with a false-bottomed container. You can create such a container by taping a false paper bottom about two-thirds of the way down inside a paper cup. Leave enough untaped area that you can slip a small object, like a short length of yarn, under the false bottom.

At first glance, of course, the cup will appear empty to Youngster. But by now her well established idea of containment should cause her to look more closely at the cup. If the false bottom is sufficiently high, she may realize that the inside depth of the cup is less than the outside height, and poke the bottom with her finger to discover the secret. However she discovers the yarn, she won't feel unfairly tricked by the false bottom. She will just accept it as something to be remembered in a world that is always producing something new and unexpected.

Whether Youngster correctly "solves" all these problems is relatively unimportant at this age.

What is important is that she is being introduced to new concepts and new problem-solving techniques that challenge her thinking skills. Besides, Youngster will enjoy the special attention involved in helping Mom or Dad to "solve" a particular problem, even though her role at this age may be primarily one of observational learner.■

What Will the Water Do?

Unstructured materials like sand and water are useful in building up Youngster's experience with shapeless quantities, the kinds he must later learn to judge, measure, and understand. If Youngster has had several months of playing and experimenting freely with sand and water, he is now ready for you to test his understanding in a few simple ways.

The following activities will require him to use his experience to predict effects. They should also give him a chance to see some new relationships.

Select three drinking glasses that have approximately the same diameter but different heights so that they hold different quantities of water. Line them up before Youngster. Fill the middle size glass with water. Then, pointing to the larger empty glass, ask him, "Will this glass hold all the water that is in this full one?" Whether he says "yes" or "no,' say, "Let's find out," then pour the water into the larger glass. "Yes, the big glass held all the water."

CONTINUED ON PAGE 156

CONTINUED FROM PAGE 155

Pour the water back into the middle glass. Repeat the question, this time with the small empty glass. Then make the test. "No, the little one couldn't hold all the water; some of it spilled out." Needless to say this would best be done with a catch basin underneath. This comparison of heights is fairly simple, and Youngster will quickly learn to make the correct judgment.

Next you can repeat the problem with containers that are the same height but of different widths. A good trio would be a 4-inch-high pan, a two-cup glass measuring container, and a small soup can. Again, Youngster will quickly be able to judge the containers by their widths and make the right decisions after a few tries.

Now combine the two sets of containers and add others to provide a variety of capacities. Fill one container and point to another, asking him whether it will hold the water of the first. Here the problem becomes much more difficult, for Youngster must take into account the height and width of a container at the same time. In fact, for all but the most obvious differences in capacity, Youngster will make the correct judgment only about half the time, which is the same likelihood as getting it correct purely by chance. But the game will give him practice in judging the capacity of one container in comparison with another.

The knowledge, built up in free play, that water can be held in a container and poured will now allow him to use water in comparing the sizes of different containers. The water is a way of measuring. It matters not to him that the yardstick may seem to change its size.

In this, as with other activities, the motivating gamelike quality will be enhanced if you take turns. If he answers a question right, he gets to pick a container to fill and then choose another for you to judge, and vice versa. This game can also be played between two children under your supervision.

A few more interesting questions can be posed for Youngster. Ask him whether the tea strainer or flour sifter in your hand will hold some water.

Fill an empty milk carton with water. If you punch a hole in the middle of it, will all the water run out? What if the hole is punched near the bottom?

Half fill a dish with sand and pour in a little water. "Where did the water go? Is it hiding in the sand? Let's tip the dish and see if the water comes out."

With a plastic glass full of water and a rock in your hand, ask, "What will happen to the water in this full glass if I drop in the rock?" Youngster can't express or understand the principles involved in these effects, but experiencing them is what counts. ∎

www.growingchild.com

Contributing Authors

Phil Bach, O.D., Ph.D.
Miriam Bender, Ph.D.
Joseph Braga, Ed.D.
Laurie Braga, Ph.D.
George Early, Ph.D.
Liam Grimley, Ph.D.
Robert Hannemann, M.D., F.A.A.P.
Sylvia Kottler, M.S.
Bill Peterson, Ph.D.

Growing Child, Inc.
P.O. Box 620
Lafayette, Indiana 47902
Telephone: 1-800-927-7289
©2005 Growing Child, Inc.

Next Month

- *Numbers and Sizes*
- *Learning to Wait*
- *Showing Respect for Feelings*

Growing Child®

Learning to Wait

The ability to delay satisfying a need, and the ability to be good-humored about the delay, are most attractive and endearing traits in a child or in an adult.

The person who doesn't get upset or angry when she can't have what she wants just when she wants it, is a pleasure to have around. Usually she is a happy person.

Further, she is probably an effective and productive person. The ability to tolerate reasonable delay is essential to being able to stick to a task, solve a problem, or complete an assignment.

This quality of personality doesn't just suddenly happen when a person reaches adulthood. It develops slowly from early infancy. And, strange as it may seem, it appears to develop better in young children whose needs are adequately satisfied. That is, the baby who is *not* frustrated appears to be better able to tolerate and deal with frustration.

A study sponsored by the National Institutes of Mental Health indicates that there is a close relationship between the degree of pleasure a baby experiences during her feedings and the gradual development of her ability to delay having her needs met.

The study found that, as a baby learns to look forward to pleasurable relief from the tension caused by hunger, she gradually begins to tolerate necessary periods of waiting—provided, of course, that in the beginning the delay is brief and bearable.

At the end of their first year, children who had their physical and emotional needs adequately met showed increased ability to pay attention to tasks and to handle testing situations well.

Introduced to activities such as fitting pegs in holes or dropping blocks into a container, these children showed interest in the tasks and pleasure when they succeeded. Further, they were not usually frustrated by failure.

In contrast, children whose feeding experiences had been less pleasurable showed less interest, less patience, and less concentration. Many showed signs of anxiety about what was expected of them.

The study was careful to point out that it is the *repeated* good or unhappy experiences that matter—not the occasional interference such as normal illness, teething, fatigue, or family stress.

As a child moves from infancy into early childhood, her ability to tolerate frustrations will continue to develop as her changing needs continue to be met.

Wise parents learn to recognize early signs of frustration in their child. Thus they are able to relieve the child's tension before there is loss of control, disorganized behavior, or temper tantrums.

This avoidance of frustration does not imply over-permissiveness. Rather it results from setting and maintaining realistic limits on behavior. A child feels secure when she knows what her parents expect of her and what she can expect from them.

Further, recognizing the early signs of frustration includes being aware of the effects of over-fatigue or over-stimulation and protecting the child from these stresses when possible.

It includes providing a pleasurable distraction at such times, such as reading a favorite story. It also includes allowing the child freedom to make mistakes as she grows into independence.

The emotional security provided by consistent meeting of her physical and emotional needs frees the child from the anxiety of uncertainty. Thus freed, she can concentrate better on a task, wait her turn, and accept the inevitable disappointments of life with reasonably good humor.

Later in her life, the social, behavioral, and learning demands of school will include the ability to wait to have a need or wish satisfied. The gradual maturation of the child's ability to wait is therefore an important preparation for later life.■

A More Independent Youngster

round a child's second birthday one can observe a shift from dependent Toddler to more independent preschool Youngster.

Since this phase will continue over the next several months and years, it is worth discussing in more detail. Parents who have an understanding of the changes that are occurring in their child will be better prepared to handle the behavior that accompanies this developmental process.

It appears that a number of factors converge to produce this shift from passive dependence to active independence. Among the most important are: (1) increased movement skills, (2) improved language ability, and (3) newly emerging social skills.

Youngster's newly acquired movement skills enable her to explore new territories. Just being able to run more easily or to climb stairs one at a time allows her to experience the exhilaration of independent discovery.

At the same time her improved language ability provides her with new opportunities to express her own independent thoughts and engage in more social interaction.

As Youngster begins to play with her peers—at first alongside them in "parallel" play and later in face-to-face play—her newly emerging social skills also help her to make the transition from dependence to independence.

Often this striving for independence on Youngster's part can be very trying for parents. She may insist, for example, on doing things for herself—like dressing—even though Mom or Dad are quite sure they can do the same things for her more efficiently and more neatly!

It is also trying on parents when Youngster constantly seems to want to "test the limits." It is often at this stage that she may suddenly decide to give up her afternoon nap—just when parents most need a midday break!

It is obvious that some adjustments in family living need to be made to take into consideration these developmental changes in behavior.

These adjustments are initially often difficult for parents to make. But Youngster's newly acquired skills and, above all, her increased independence will eventually contribute to having a happier child in the home.

Ultimately her new behaviors will become a source of pride and joy for the parent who has learned to observe and handle this exciting developmental change.∎

Toy Safety

 2-year-old is an imitator and an experimenter. Not only does she imitate, she is continually experimenting with her toys—poking, pulling, prying, pinching. There appears to be no end to her curiosity.

This is a time for you to be particularly aware that some toys can be dangerous for your child.

Some stuffed animals, for example, have cute button eyes that pull off easily, exposing the sharp points which fasten them on. These points sometimes do not lock like staples but are just pushed in like a double- or triple-pointed thumbtack. Such toys should be inspected carefully to avoid those that are dangerous.

This type of stuffed animal is apt to be found in souvenir shops or carnivals. They are often attractive to children and may be bought casually or given as a spur-of-the-moment gift.

Your 2-year-old can be rough on toys. She experiments by dragging them, banging them, and even sitting on them. Avoid letting her play with anything that has sharp or rough edges which will cut or scratch.

Be sure to read age-related information on toy packages. Those with small parts should be labeled "Not Recommended For Children Under 3 Years."

Avoid toys or objects with small removable parts that can be swallowed or—perish the thought—pushed into an ear or even up a nose. No one knows why a child will push a small object up her nose—but we know that children do such things and the consequences may be serious. Other points to check for toy safety:

• If a toy is painted or has painted decorations, be sure that the paint is non-toxic. Imported toys may contain lead-based paint which can cause lead poisoning.

• Some plastic toys may be flammable if exposed to heat.

• Decorative beads, beans, or seeds may also be poisonous.

Although there are laws and regulations to protect young children from toys that may be dangerous, accidents that were avoidable are reported every year.

It is therefore wise for you to assume direct responsibility for checking the safety of any toy or other object with which your child may play.∎

Let's Read a Story

umerous research studies have indicated that children whose parents regularly read to them during the early childhood and school years will generally do better in school. That is why we continue to encourage parents to read aloud to their children. A child's parents are generally his first educators and his most important resource for developing a love of reading.

Let's consider some of the things your child can learn while you read a story aloud:

Vocabulary. As you read, your child is acquiring new words. Let him see the pictures in the book. Point to an object as you read its name. See if he can point to some objects which you name.

Information. Your child is also acquiring new knowledge and expanding the horizons of his mind. Reading helps to open a whole new world for him.

Comprehension. From books a child acquires new understanding of his world. He perceives new relationships between words and can relate new knowledge to what he already knows.

Listening and attention skills. Reading helps to sharpen your child's listening skills and improve his attention span.

Mental awareness. As a result of your reading to him, he will also likely become more aware of and take greater interest in his everyday surroundings.

Sequencing. From your reading he can learn about sequencing in time ("Once upon a time ... ") and in space ("In the first place sat ... ") which are important skills for school learning.

Emotions. As he identifies with the characters in the story, he can sometimes gain a better understanding of his own emotions.

Love of books. As you read to your child, you are imparting an important value in your life, namely, your own love of books.

Personal love. Above all, by setting aside uninterrupted quiet time for reading, you are letting your child know how important he is to you. You are thereby conveying your own personal love for him.■

Reading Together

ere are some suggestions that will help you and your child get the most enjoyment out of reading together:

1. Try to make reading time a fun experience, both for you and for your child. So choose a time for reading that is good for you and for your child. Don't try to "impose" reading time—as though it were a daily duty—if you and/or your child are feeling tired.

2. Give Youngster your undivided attention while reading to him. If you have an answering machine for your telephone, use it. Also, turn off the radio, stereo, and television.

3. Become aware of the kinds of books your child enjoys the most. A trip to the public library will enable him to know more about the different kinds of books available.

4. Encourage your child to make his own choice of books. Ask him what he likes about the books he chooses.

5. Involve your child as much as possible in what you are reading. Here are some suggestions:

• Point to pictures in the book as you say a word or ask your child to point to objects he recognizes.

• Get him to join you, if possible, in reading recurring sentences. ("Run, run, as fast as you can. You can't catch me, I'm the gingerbread man.")

• Ask him open-ended questions about the story. ("What do you think will happen next?")

• Help him to relate the story to his own experiences. ("Has that ever happened to you?" "What would you have done?")

6. Help your child develop a sense of sequencing in space and time. ("What happened first, second, next ... ?")

7. Relate the pace of your reading to your child's interest in particular aspects of the story. Children often like to create their own "side-road" stories, becoming more fascinated with what happens along the way than with the story's ending. Parents, on the other hand, are often the ones who are most eager to reach the story's ending.

8. Let your child cuddle up beside you or sit in your lap while you read with your arm around his shoulder.

The warm, loving feelings you convey are as important to your child—and often even more important—than the content of the story you are reading.■

Expressions in Play

What an active period! Youngster touches, explores, and investigates everything everywhere. Her inquisitive nature and growing interests are limitless. Every obstacle, crumb, crack, or crevice is her immediate business.

In order to satisfy this enormous curiosity, she needs games, toys, and other objects.

However, don't give her too many toys, nor too expensive ones. Excessive generosity doesn't help her learn respect for her possessions. She may only learn that she can have more toys or better ones if she breaks them or becomes bored with them.

Too few toys, on the other hand, will not provide the mental nourishment she needs.

Games or toys made at home are an excellent learning resource. We encourage you to develop your own ideas related to your child's interests and abilities. Here are some examples:

(1) An old handbag for make-believe. Fill it with old keys on a key chain, a pocket flashlight (the kind which is sealed against removal of the battery or lamp), a hairbrush, and a comb.

(2) A cardboard box to help develop form perception. From the lid cut out various simple shapes (square, circle, diamond) through which she can deposit a matching object.

This box is more than a formboard. When she drops the object, she can watch it disappear, hear it land in the bottom of the box. Then she can remove the lid and observe where it went.

Further, after several trials, she will discover that the ball will go into the round hole while the cube will not.

(3) Tin cans for nesting or stacking. Remove the lids from fruit, vegetable, or juice cans. For safety, check the cans for sharp edges.

Having collected a variety of sizes, cover the exteriors of the cans with colorful adhesive paper.

Now Youngster can build towers to demolish. She can hide small cans inside large ones and discover some of the mysteries of space relations ("near" and "far," "up" and "down"). She can also learn about gravity, such as what happens when objects fall or drop off tables.

(4) A sandbox and basin of water for discovey. Give your child some different-sized containers from which to "pour" either sand or water.

By transferring sand or water from one location to another Youngster learns the various properties of these substances. (The water that was spilled on the ground just disappeared!)

(5) Plastic containers and lids for the development of size discrimination. Use an assortment of different-sized containers and lids, preferably ones made of non-breakable plastic. Screw one container securely to a board. Then let the child attempt to place the appropriate lid on the container.

For variety and complication, change the container on the board or change the location of the board.

In each of these activities your child enjoys a new learning experience. From new experiences emerge new ideas, new concepts, new understanding of the world around us.

In this way her enormous curiosity is being put to good use. Best of all, these new learning experiences are really fun.■

The Injuries of Childhood

Injuries, like illness, are a part of growing up. Knowing how to prevent and treat them is part of being a well-prepared parent.

Bumps and bruises happen to every active child every day, beginning with his first roll as an infant and continuing with the tosses and tumbles of later years.

Bumps and bruises happen when the child trips, falls, or collides with something as he walks or runs about. Occasionally injuries can happen in a tussle with a playmate.

Regardless of the cause of a bruise, the result is the same—a painful swelling that at first is red, then becomes blue, and after several days turns yellow or green.

Naturally parents try to prevent injury by developing good safety habits. But when injuries occur and a bruise develops, several first aid measures can be employed.

First, cool compresses or an icepack can be applied to the hurt area. This will decrease the pain and stop the bleeding that is occurring beneath the skin.

Wrapping a piece of ice in a cloth or paper towel may help relieve the discomfort. Getting Youngster to hold the ice in place is often more successful than having a parent try to do it.

The pain of a bruise usually lasts only a short time (20-30 minutes and then, although it may appear serious, seldom

CONTINUED ON PAGE 161

Numbers and Sizes

Over the last few months Youngster has probably had lots of experience with filling and emptying containers.

Our suggestions for learning activities have included using containers of different shapes and sizes with a variety of objects to fill them.

Now we can use Youngster's knowledge of container-object relationships and his growing understanding of "more" to take another step toward awareness of numbers.

First, though, Youngster needs to know what it means for a container to be full. For our purposes, "full" means that a container holds as many objects as possible while still permitting the cover to be put on without forcing. With this understanding established, a game can be played involving sizes and numbers.

Find two shoe boxes, coffee cans or other containers that have large openings and thus are easy to fill and empty.

You and Youngster each take one container. Then gather up a number of toys and durable household objects and place them in a pile between you and Youngster.

The objects should cover a wide range of sizes. The largest

ones should be big enough that three or four of them will completely fill a container. The smallest could be as small as a clothespin. Try to have a few objects for each of several different sizes.

Take turns selecting an object, with each one putting the object selected into your own container. The goal is to fill one's container with as many things as possible. When each of you has filled your container as described, compare the number of objects in each one.

How can this be done since Youngster can't count? Pour out the contents of each container and arrange the objects from one of the containers in a straight line. Then form the other container's objects in a parallel

straight line so that each of your objects lines up with each of Youngster's. This is called one-to-one correspondence.

If you have more objects, as will probably be the case, your line will be longer and it will be easy for Youngster to see that you have more objects.

If there are 10 or fewer objects in your line it would be good to count each one out loud as you point to it. Then do the same with Youngster's line. This will give him experience in hearing someone count. (Soon he will be able to do it, too, although such behavior right now would probably be a result of rote learning rather than a true understanding of the counting process.)

The main purpose of this game is to show Youngster that there is a relationship between the size of the objects and the number that can be placed in the container.

In technical terms the number of objects that will fill a space is inversely proportional to their size. In more down-to-earth language, the smaller the objects, the more can be put in the container.

While Youngster can't express the idea even that simply, he should grasp it intuitively after playing this game a few times. Don't give away the winning method by selecting only the very smallest objects. Try to be just slightly better than he is and see if he finds his way to the correct method as he gains more experience.

As Youngster begins to grasp the principle, you can anchor his understanding by using new containers and new objects. His judgment of size will improve if you reduce the difference between the sizes of the objects to make them more alike.

This little game is a small but fun step on the long road to learning about numbers and sizes and their practical application.■

———— CONTINUED FROM PAGE 160 ————

interferes with play.

If the bump continues to enlarge or becomes increasingly painful, it may mean there is continued bleeding. In such cases the cool compresses or icepack should be reapplied and your physician notified.

Most bruises are gone within seven to 10 days although a little blue, yellow, or brown color may remain for two to three weeks. There may also be a "knot" under

the skin. This should get smaller and smaller as the weeks go by. If it does not, or if it becomes tender or inflamed, your doctor should be consulted.

Additional care and observation is necessary for head injuries. In the case of an injury around the eye, an icepack may be applied , but *never* directly on the eye. If the eye itself is injured, consult your child's physician immediately.■

Showing Respect for Feelings

Both research studies and experience with child rearing reveal what marvelous imitators children are— "child see, child do." It is therefore essential to start right now to model the positive traits you want your child to possess. For example, if you demonstrate respect for her feelings, she will grow up to exhibit this same quality.

At this age Youngster is likely to experience feelings of inadequacy with regard to her speech. The late Dr. Haim Ginott championed an approach, a feedback technique, which not only helps the child overcome this sense of inadequacy but also helps to build a strong self-identity.

Let's consider an example. You're having morning coffee with a neighbor when Youngster rushes in to tell you something that is important to her. Since she's not yet a fluent speaker and she's speaking in a hurry, you don't know what she's trying to tell you.

First, let's talk about what to do:

(1) Echo what she has said as best you can and replace the part you can't understand with one of the "wh" words. For example:

Youngster: "Sam broke too me ever."

Parent: "Sam broke what?"

(2) Assure her that you truly understand her feelings (even if you do not understand her speech). Reflecting her feelings back to her is very reassuring to a child and helps her develop self-confidence.

None of us ever outgrow the basic need for emotional support. For a child, this can be expressed by a hug or a squeeze accompanied by some simple feedback: "I know you are upset right now. I understand how you feel. Let's sit down and talk about it."

Treating Youngster as an individual with her own personal dignity will enable her to overcome her feelings of helplessness or inadequacy. It is also the best way to help her gain self-confidence and thereby build a positive self-concept.

Now, let's talk about what *not* to do.

(1) Don't belittle the child with criticism, e.g.,"Who can understand you when you talk like that?"

(2) Don't threaten her, "If you don't talk better I'll have to send you to your room."

(3) Don't bribe her, "If you say it nicely, you can have a cookie."

(4) Don't command her, "Say it properly so we know what you mean."

(5) Don't overprotect her, "You poor girl—you haven't yet learned to talk."

In summary, by knowing how to deal appropriately with your child and by knowing what not to do, you can help to build your child's self-esteem and develop greater self-confidence.■

www.growingchild.com
Contributing Authors

Phil Bach, O.D., Ph.D.
Miriam Bender, Ph.D.
Joseph Braga, Ed.D.
Laurie Braga, Ph.D.
George Early, Ph.D.
Liam Grimley, Ph.D.
Robert Hannemann, M.D., F.A.A.P.
Sylvia Kottler, M.S.
Bill Peterson, Ph.D.

Growing Child, Inc.
P.O. Box 620
Lafayette, Indiana 47902-0620
Telephone: 1-800-927-7289
©2005 Growing Child, Inc.

Dear Growing Child:

"I'm so happy with your newsletter! Seeing that envelope in our mailbox brings a smile to my face.

"I read the newsletter and then pass it on to my parents (baby's caretakers). Things have changed so much in 25 years that this gives them a new insight with my daughter."

Teresa P.
Green Bay, WI

Next Month

- ■ *Learning to Make Decisions*
- ■ *Problem Behaviors*
- ■ *The Ebb and Flow of Time*

Growing Child®

'The Operator'

Your young "almost-2 1/2-year-old" is rapidly extending her range of operations. And, she is an "operator."

By now she walks with a smooth heel-toe gait. Sometimes she combines walking with pushing, pulling, carrying or dragging almost anything movable.

When not engaged in this sort of "work," she hurries from place to place as if afraid she might miss something.

Her running is still somewhat stiff and awkward. Although she is fairly sure-footed, she still has trouble turning sharp corners or coming to a quick stop. This means that she frequently trips, runs into things, or knocks them over.

She is curious about everything—what it is, what it does, how it works. As yet she has not begun asking many questions. Sometimes her vocabulary isn't equal to the task. So she continually must try things out for herself.

She may stand on tiptoe to see something or to pull it down to her level. She will also try to climb anything climbable.

Earlier she climbed just for the sake of climbing. She was interested in exploring all the space around her—vertical as well as horizontal.

Now she climbs with a definite purpose. She wants to see better or to reach something otherwise unreachable.

Her determination can be surprising. She will pull, push, and tug anything on which she can climb, such as a chair, to the right place for its effective use. A drawer in a chest of drawers can be pulled out to make a convenient step.

Once she has reached the object of her momentary heart's desire, guess what? She probably can't climb down again!

You may find her in strange places—in a dry bathtub, on top of a chest of drawers, in the middle of a table—or sitting quietly in a chair "reading" a newspaper!

Youngster has also learned to jump up, getting both feet off the floor. She usually makes a pretty big production of it. She bends her knees, then bends some more and swings her arms most energetically. With great effort, she clears the floor by an inch! Of course, our high jumper expects applause for such an enormous effort.

Youngster is busy learning many things and beginning to show more independence every day. If you haven't yet heard "Me do it!" you'll be hearing it soon—and often.

Be patient. This is a child's "Declaration of Independence"— a sign that Youngster is beginning to see herself as "Me," an individual, someone who can learn to cope effectively with this big, wide, wonderful world.■

Funny Sounds

Youngster's expressions are becoming increasingly funny. He reverses sounds in words so that biscuit sounds like "biksit," elephant is "efilant," bunny rabbit is "runny babbit."

If he doesn't know the precise words to express an idea, he creates his own. (By now you probably know that "hockle bockle" means hot-water bottle!)

From now until he is about 3 years old, Youngster will acquire approximately 50 new words a month.

In some cases you may not recognize them as bona fide words—"mardapane" for marmalade, for example—until you hear him use them repeatedly in similar situations.

Youngster is also hard at work using many different parts of speech. While his first words were interjections ("hi," "bye," "ouch"), nouns are presently the words he uses the most, followed by action verbs ("go," "carry," "eat"), and prepositions ("up," "out," "in," "again").

His chatter is constant. It is as if his use of new words helps him to think aloud. Words help direct his perceptions and his motor activity.

CONTINUED ON PAGE 165

Learning to Make Decisions

ne of the most important skills a person can develop is the ability to make intelligent decisions. Throughout our lives our decisions will range from big ones like the choice of a mate or a career to small ones like deciding whether to buy something now or wait until it might be on sale.

Sometimes one decision is important because as a direct consequence it leads to a particular set of choices later. Some decisions cannot be reversed. Thus, when one buys a new car, the decision cannot be undone for it can only be sold as a used car with a corresponding drop in value.

The question then becomes how long to keep the car, weighing reduced depreciation over the years against increasing maintenance costs. In this case there is generally no right or wrong decision, just a matter of personal preference.

Other decisions require careful reasoning and good judgment. These qualities are not universal. We all have known people who seemed to be lacking in good judgment or even "common sense."

Decision-making ability has its roots in early childhood. Like personality, it is usually well-formed by the time a child enters school. By elementary school age, the quality of a child's decisions as well as the style of his decision-making—reflective or impulsive—are fairly predictive of the way he will make his choices as an adult.

His decisions, like those of an adult, are based on how he views the chances of being successful and the consequences of success or failure. But since his judgments of the chances and the consequences are likely to be inaccurate, his decisions are often the wrong ones.

He might toddle into a closed door in the dark because he is used to its being open. He needs to learn about the injury he could suffer by bumping into something.

Similarly, a young child might dart into the street without looking because he is unaware of the possibility of a car coming. The likelihood and the consequences of being hit are too abstract for him to fully grasp.

So we see that a child must be able to take into account both the probabilities and the consequences of an event in order for him to make wise decisions.

You can stimulate Youngster's decision-making powers with a little game. Here's how it works:

Cut a hole in the top of a cardboard box, a hole that is large enough for toys of a certain size to be dropped through.

Then gather up several toys, some that are smaller than the hole, some the same size, and some that are too large to go through the hole.

Point to each toy in random order and ask Youngster if he thinks it will go into the box.

After he has answered, let him try the toy in the hole to see if it will go through without forcing.

If he correctly judges that the toy will or will not go through, you can give him a little reward such as a piece of cheese or fruit and a verbal reward, "good choice" or "good decision."

As the game progresses, Youngster will tend to say yes to any toy that appears to have any chance of going through the hole.

The next time you play the game, change the rules slightly. Tell him that for every judgment he makes correctly he will receive a reward. But if he makes an error by saying, for example, that it will go through the hole and it doesn't, he will lose one of the rewards he previously earned.

As soon as he understands the scoring system, you will notice he makes his judgments with greater care, for now the consequences of a wrong decision are greater.

In judging the size by eyeball comparison he is learning to make size discriminations as well as learning to judge the probability of success in each case.

You will need to change the toys or the hole size often so he doesn't merely memorize which toys fit. The shape of the hole can also be changed: round, square, rectangular, slit-like.

Other activities can be used, provided Youngster is capable of making the appropriate decisions and understanding the consequences of each decision.

With any of these games, Youngster is likely to be reckless and inaccurate at first. But after he gains some experience, you can almost hear the wheels turning in his head as he weighs the elements that go into making a decision.

At this age tangible rewards will provide your child with the motivation needed to stay with a task.

Later in life, after he has learned to experience success, success will provide its own reward.

In choosing rewards for your child, it will be helpful to keep the following in mind:

1) What is rewarding to one child (for example, a 15-minute visit to a playground) may not be considered rewarding by another. So, try to be sensitive to your child's likes and dislikes.

2) Rewards that are immediate ("Right now you will receive ... ") are more effective at this age than rewards that are long-term or delayed ("Sometime next month you will get ... ").

3) Rewards should be tangible and concrete (for example, a favorite treat).

4) Rewards can be strengthened by praise ("You did a good job!").∎

The Ebb and Flow of Time

Time is something Youngster is learning about. We don't mean he is learning how to "tell time" or even "what time it is." But he is learning that time is always flowing, that there are rhythms and patterns in time and that there is a "before," a "now," and an "after."

When Youngster notices that "getting-up time" is different from "going-to-bed time" he is experiencing events as they unfold over time.

Time is also a part of activities that involve rhythm. Rhythm is actually a *pattern* of things which happen *in time*. For instance, when you clap your hands in rhythm, you are actually organizing movements in time.

Rhythm also is involved when a child learns to creep on all fours. This activity demands that the infant make organized movements. The right hand goes forward and then the left knee. Next in time the left hand goes forward and then the right knee.

If the infant learns to creep well, he has also learned to organize his movements over time.

In teaching him about the regularity of events in his daily life, you are helping him structure his own personal time world.

If a youngster lives in a confused time world where things do not happen with dependable frequency, he may become confused about time itself.

What can you do to assure that your youngster develops good organization of his time world? The following practices will be helpful:

1. Give Youngster a consistent schedule. There should be some dependable landmarks in every youngster's typical day—certain things should happen in a certain time order so he can learn about time itself.

2. Going to bed and getting up should happen on schedule. That is, there is a time to go to bed and a time to get up.

3. Another important part of his schedule is the time for eating. Meals—breakfast, lunch and dinner—should occur at dependable times each day. As he learns about eating, he also learns about time.

4. There should be a time for getting undressed, having a bath, and going to bed. These important events should happen with dependable regularity.

5. You can add much to his time learning by talking to him about time throughout the day. "Hey, John, you just got up. This is your *first* meal *today*.

"After *breakfast* you'll play until *lunch*. *After* lunch, you'll have a nap.

"*Then* we'll play some more and after a *while* we'll have *dinner*.

"*After* dinner you can play with Mom and Dad.

"*After* that you can go to bed and sleep until *morning*.

"*Then* we'll have another nice breakfast."

Note that the words emphasized are all *time* words. You may want to use different ones. Just be sure to use words which help him learn about time.

6. Be careful to monitor his experiences with time.

For example, many television programs create an artificial time frame. In some the action unfolds over a number of years while the actual time space is just 30 minutes. Such experiences are likely to be confusing to Youngster.

As a general rule, we think Youngster should have limited exposure to television except for educational programs designed specifically for preschool children.

7. Help Youngster understand that the same time span (such as 15 minutes) may appear short or long, depending on the circumstances. If Youngster really enjoys what he is doing, he may lose all sense of time passing.

On the other hand, if he has to wait for something he wants immediately, then a few moments may seem like an eternity.

Use these opportunities to talk with your child about his time world so that he will be able to deal effectively with the ebb and flow of time which confronts every human being. ∎

———— CONTINUED FROM PAGE 163 ————

In addition, words help him to associate what he cannot see with what he can see; to relate past experience to what he is presently doing so that what is out of sight is not out of mind. Thus words help build up a time world in which he can develop time concepts and the specific vocabulary to represent them.

It is often tempting for a parent to intervene by trying to redirect the child's chatter. However, parents can learn to understand their child better by listening as he talks to himself.

It may sound something like this if he is playing with a ball: "Ever you be, ball?" Or, looking through a picture book, he finds a picture of a dog. Then he closes the book and asks, "Ever can Lassie be?" ∎

Problem Behaviors

 o one will deny that a 2-year-old can exhibit a very strong will, such as refusing to eat or to go to bed. But parents ought to recognize that problem behaviors are not always Youngster's fault. They may occasionally be precipitated by a parent's lack of understanding of the child's behavior or by ineffective discipline techniques.

A good starting point for establishing good discipline is to set reasonable limits for Youngster's behavior. These limits must be specifically defined and clearly explained to the child.

It should be noted that, for successful discipline, the limits must be *reasonable*. In other words, there won't be an unreasonable number of "no-nos," "stop that," or "don't touch this."

Parents who use physical punishment may accomplish short-term compliance with their wishes. But in the long-term they may be creating new problems for themselves since children have been found to learn aggressive behaviors from parents who are aggressive.

Thus parent and child may be feeding the flames of each other's passions by temper tantrums, followed by physical punishment, leading to more temper tantrums, etc.

Other parents may try using psychological or emotional punishment—"I don't love you anymore" or "You make me sick" or "Why can't you be more like your brother?" In these cases, the scars left by the parent's rejection may produce more serious consequences than the child's initial acts of misbehavior.

But there are effective ways to handle problem situations. Parents who respect their child's feelings and take into account her individual tempo can develop great skill in deflecting anger.

They can become experts in

defusing potentially explosive situations. Or they may provide their child with emotional release by reflecting her feelings back to her: "I know you feel angry because your brother just broke your favorite toy."

Even though no discipline technique can ever restore the broken toy, the caring/understanding approach can help a child gain the self-control needed to deal with a difficult situation.

A common problem situation faced by parents and child is the hassle over going to bed. Here parents have an opportunity to apply the principle of "reasonable limits."

Once these limits have been specifically defined, they should be clearly explained to the child—along with the consequences for any misbehavior. Then the parent must adhere consistently to those limits and consequences.

A child will occasionally "test the limits" to find out what are the *real* consequences for misbehavior—as distinct from a parent's *threatened* consequences. Here is where parents need to be thoroughly consistent.

A child will inevitably become angry if parents apply one rule at one time and another at a different time. If temporary changes need to be made in the rules or in the consequences—because of special circumstances—the child should be alerted in advance

about these changes.

Anticipation on the part of the parents is a most effective way to prevent problem behaviors in the child.

For example, before bedtime a parent might announce: "You have just five more minutes to play before it's time for bed." In this way the announcement about bedtime doesn't come as a sudden shock.

Similarly, a parent might say: "I will play one game with you before bedtime," or "I have time to read you one story before you go to sleep."

The same technique can be used before it is time to leave the playground, the park, or end some favorite activity.

If a parent anticipates that Youngster may not go to sleep immediately or may awaken early in the morning, it is wise to provide her with some soft toys she can hold before she falls asleep. The same soft toys will also be at hand for her amusement in the early morning.

Anticipation can also prevent many other problem behaviors. If the last trip to the supermarket was disastrous in terms of Youngster's misbehaviors, it is time to think through those problems and rehearse that situation.

Before leaving for the supermarket, sit down with Youngster to explain acceptable and unacceptable behaviors in the store. You might even promise a specific reward for good behaviors at the end of your trip to the supermarket. And if Youngster behaved well on this trip to the store, be sure to tell her in very specific terms what it was she did that particularly pleased you.

By focusing attention on positive behaviors—rather than their opposite negative behaviors—you are taking a most important step toward avoidance of future problem behaviors. ∎

New Play Materials

inger painting. This is a favorite of most 2-year-olds. Here is a recipe for homemade finger paint.

Thoroughly dissolve one tablespoon of cornstarch in 1/2 cup cold water. Stir constantly while cooking over medium heat until mixture comes to a boil, loses whiteness and starts to thicken. Lower heat, and continue stirring for about two minutes until mixture is very thick and smooth.

Let it cool slightly. Color by stirring in powdered or liquid tempera, or food coloring. One color at a time is enough for a beginner. Leftovers can be stored in a covered jar in the refrigerator. The cornstarch mixture may be divided into separate jars, and a different color mixed into each one if you wish.

The surfaces for finger painting are numerous—plastic, aluminum or steel trays, oilcloth over floor or tabletop. If a permanent record is desired, shiny shelving paper or finger paint paper may be used.

To begin, moisten the surface—tray, oilcloth or paper—with a sponge because the surface must be damp.

Deposit a tablespoon of paint and encourage your Youngster to cover the area with the palm of her hand. Continue to provide spoonfuls, one by one, until the entire surface is coated.

Now she can do her own thing—painting with knuckles, fingertips, front or back of hands, and wrists.

When finished, she can assist with the cleanup which requires only a wet sponge and some paper towels.

Use finger painting as another language experience for Youngster, describing to her what is occurring: "How *red* the paint is!" "Your hands go *round* and *round*." "The line is *long*—it goes all across the tray."

Clay. Working with clay resembles finger painting because it allows direct contact with the material and permits a child to make a mess in a constructive pursuit.

If a child needs a release from too much excitement or stress, clay play is a good way to "blow off steam." She can pound, hit, squeeze and punch without fear of destroying something and without fear of punishment.

A water-based clay sold as moist clay is preferable to more colorful modelling clay. Modelling clay is frequently too hard for Youngster's hands to mold. She must therefore depend upon an adult to soften it for her.

Water-based clay may be stored in a plastic bag to prevent it from hardening. A wet cloth placed on top of the clay will keep it in good condition.

Play dough is a good substitute for clay. Here is an easy and inexpensive recipe:

Mix together in a large bowl 2 cups flour and 1/2 cup salt. Keep stirring while gradually adding 1 teaspoon salad oil and approximately 3/4 cup water.

Add the water very slowly at the end so the mixture doesn't get too wet. Knead together until a consistency similar to bread dough is obtained.

When you introduce the clay, work a piece of it yourself, without making anything specific.

Now, here's another opportunity for language learning because adjectives appear so automatically. For example, you might talk as you play together: "My, that's *round!*" "Look how *long* the clay can be pulled." Or, "Feel how *smooth* it is."

Cleaning up should include Youngster. She can roll up the clay into a ball and place it in a container. Then she can use a wet sponge to wipe off the tabletop.

Play dough may be stored in a tightly closed plastic bag in the refrigerator. If it is too sticky the next time it is to be used, roll it in flour and re-knead to the original consistency.■

Travel Tips

fter making several long distance journeys by car with their young children, parents usually begin to think about how to make traveling more enjoyable. Here are some travel tips that may help:

Plan ahead of time. Trips that are well planned are usually more enjoyable for young children. So take the time to plan the details of your travel: how far you will travel each day, where you will stop for lunch, etc. Having made your plans you can then be flexible if any changes should be necessary along the way.

Try to involve your children as much as possible in making these plans. Even though a young child is not capable of reading a map, she will enjoy being shown the line on the map that indicates where you will be going. She will also enjoy hearing the sounds of the places through which you will be passing. Her imagination will help her to conjure up fairyland visions of where these travels will take her, especially if you have travel brochures with pictures, which are usually available from a tourist office or convention bureau.

What to bring? Once you

CONTINUED ON PAGE 168

CONTINUED FROM PAGE 167

have completed your initial plans for the trip, it is now time to consider what to bring with you in the car to make the journey more enjoyable.

A first consideration would be a basic first aid kit—adhesive bandages, thermometer, medicines, etc. that you regularly need at home.

Have your child pack a bag of some toys to bring. Monitor the selections, pointing out to her why one toy would be more appropriate for the car than another. Just make sure that she is involved in the final selection.

It is also wise to bring a pillow as well as a child's favorite stuffed animal. That way, even though she will be sleeping in a strange room, she will have the comfort of a familiar friend.

Be sure to bring some snacks which might include fruit or fresh vegetables as well as something to drink. In the summertime especially, young children can become dehydrated inside a hot car.

It is also wise to pack a picnic lunch so that children will have more freedom to stand, stretch and exercise than would be possible inside a restaurant.

On the road. Now that all the preparations have been made, you are ready to take to the road. The first step is to make sure that everybody is wearing a seat belt or is in a safety car seat. Statistics on safety have documented the wisdom of wearing seat belts—so that it is now the law in all states.

It will be most beneficial for young children if adults perceive the journey by car as a part of, not a prelude to, the whole vacation. Parents will learn that traveling long distances without a stop may result in "making good time" but it will also result in having a carload of very unhappy and unpleasant children.

Rest stops should therefore be planned at regular intervals along the way, preferably at locations where children can run and play.

The closer parents can adhere to a child's normal schedule for eating and sleeping, the less aggravated the child will become while away from home. Even though a child may not be able to eat or sleep well because of excitement, it is best to try to restore and maintain the child's normal schedule.

A good way to pass the time on the journey is to play some simple games together, such as counting trucks or identifying colors. As the child grows older these games can become increasingly more sophisticated—even to the point where the child performs better than the parents! Some parents like to bring a tape recorder and some sing-along tapes or a songbook whenever they travel.

Whatever you do, try to make this time on the journey quality time together as a family. The more enjoyable you make the journey, the happier your children will be. And, vice versa, the happier your children are, the more likely you too will enjoy the journey.■

Dear Growing Child:

"My son is a treasure to me, but I don't really know that much about how babies develop, grow and learn. I want to provide him with a stimulating environment and teach him what he needs to learn when he's ready.

'Growing Child has given me confidence in my ability to raise a happy, intelligent baby. Thank you."

Dawn P.
Stanford, ME

www.growingchild.com

Contributing Authors

Phil Bach, O.D., Ph.D.
Miriam Bender, Ph.D.
Joseph Braga, Ed.D.
Laurie Braga, Ph.D.
George Early, Ph.D.
Liam Grimley, Ph.D.
Robert Hannemann, M.D., F.A.A.P.
Sylvia Kottler, M.S.
Bill Peterson, Ph.D.

Growing Child, Inc.
P.O. Box 620
Lafayette, Indiana 47902-0620
Telephone: 1-800-927-7289
©2005 Growing Child, Inc.

Next Month

■ *Childhood Fears*
■ *Sibling Rivalry*
■ *Vision Problems*

Growing Child®

Childhood Fears

ne of the problems of dealing with a youngster's fears is recognizing when he is scared. When he cries, clings, hides, resists—or is generally "being impossible," it may be that he is frightened.

Why?

He may often be unable to express his feelings clearly because of his limited vocabulary.

Then, too, he may not yet recognize or identify his own feelings as "fear." He just knows that something is wrong. He feels upset inside.

Dealing with these behaviors can be very frustrating for parents. It is easy to think a child is just being stubborn or having a tantrum. Even if a parent does recognize that the reason for such behavior is fear, it is often difficult to decide just how to cope with this fear.

A good first step is to try to gain a better understanding of this emotional response.

Fear is a normal human emotion—a natural means of self-protection. Certain fears appear to be inborn, such as a newborn's response to loud and sudden noises. Such responses are usually reflex reactions.

Some fears we consciously teach a child because he needs to be wary of persons, objects, or situations which are potentially harmful to him—such as strangers, fire, or a busy street.

Some fears a child learns on his own. For instance, if he sees another child fall from a swing, he realizes that he too might fall. The next time he rides on a swing

he will likely hold on tightly! Fears such as these are healthy because they tend to protect the child from real dangers.

Parents need to avoid two extreme reactions when dealing with a child's fears. One extreme is to express alarm at every sign of childhood fear. The other is to ignore completely all manifestations of fear by the child.

In between these two extremes lies a happy medium that involves giving thoughtful consideration to a young child's fears because they may indeed be a parent's first indication that all is not well with the child.

Parents will want to help their youngster overcome unrealistic fears, both for his benefit and their peace of mind. Recognition of a fear and reassurance to the child are important parts of dealing with a child's fear. Without this reassurance, a child may become more confused and even more fearful.

When coping with Youngster's fears it is important to remember that no matter how unreasonable, even ridiculous, his fear may seem to you, it is very real to him. It is important, therefore, to respect his feelings and reassure him gently that he need not be afraid.

Some of the more common fears include fear of certain animals, loud visitors in the home, the dark, going to bed, going to sleep, and separation from parents.

Fear of animals may have its beginnings in an alarming experience with a neighbor's pet

or a fright while visiting a zoo. This initial experience may lead to avoidance of even stuffed animals or those pictured in a book.

If he shows an abnormal fear of animals, introduce him gradually to their presence. When you're driving, point out dogs and other animals you see. When possible, stop and let him watch from the safety of the car.

Several visits to a children's "petting zoo" also may be helpful. Don't force your child to go near the animals. On the first visit just walk casually around the zoo and let him look. If he shows anxiety, quietly and gently pick him up and hold him.

Somehow it is harder to be afraid of something that you can look down upon. Let him watch other children play with and pet the young animals. Talk with him about baby animals and their mothers.

An over-enthusiastic relative or friend who greets a child with loud laughter and smothering hugs also may arouse considerable anxiety and fear in a toddler. In fact, he may not only hide from that person but show increasing fear of everyone outside the immediate family circle.

It is pretty hard to tone down loud and over-demonstrative relatives but sometimes visitors can be told in advance that your youngster is just learning to adjust to persons outside the family. They also can be asked to wait until your child approaches them on his own.

——— CONTINUED ON PAGE 174 ———

Sibling Rivalry

In previous issues of *Growing Child* we have talked about the idea that during these formative years, young children gradually develop a sense of who they are and what they can become.

In this process it is not uncommon for them to experience feelings of jealousy toward another child.

Parents frequently are upset by a particular form of jealousy known as *sibling rivalry*. This rivalry involves expressions of hostility between children of the same family who look at themselves as rivals competing for the love and affection of their parents.

Sibling rivalry most commonly occurs with the arrival of a newborn baby. It is important for parents to recognize that—even though the older child's behavior may be considered obnoxious by them—it is a common and normal reaction on the part of the child. The older child is expressing distress and anger at being knocked off the pedestal on which he had previously stood.

The author Judy Blume humorously reflected these feelings of distress and anger when she described Fudge, in the book *Superfudge*. Fudge tries to "sell" his new baby sister, Tootsie, whenever there is company in their home. "You like the baby?" he asks. "You can have her for a quarter."

When that doesn't work, he even tries to pay people to take her away: "I'll give you a quarter," he says to strangers on the street, "if you take her to your house and never bring her back."

Sibling rivalry is most likely to occur if parents show favoritism toward the new arrival and don't give adequate attention and affection to the older child.

It also will develop if a parent is over-indulgent toward one child while being over-strict with

another. A young child also may feel slighted if parents are heard to compare one child with another.

A child's feelings of jealousy may be expressed either by aggressive or regressive behaviors. The child's aggression may be expressed either directly toward the parents or toward the "intruder" in the family.

Regressive behaviors, on the other hand, involve a return to babyhood activities, such as thumb-sucking, bedwetting, or soiled pants.

There are many things that parents can do that will lessen or prevent sibling rivalry.

The first step is to prepare the child for the new baby's arrival *before* the event occurs. It is most helpful to communicate this information in a way that is personally meaningful to the child, for example, "*You* will soon have a baby brother or sister."

Even though a young child may not understand all that a parent tells him, it is most important to take the time to talk about any changes that may occur in his life and to talk openly about the feelings that may accompany those changes.

The second step is to involve the older child as much as possible in the preparations for the new baby. This might include preparing the baby's crib or getting the diapers ready.

Even though a 2-year-old is very limited in terms of what he can do to help, it is important that his contributions be perceived as an integral part of the family's preparations for the new baby.

The third step is for the parents to set aside some time exclusively with the older child after the new baby arrives. This can often be arranged while the baby is taking a nap.

Such interaction time provides reassurance to the child that he is still loved as much as ever by his

parents, even though they now have to devote much time to caring for the baby.

It is important to realize that feelings of jealousy toward a newly arrived baby are a normal reaction on the part of an older child. Even if parents are unable to totally *prevent* sibling rivalry, the same procedures—talking with the older child, involving him in activities to care for the baby, and providing him with exclusive time for love and attention—also are the most effective ways to help him *adjust* to this new family situation and thus keep sibling rivalry at a minimum.

Even apart from the birth of a new baby, children in the same family will most likely continue to experience some sibling rivalry during the preschool years. It is as though they think of parental love as being limited in quantity: if you show love for my brother or sister, you will have less love left for me!

It is important for parents to be aware that because children's personality characteristics differ, parents may express their love differently for each of their children. For example, one child may like hugs whereas another may enjoy praise but dislike being hugged.

It is a good idea to explain these differences to children. This will help them to avoid feelings of jealousy and will ultimately help prevent sibling rivalry.■

Motor Skill Development

When parents see the title "Motor Skill Development," they might ask: "Haven't we already dealt with that topic in previous issues of *Growing Child?*" Of course, the reason the topic keeps recurring is because motor skills are developed at different stages of growth. In this issue we will discuss the specific gross motor skills and fine motor skills which children normally develop between two and three years of age.

Parent Involvement

Can parents stimulate their child's development of motor skills? Before answering that question we need to clarify two issues related to the purpose of stimulating a child's development.

It seems that there will always be some parents who want to know if "being ahead" in some area of development means their child will be a whiz in school or will some day become a professional athlete.

To those parents there is a straightforward answer: It is not possible to predict later success based on performance at this early age. The earlier the prediction is made, the more likely it will be wrong.

The purpose of stimulating a child's development is not aimed at "getting ahead" of one's peers but rather to ensure that *normal* growth and development will take place. Being aware of what constitutes normal development also enables parents to keep an eye out for possible coordination problems which they could discuss with their pediatrician.

A second question related to stimulating development is: "Am I challenging my child enough or too much?" In responding to that question, two considerations must be kept in mind: (1) Young children like to be challenged and will get bored if they are "stuck in a rut"; (2) When faced with new challenges, young children need to

experience some degree of success in order to be motivated to do their best. If the challenge is too difficult, or if parents push too hard, children are likely to become discouraged and their development may even be impeded. The secret is finding a happy balance.

Having addressed both of these issues, we can now answer the question about parent involvement by saying that parents have a most important role in a child's development of better motor skills.

The first secret is to focus on the here-and-now without being preoccupied with predicting the child's future.

The second secret is for parents to strive for a happy balance between providing appropriate challenges while ensuring some degree of success for the child.

Keep in mind that what children need are exciting challenges, opportunities to succeed, encouragement in defeat, and some involvement in selecting the activities which they will perform.

It's usually a good idea for parents to perform the same activities as the child. Parent participation in movement activities has several advantages: 1) It lets the child know that motor activities are important; (2) The parent can serve as a role model for new physical challenges; (3) It provides good exercise for the parent as well as the child: (4) It adds to the fun for both.

As parents participate in motor activities with their child, they will also become aware of adaptations that may be needed for a child to succeed. Adaptations might include simplifying a task by breaking it into simpler components, slowing the pace of the movements such as the tempo of a musical activity, and using materials or equipment which are more appropriate for the child to work with.

The key is to initiate an activity at a level which enables the child to participate safely and successfully. Once a child becomes competent

and comfortable at that level, it's time to move on to new challenges which not only increase the skill difficulty but should also add to the child's enjoyment of the activities.

Benefits of Movement Activities

Movement activities help 2-year-olds to develop not only motorically, but also cognitively, emotionally, and socially as well. Playing interactive games, for example, can involve such cognitive skills as counting, sequencing, vocabulary development, and color identification.

In motor development play activities, children also experience and learn to deal with emotions such as happiness and sadness.

Participation with peers inevitably involves social interaction and social communication. When a number of children are involved, the emphasis should be on cooperation rather than competition. So, even when the focus is on the development of motor skills, these movement activities foster cognitive, emotional, and social development. In other words, the whole child—not just arms and legs—will benefit.

Expensive equipment and materials are not necessary for a child to participate in motor skill development activities. Gross motor activities can include simple stretching, bending, and lifting, as well as walking, running and jumping. Fine motor activities include drawing, scribbling, stringing beads, or using play dough, for example.

An obstacle course can be constructed very simply with rope, an old tire, and a cardboard box. Children can practice jumping over a rope or crawling under it. They can climb through an old tire or into a cardboard box. The items in the obstacle course can be selected to match the child's interests and level of accomplishment.

CONTINUED ON PAGE 172

CONTINUED FROM PAGE 171

Gross Motor Skills

Here are some activities which are appropriate for children between two and three years of age to develop gross motor skills:

Walking: In walking, what was once a stiff, jerky gait is now becoming a smoother stride. Steps become more regular and feet are not planted far apart as they used to be. But children this age prefer short, quick little steps rather than a longer stride, which means they grow tired more quickly.

Running: As walking becomes smoother, running begins to appear. It starts out more like fast walking until it eventually becomes true running.

Galloping: Many 2-year-olds prefer to gallop than to run. The uneven clip-clop rhythm of galloping seems more attractive and playful than straightforward running. When children are particularly happy, they like to gallop up and down with joy, without really going anywhere.

Stopping: Once a child gets going, whether running or galloping, the next problem is learning how to stop. In the meantime, until they master the skill of being able to stop, children usually become adept at finding a soft landing spot.

Jumping: Two-year-olds generally like to try out their jumping abilities. As we watch an Olympic gymnast perform a perfectly graceful dismount, it's important to realize that those wonderful skills began by jumping as a 2-year-old from one step to the ground.

Jumping down a step is easier than jumping upward or across a flat surface. By about 3 years of age, children learn to use their arms to propel themselves forward, but a broad jump of a few feet will not be accomplished until about 5 years of age.

Throwing: At first children throw all balls in the same way—generally with a two-handed forward lurch—irrespective of the size of the ball. As their skill develops with practice, they will begin to throw a small ball with one hand and with more wrist action. With a bigger ball, they will bring it over their head in order to get a longer arm movement. But control of the throw will only come with practice.

Catching: Catching usually begins by having someone drop a ball into the child's outstretched arms. As the person throwing the ball moves a little farther away for the throw, many young children close their eyes as soon as they see the ball coming toward them.

Once they have overcome this reaction, they eventually learn to close their hands and fingers around the ball to prevent it from popping out of their outstretched arms. It's another motor skill that will improve with practice.

Fine Motor Skills

Between 2 and 3 years of age, children show progress in fine motor coordination. This depends not only on the development of new physical skills but also on the way a child's brain develops. For example, prior to 24 months, when faced with the task of placing a wooden square block in a square hole of the same size, a child will likely use a trial-and-error approach, pounding on the block if it doesn't fit right away—as though sheer physical force and will power will make it go in the hole.

Sometime before thee years of age most children gain a cognitive insight that the side of the block must be aligned with the side of the hole in order for the block to fit in the hole. And they now have the fine motor skills to act on this new cognitive insight. Each new discovery like this brings a new sense of excitement and interest to the child's explorations.

Most public libraries have simple puzzles appropriate for children of this age. Children seem to love the challenge of a puzzle they haven't seen before. But once they have mastered how to do it, they are ready to move on to a new and more challenging task.

One of the fine motor activities which all children appear to enjoy is drawing—which, at this age, might more accurately be described as scribbling. They enjoy experimenting with crayons, pencils, paintbrushes or markers.

Although the drawings may appear to an adult to be meaningless scribbles, to the child they may represent a particular person ("That's my mommy.") or object ("That's my house.) or feelings ("Joey is sad."). Young children show great pride when their artwork is displayed in some prominent place in the home such as on the refrigerator door.

Fine motor skills are also involved in many routine activities throughout the day, such as getting dressed, washing hands, brushing one's teeth, eating with a spoon, or turning a doorknob.

With some tasks a child may need some help just to get started. For example, when zipping or unzipping clothing, a parent may have to take the initial step, then let the child take over the task. The more practice children have with these activities, the sooner they will develop the skills.

In summary, motor skill development isn't something that happens all at once. It takes place over a long period of time. As new skills are developed, new challenges can be faced, leading to new learning opportunities. From these motor activities the whole child benefits.■

Vision Problems

During the early childhood years good vision develops as a result of normal and proper use of the eyes. For example, while a young child plays with blocks or uses finger paints, many important visual skills are being developed.

When vision problems occur, treatment is more likely to be successful the earlier the problem is detected. Parents who are well informed about some of the most common eye problems of young children will better know when to seek appropriate professional help.

When vision problems occur, treatment is more likely to be successful the earlier the problem is detected.

An eye examination is generally part of a physician's routine physical examination of a child. It is recommended that all children have a thorough eye examination at least once before their fourth birthday by a physician or by an eye specialist. By that age, a child's vision can usually be measured fairly accurately.

Because vision is so important, parents should know something about how it is measured. Normal vision is labeled as "20/20." The first number indicates the distance in feet from the eye chart to the eye being tested. The second number refers to the distance at which a *normal* eye can clearly identify a certain sized letter or picture on the chart.

"Twenty/twenty" vision, then, means that the eye being tested sees at 20 feet what a normal eye should see at that distance.

"Twenty/forty" vision, on the other hand, means what a normal eye is able to see at 40 feet can only be seen at 20 feet by this eye.

One common finding in vision screenings in preschool children is *hyperopia*, or farsightedness. Here, the eye must exert increased focusing to keep things clear.

While farsightedness may cause problems for an adult, particularly while reading, it rarely produces any symptoms in preschoolers.

If a child has to come closer than 10 feet to recognize what a normal eye sees at 20 feet, a check for *myopia*, or nearsightedness, by an eye specialist is in order. A nearsighted child will sometimes squeeze his eyelids together to produce a slit or pinhole effect (like a camera) in order to get a sharper focus.

Another vision problem to watch for in a young child is *strabismus*, a disorder which involves the inability to direct both eyes simultaneously to the same object.

When the eyes seem to be looking at the nose, the condition is called "cross-eye;" when they both appear to be looking to the opposite sides, it is known as "wall-eye."

The eyes may be crossed or divergent from birth, even though this may not be obvious until later. But strabismus can occur at any age.

In infancy a pediatrician watches for this condition. But as visits to the doctor become less frequent, it is possible for the problem to occur unnoticed.

You can check for this problem by watching Youngster's eyes while she is playing. It is especially important to do this when she is tired, for that is when crossing or divergence will most likely occur.

An eye that turns in or out during the early childhood years may sometimes lose its vision unless treated. Therefore, if you suspect that your child's eyes may be crossed or divergent, you should consult an eye specialist.

A problem occurs when one eye noticeably deviates outward or inward and then stops working to avoid causing double vision. This is what is known as *amblyopia* or "lazy eye." The eye really does not stop working. The brain simply ceases to receive the image from the deviating eye.

This is similar to the ability of some people who can look through a microscope or telescope with one eye while keeping the other eye open. The vision in the unused eye is "suppressed" by the brain.

If the use of one eye is suppressed for a period of months or years, its ability to see sharply will decrease. It can only be restored by treatment such as putting a patch over the good eye for several weeks or months to force the defective one to resume its function.

The earlier this is done, the more likely the "lazy" eye will develop normal vision. That is why it is important to identify eye deviations and amblyopia as early as possible.

Parents need to be aware that a child will generally not "outgrow" vision problems. These problems require professional treatment, such as eye muscle exercises, covering the good eye, wearing glasses, or other measures.

A little watchfulness by parents will go a long way toward early detection of vision problems. This watchfulness is especially important if there is a history of vision problems (e.g. crossed eyes) in either of the parents' families.

If vision problems are discovered early, a lot can be done by a skilled eye specialist. That is why early examination and diagnosis are so important.■

CONTINUED FROM PAGE 169

Another method is to pick up Youngster and hold him as you greet your visitors. This includes him in the eye-level greeting and gives him the additional security of your arms.

If he struggles or cries, comfort him. Then try to interest him in something else. A young child is naturally curious and will usually overcome his fear if visitors keep their greetings low-key and if he is allowed to exercise his own initiative in approaching them.

Fear of the dark, fear of going to bed, and fear of going to sleep usually are interrelated. They also usually involve fear of separation from parents.

Here are some actions you can take that will help calm these fears.

Begin by letting your child help you choose an attractive child's nightlight—a clown, star, or happy face. Let him handle and examine the light so that he will be familiar with it. Children's nightlights should be fully enclosed in plastic for safety. They should also be dimmer than the ordinary nightlight, if possible.

A half hour of quiet play and a warm bath are recommended to relax a child before bedtime. This routine will be a source of security to an anxious child.

Youngster must learn trust. When you put him to bed, reassure him, if necessary, that you are near and that you will be there in the morning when he awakens. He needs to know that his parents will be there when he really needs them.

Once he has been reassured, you must then be firm with bedtime rules. Firmness in carrying out reasonable bedtime rules will eventually help a child to overcome fear of the dark or fear of going to bed.

When you leave him in someone else's care, be sure that it is someone he knows and trusts. Explain the nightly routine carefully to that person so that your child will feel more secure as the same routine is followed, even if you aren't there.

Don't forget that in dealing with childhood fears, an "ounce of prevention" goes a long way. If your child must undergo a potentially frightening experience, such as a visit to the dentist or doctor, prepare him for it carefully by talking about it calmly and reassuringly. Control your own fears.

Above all don't punish your child in fearful ways, such as locking him in a darkened room, or threatening to have the doctor give him a "shot."

When in doubt about how to handle your child's fears, discuss the problem with your pediatrician, physician, or mental health professional. He or she is interested in your child's emotional health as well as his physical well-being.

A physician, for example, will know if it is appropriate or necessary to refer your child to another professional with specific expertise in dealing with childhood fears.■

www.growingchild.com

Contributing Authors

Phil Bach, O.D., Ph.D.
Miriam Bender, Ph.D.
Joseph Braga, Ed.D.
Laurie Braga, Ph.D.
George Early, Ph.D.
Liam Grimley, Ph.D.
Robert Hannemann, M.D., F.A.A.P.
Sylvia Kottler, M.S.
Bill Peterson, Ph.D.

Growing Child, Inc.
P.O. Box 620
Lafayette, Indiana 47902
Telephone: 1-800-927-7289
©2005 Growing Child, Inc.

Next Month

- *Good Manners: Are They Important?*
- *Parenting Styles*

Growing Child.

Courage–Now and Later

As a parent you know some of the problems and heartaches life can bring. In a quiet moment you may have wondered what the future holds for your child. Will your child meet whatever life brings with courage, sensitivity, and tenderness? How can you help your 29-month-old develop the inner toughness—and tenderness—she will need?

You have already made a good start in this direction. When you recognized your Youngster's drive to learn about her world and made it possible for her to explore it safely, you were helping her to develop self-confidence and courage.

Your quiet observation of your exploring child has provided her with protection while allowing her to develop independence and the ability to meet and conquer new challenges. As your child successfully overcomes small problems, she develops the confidence to tackle and solve larger ones.

Even children who demonstrate self-confidence and courage, however, may suddenly display unexplainable fears. A parent's first reaction is usually in the form of reassurance. But a child generally will not overcome her fears just because we tell her there is nothing to be afraid of.

Fear of water is a case in point. Every child is familiar with water—but usually with the limited amounts found in bathtubs or puddles. The new, large, and to her, seemingly endless amount of water in a swimming pool, lake, or river is different. She wants to approach it gradually, to explore it on her own terms and in her own good time. Fear of water is not a shameful emotion in a young child. It is a natural feeling that needs to be understood and respected by parents.

Nothing is more certain to produce lasting fear of water than a parent's determination that *his* child—or *her* child—will overcome that fear immediately.

No matter how confident an explorer your child has become, she may be hesitant and wary when she finds herself in a new and strange situation. An unknown relative who snatches her up for an energetic hug may reduce your child to tears. A large, friendly-but-noisy dog may instill panic in a child whose previous experience has included only a small, quiet dog.

Such fears, though they may seem trivial to an adult, are entirely sensible from the child's point of view.

If we are to help a child be brave we must begin by respecting her worries and fears. Accept them for what they are—questions about her own safety and security. "What is this? Will this hurt? What should I do?"

Talk to your child calmly. Don't pressure her to hug Aunt Mary or pet the nice, big doggie. Give her a chance to recover her balance. Then over a period of time give her frequent opportunities to learn more about the feared object or situation.

Work gently but persistently to help her conquer any fear which may hobble her independence.∎

A Sense of Order

Youngster has been busy for the past few months acquiring new information, developing new skills, and processing new knowledge. In a very real sense she is putting things in order in her mind.

As she attempts to order her mental understanding of the world around her, it will help her greatly if she can readily find order in her immediate physical environment. A sense of order will also help to make Youngster's learning environment more predictable—which, in turn, will help her develop a greater sense of security and of trust.

We know that many families cannot arrange their affairs in such a way that every object is always in its proper place or that every event always happens on schedule. What we are describing is an *ideal*—something to work toward.

By trying to get things in their proper place, and by trying to work out a schedule where events in your family's day occur with dependable regularity, you will be providing the stability and

——— CONTINUED ON PAGE 180 ———

Good Manners: Are They Important?

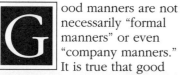

Good manners are not necessarily "formal manners" or even "company manners." It is true that good manners, in part, consist of the simple courtesies—saying "please," "thank you," "excuse me." These pleasant words help to make an increasingly impersonal world a little more personal, a little more gentle.

However, the key to good manners is not rigid obedience to social rules. It is our attitude toward others. It involves a respect for the rights, ideas, and feelings of others, even of those with whom we disagree.

When we look at good manners from this point of view the importance of certain social conventions becomes a little clearer. A few are essential. Others are trivial. Most lie somewhere in between, depending on circumstances and your own family customs.

But whatever courtesies you decide are important, it is the qualities of caring and consideration expressed through the courtesies which are important for children to learn.

"Thank you" can express gratitude and appreciation. It also can be said in such a way as to offend or even hurt. What matters more than the words expressed is the attitude toward others which underlies those words.

A child's manners not only reflect his feelings toward others, but also help him develop new, desirable attitudes. The young child who is trained to parrot "please" and "thank you" may not, at age 2 or 3, be any more considerate than a child who has not been taught these courtesies. But as his good manners bring him praise and smiles, he becomes pleased with himself. This in turn makes him feel more friendly toward others.

Through the practice of good manners he begins to develop the new attitudes which courtesy should reflect.

These attitudes and the learned courtesies are further reinforced as the child sees them practiced by his parents. He accepts his parents' valuation of others as being individuals worthy of care and consideration and he adopts the outward forms which are the reflection of this attitude.

Thus the child learns to make his desires known in ways which are considerate of others and to express his appreciation in an appropriate manner.

He learns good manners in much the same way that he learns to take turns or share with others, all of which become ways of expressing positive attitudes toward others.■

Tips for Effective Parenting

The following suggestions are from "The Hidden Hinge," by Rosa Covington Packard, published by Ballantine Books. We think they're excellent.

1. **Be objective, not personal in your instructions**. "Books go in this bookcase," rather than "I want you to be sure to keep your books in the bookcase."

2. **Be positive, not negative.** "Use the tricycle, it is your size," rather than "You are too little to ride the bicycle."

3. **Give the social reason for rules rather than flat authority.** "Hang the coat up before the baby steps on it and wrinkles it," rather than "Hang it up."

4. **Give a solution to a problem rather than mere prohibitions.** "Please move to this side of the table, John, so that Mary will be able to see," rather than "Don't stand in Mary's way, John."

5. **Be specific.** Give concrete information using concrete names and commands: "If you hold the card by its edge, it will stay clean," rather than "Don't mess up the cards."

6. **Match objects and actions to your words.** "Trays (pause and show) are held in the middle (pause and show)," rather than "Do it this way."

7. **Give awareness of consequences.** "Hitting hurts Peter," rather than "Don't hit Peter."

8. **Act as an individual to defend the common law in specific instances.** "I will not let you hurt John with the stick," rather than "We don't hurt people."

9. **Recognize the validity of emotions when you limit destructive actions.** Some examples: (a) "I know you are angry but you may not hurt Mary," rather than "Why did you hit Mary? She is your friend." (b) "I know that you are afraid but you must have the scratch cleaned," rather than "You are a big girl and that little scratch doesn't hurt." (c) "I know you don't want to wear shoes but you must protect your feet when you walk on city sidewalks," rather than "You don't want your feet to get all dirty and hurt, do you?"

10. **Use simple and scrupulously courteous manners to children and other adults.** (a) "Good morning, John, I am glad to see you (hand offered and withdrawn if not taken)," rather than "Can you say 'good morning' to me, and shake my hand, John?" (b) "Thank you, Aunt Jane, for remembering Susan's birthday," rather than "What do you say to Aunt Jane, Susan?"■

Parenting Styles

In the previous article, "Tips for Effective Parenting," we offered you some suggestions for becoming a more effective parent. Now we need to look at some behaviors that parents need to avoid. We hope that so far you have been able to wisely avoid these inappropriate parental behaviors which unfortunately are all too common in our society.

The first of these is the half-hearted, monotonously repeated warning issued by the parent whose attention is elsewhere.

Such warnings are usually non-specific: "Karen, don't do that."

These vague warnings are meaningless to the busy child. Don't do *what?* Since Karen isn't certain what she shouldn't be doing, she continues to pursue her interest of the moment.

Next comes a parent's shriek: "Karen, I said *stop* that!" But stop what? By this time perhaps, Karen, chair and all have toppled with a crash and a wail.

Then follows parental anxiety. Maybe even anger expressed by a smack or a shake. Karen is left resentful and confused. There is little consistency or security in her world. She is sadder, but no wiser.

There are other parents who overdramatize, overprotect, over-explain. Every possible hazard is described in gory detail, every act cautioned against.

Grass should never be walked on because it may be full of rusty nails lying in wait for bare feet. Dogs are always noisy, rough, dirty, and apt to bite. Doors and drawers are just traps for fingers. Rain means there will be thunder and lightning—or the rainstorm might even turn into a tornado.

Johnny is cautioned, "Don't climb that. You'll fall." "Let me carry the glass. You'll break it and cut yourself!" "Don't"—"Be careful"—"Watch out."

Johnny is soon so full of horror stories, so overloaded with words, so smothered by protection that he becomes a passive onlooker at life, afraid to commit himself to any new experience.

We mention these parental behaviors because they are observed so frequently in our society. For that reason it is probably good to repeat some of the most basic principles of effective parenting:

1. Be prepared.

Try to anticipate problems if possible. Many unpleasant situations could be avoided if appropriate preventive measures had been taken. For example, if you anticipate bad behavior from Youngster while shopping in the grocery store, be sure to talk with her about what is acceptable behavior *before* you leave for the store.

2. Be specific.

Even though a parent knows what bad behavior is, a child may not. Therefore, be as specific as possible in describing these actions.

3. Be fair.

As far as possible, make known to the child in advance what specific reward will be given for good behavior and what specific punishment will follow bad behavior.

4. Be consistent.

Although a parent may be in a good mood one day and in a bad mood the next, children are not able to "read" these feelings. So it is important for parents to maintain consistent behavior from one day to the next and from one situation to another.

Developing effective parenting skills is not easy. It is an endeavor that demands constant effort. But the effort is worthwhile because it will help a child become socially well-adjusted. It will also increase the joy of parenting.■

Make-believe

Make-believe play is one of the best ways for a child to practice language skills.

Pretending also helps him understand events by re-creating them and then talking about them. He can alter a stressful memory by imagining a pleasant one. He can play out the roles of different family members. This kind of activity is vital in establishing his own identity and learning to be a member of his family and society.

While he pretends he also discovers how to manage some of his hostile feelings, particularly those which do not receive parental approval. He may even be heard "reprimanding" a stuffed animal for misbehavior in a tone of voice that sounds remarkably like Mom or Dad!

What props are useful for make-believe? Clothes (hats, scarves, gloves), a toy telephone, heavy cardboard boxes (they can become shelves, counters, cars), an old sheet, blanket or bedspread for draping over a card table, kitchen equipment (wooden spoons, bowls, pots and pans, empty plastic bottles or containers), eyeglass frames (without glass), tool chest, lunch box.

This is just a suggested starter list of ideas. It is not meant for just one day but for many make-believe performances. As parents watch their child engaged in make-believe play they can become very creative in providing new props to stimulate these activities.

Later on Youngster may want a child-sized ironing board and iron, broom, vacuum, and play foods. Household furnishings scaled down to size are basics. Meanwhile, offer empty cans (after checking the edges for safety), boxes, containers, paper sacks.

——— **CONTINUED ON PAGE 180** ———

Selecting Good Toys

What are desirable toys for the 2 1/2- year-old? A sandbox with bucket, shovel, and spoon plus other containers of assorted sizes will provide hours of fun and lots of learning experiences.

Large peg boards also provide good learning experiences. Jumbo pegs are easy for small hands to grasp and push into the holes and they are too big to be swallowed.

The "peg board" is usually a 1/2- to 3/4-inch thick piece of crepe foam rubber which is easy to handle and soft enough that its edges won't nick the furniture.

Big sturdy cars and trucks— not the small plastic type that are easily breakable—will be much used by 2-year-olds as they travel many miles over the floors in your home.

A good sturdy wagon will last through several years of loading, hauling, and unloading.

At age 3 many children can ride a tricycle, but steering and pedalling are a little too much for one who is "just past 2."

Tip-proof kiddie cars without pedals—little riding toys which the child moves by using feet and legs—come in a variety of forms. Just be sure the wheels are far enough apart for good stability.

The kiddie car gives practice in steering and in going both backward and forward but doesn't require the coordination

Toys with which a child can actively interact will provide more fun and more educational benefit than mechanical toys (such as an electric train) that require him to be merely a passive spectator.

needed for pedalling.

A low rocking horse is a toy that provides exercise and excitement for a budding buckaroo. For safety's sake be sure the toy is stable with a low center of gravity and that your child can mount and dismount unaided.

A small table and chair will afford hours of entertainment as children imitate the family meals. It is nice to have child-size chairs and table that fit them since everything else seems to be made for adults.

Children also enjoy using a small table and chairs for other activities—arts and crafts, pretend play, etc.

The use of large crayons will stimulate an interest in colors. You can help your child differentiate between colors by naming the ones he chooses.

Scribbling with crayons also helps a 2-year-old improve eye-hand coordination. At this age a blank sheet of paper is better than a page from a coloring book. Just be sure to let your child make free and easy gestures—even if the final product may appear to you to be "messy."

Simple, well-made musical instruments—drum, toy horn, toy autoharp, xylophone or piano—will be enjoyed by Youngster while he experiments with different sounds.

Generally speaking, toys with which your child can *actively* interact (such as the ones we have just described) will provide more fun and more educational benefit than mechanical toys (such as an electric train) that require your 2-year-old to be merely a passive spectator.

Through his play with toys he discovers more about the physical world. He perceives similarities and differences between things in terms of color, weight, size, shape, odor, and taste. Yes, taste! Tasting or

mouthing is still an avenue for exploring the unfamiliar, although he uses this method much less frequently than last year.

He also uses sorting to help him classify things into a system—size, number, color. Just watch as he builds with blocks, kitchen equipment, or construction materials. He orders and controls them.

What emerges is what he has constructed; from his own head he has built what he thinks things should be like.

Be sure to leave him his creative freedom to reconstruct his world *as he perceives it*, rather than require him always to imitate your "real" world.

Since toys not only provide fun but also stimulate development, be sure to choose them carefully and wisely.

In choosing a new toy for your child keep these questions in mind:

(1) "Is this toy safe for a child under 3 years old?"

(2) "Is this toy appropriate for my child's age?"

(3) "Does this toy require my child's active involvement?"

(4) "What will my child learn from it?"

(5) "Is the toy attractive? Will it attract my child's attention?"

(5) "Will my child have fun with it?" ∎

Content and Process

Everything Youngster learns (and everything we learn, also) can be considered to be either content or process.

Content. Children learn specific facts or skills. For example, they learn the specific *fact* that it gets dark after the sun goes down, and they learn the specific *fact* that a ball bounces when you drop it.

They learn the specific *skill* of stacking one block on top of another, and they learn the specific *skill* of making marks on surfaces like walls (which sometimes makes you wish they wouldn't learn certain things!).

All this learning of facts and skills is called *content* because it is seen as an assortment of facts and skills which makes up the content of the child's "learning bag."

Process. Youngster learns more than specific facts and skills, however. She also learns process.

This kind of learning is much more advanced. We urge you to help your Youngster develop her "process learning."

What is "process learning?" Stated simply, this involves learning to apply general principles to solve practical problems.

Before we suggest specific ways of developing this extremely important ability, we will consider a concrete example of "process learning."

Let's say that Youngster has learned the specific skill of stacking large blocks on top of each other. One day she notices that you have put the cookie jar in a kitchen cabinet which is higher than she can reach. She wants a cookie, but the cookies are up high and she cannot reach them.

She moves a chair next to the kitchen counter, climbs onto the chair, then onto the counter,

opens the cabinet door, reaches into the cookie jar, and takes out a cookie.

It is precisely at this point that your Youngster has demonstrated that she is learning about *process*.

She first learned the specific skill of stacking blocks. Then she applied the same *general principle* so that she could reach the cookies by climbing from the chair to the counter to the cabinet. It is this kind of learning which we want to help Youngster expand.

How do you expand process

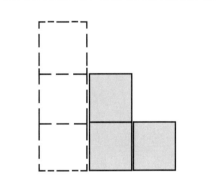

learning? Here are some ways of going about it.

Build an incomplete stairway with blocks. The first step has one block, the second has two blocks.

Give Youngster about four or five blocks and tell her to build the next (third) step in the stairs.

To do this she must be aware that her (third) step must be higher than the second step.

At first she may fail to make her step high enough. Or, more likely, she will want to use all of her blocks and will therefore make the step too high.

You can explain to her that if one of her dolls wants to walk up the stairs, the steps must have an ordered (1, 2, 3) number of blocks.

It may take many sessions

over several days before she can build the stairway accurately. The next time she climbs the stairs in your home or in some other building she may note something that she had never noted before: The steps are each the same distance apart.

If you find that you have to demonstrate the solution to Youngster, first make sure that she can imitate what you have demonstrated.

Next, you can extend the problem by building the first three steps.

Give her five or six blocks and tell her now to build the next (fourth) step.

If you observe her making mistakes, don't rush in too quickly to solve the problem. A child can sometimes learn more by trial-and-error than if a parent has provided the immediate solution.

After this task is mastered, it will be time to move on to another interesting activity.

Get three similar glasses and fill them with varying amounts of water.

Then have Youngster point to the glass with the least amount of water, then the next least until finally she points out the one with the most amount of water.

After she has mastered the task of identifying the three glasses in order, you can extend the problem with a fourth glass which has even more water it in.

In each of these "process learning" tasks Youngster has had to identify some general principle which she could apply to solve a specific problem.

There is no need to be unduly concerned, however, if your child doesn't appear to immediately learn all about content and process. Every child needs a great deal of experience and practice for learning to occur.

Sometimes her learning will take place when she is practicing alone after you have interacted with her.■

CONTINUED FROM PAGE 175

security that will enhance your child's intellectual and emotional growth.

There are a number of ways in which parents can create an orderly environment in the home:

(1) **Provide some order for your child's clothes.** Have a special place for Youngster's clothes. Even though she won't immediately imitate the good habits you are teaching, you are using this opportunity to help her learn little by little about order.

(2) **Provide some order for toys**. Make boxes and shelves available for playthings to be sorted and separated. Just as you organize your own cupboards and closets, so Youngster's "tools" should be organized and not junked together randomly.

(3) **Toys that are not currently in use should be stored out of sight in a box.** A child gets bored easily if she sees the same toys every day. But she will be thrilled when you bring back an "old friend" that has been hidden in the storage box.

(4) **Provide for the order of space, particularly if you have more than one child and limited area.** Decide what goes where—doll corner here, clay play there. You will find fewer conflicts when the territory is divided in advance. After all, in your own world you have a place for cooking, another for watching television, etc.

(5) **Provide for the order of time.** You teach your child the order of time by providing some regularity to her daily life. Plan your meals at the same time each day so that the family eats together and meals are pleasurable. This will help Youngster become sensitive to time order so that she can learn to anticipate events, to plan ahead, or learn to postpone until later what she is currently involved in.

Bedtime is consistently the same as is the sequence leading up to it—the bedtime story helps her to anticipate a happy experience. Such well-established habits will make Youngster's days more predictable and secure.∎

CONTINUED FROM PAGE 177

Also real foods like carrots, apples, potatoes, and onions can be "purchased" in the child's "store," cooked in the child's "oven," and then served at mealtime.

Youngster will be very "busy" in these activities. He also will be very serious about this "work" he is doing. It is important for parents to let him enter fully into his activity without making fun of him.

If you doubt the value of make-believe, just watch the serious expression on a 2-year-old's face as he helps "wash" the family car.

It is by participating in this world of make-believe that Youngster learns to participate later in the world around him.∎

Dear Growing Child:

"I've been receiving Growing Child for two years now and I've thoroughly enjoyed it. The articles have really helped me through some questioning times.

"It has also helped me to see the important role that we as parents play in raising a positive, responsible, and loving child. This insight has helped me have a more positive, loving, and encouraging attitude toward my son. Thank you!"

Sheila T.
Clayton, NC

www.growingchild.com

Contributing Authors

Phil Bach, O.D., Ph.D.
Miriam Bender, Ph.D.
Joseph Braga, Ed.D.
Laurie Braga, Ph.D.
George Early, Ph.D.
Liam Grimley, Ph.D.
Robert Hannemann, M.D., F.A.A.P.
Sylvia Kottler, M.S.
Bill Peterson, Ph.D.

Growing Child, Inc.
P.O. Box 620
Lafayette, Indiana 47902
Telephone: 1-800-927-7289
©2005 Growing Child, Inc.

Next Month

- *Unpredictable Is the Word for Two-and-a-half!*
- *"I Had It First"*
- *Hang On—But Don't Get Hung Up*

Growing Child.

Unpredictable Is The Word for Two-and-a-half!

Many people who study and work with young children agree that the period around 2 1/2 can be very exasperating. You are no doubt finding it also to be one of the funniest. Just keep your sense of humor well shined-up, draw on your hidden reserves of patience and objectivity, and both you and your child will weather this stormy period successfully.

Two-and-a-half has a well-earned reputation for going to extremes—sometimes shifting without warning. Contradictory as this may seem, Two-and-a-half has her own reasons for being so changeable. This is a *transitional* age. Youngster is just discovering opposites and alternate choices of action. Her understanding of commands such as come and go, run and stop, give and take, grasp and release, push and pull, attack and retreat is still so evenly balanced that she is as yet unable to decide which way to go.

Her capacity for voluntary choice is weak. She is too inexperienced to make a reasonable choice and stick to it. She learns by doing—so she may sometimes try to go both ways at the same time. This is not stubbornness. She just cannot yet weigh the relative advantage of one choice to the exclusion of the other.

This same quality characterizes her physical activities. Two-and-a-half doesn't yet have good control of opposing groups of muscles. She tends to squeeze too tightly,

and let go too suddenly. When being very cautious, as in building a tower of blocks, she may place one block carefully, then release it suddenly by spreading her fingers very wide. She enjoys building *and* knocking down!

Two-and-a-half has not learned to unwind or relax easily before going to sleep. She may demand a long and complicated bedtime ritual in order to prepare for sleep. Once in bed she may talk to herself for some time before falling asleep.

This same difficulty is exhibited in toileting. At 2 1/2, a child may not easily relax her bladder sphincter voluntarily—and then may withhold too long. A child who has generally been "dry" during the day since age 2 may begin to have "accidents." She may play so intently that she ignores the mounting bladder pressure until it is too late.

Characteristically, Two-and-a-half cannot modulate her social

behavior. She is going through the growing pains of learning about opposites, and the developmental method of learning is to try *both*. She is a sort of pre-school edition of a confused adolescent. Yet by this very process, Two-and-a-half is finding her way. She is learning to choose *one* by trying *two* or more.

Our lives are a series of choices—some simple, some complex. For example, Mommy may try on a number of dresses before choosing the one that feels right. Youngster is taking her first tentative steps toward meeting life's challenges. She does this by learning to choose between opposites, and to choose she must sometimes try *both*.

These characteristic behaviors are not equally marked in all children. They are particularly pronounced in very active children, but less conspicuous among more placid children. It is relatively normal for a child of this age to show swings between the following extremes:

From intense activity to quiet passivity, sometimes accompanied by thumb sucking.

From boisterousness to shyness.

From a keen desire to possess an object to sudden indifference once she has obtained it.

From loud demands for food to rejection of it when offered.

From loud laughter, shrieks

CONTINUED ON PAGE 186

Language and Music

It shouldn't be necessary to structure every moment of Youngster's play. However, in bad weather, cold climates or periods of illness, when children are indoors a lot, they sometimes need ideas for constructive play.

The 2- to 3-year-old loves to listen to music, particularly cassettes or CDs. His preference will likely be for music with a strong, definite beat to which he may respond with total body movement.

It will not be unusual for him to want to hear the same music or stories-to-music over and over again.

If you happen to play the piano, guitar, or autoharp, you will become his favorite entertainer.

Here are some ideas you can use for creating different songs:

I. Improvised songs

These are songs you "make up" to fit a situation or a need. The words are made to fit tunes borrowed from other songs.

(1) Washing Tune: Mulberry Bush—This is how we wash our face, wash our face, wash our face;

This is how we wash our face, Before we eat our dinner.

(2) Bedtime Tune: Hey, Betty Martin—Hey, little sleepy, sleepy, sleepy;

Hey, little sleepy, it's bedtime now.

II. Counting Songs

Tune: This Old Man

This old man, he played *one*, He played knick-knack on his thumb,

Knick-knack paddy whack, give your dog a bone,

This old man came rolling home.

This old man, he played *two*,

He played knick-knack on his shoe, etc.

This old man, he played *three*, He played knick-knack on his knee, etc.

This old man, he played *four*, He played knick-knack on the floor, etc.

This old man, he played *five*, He played knick-knack on his hive, etc.

III. Chants (to be clapped, beat out, or played with homemade instrument).

Teddy Bear—originally a rope-jumping chant.

Teddy bear, teddy bear, turn around,

Teddy bear, teddy bear, touch the ground.

Teddy bear, teddy bear, show your shoe,

Teddy bear, teddy bear, better skiddoo!

——— **CONTINUED ON PAGE 186** ———

Music as Education

Music is more than just fun; it is education. As he sings along, dances, or "plays" an instrument, here are the sorts of things Youngster learns:

1. New vocabulary. Many songs, particularly folk songs and nursery tunes, repeat words or refrains over and over again.

For example, "We swing our arms so gayly, gayly; We swing our arms so gayly, all on a Saturday night."

This type of repetition strengthens associations between newly acquired words and their meaning.

2. Time sense. When swinging the arms, moving the body, or tapping an "instrument" to music, the child is exposed to time relations between musical notes. He becomes aware of order—this comes first, this comes next and this comes last.

This kind of order is important in both understanding and using speech. It is also extremely important later in learning to read. This is demonstrated by what happens to a sentence when just one word is put into a different order—"*Now*, I want to go"/"I want to go, *now*."

In addition, changes in the length of utterances, such as pauses within them, produce different patterns and thus different meanings.

For example, remember a song of the '40s, "Maresy Dotes and Dozey Dotes" ("Mares Eat Oats and Does Eat Oats"), or the prayer, "The Cross-eyed Bear" ("The Cross I'd Bear")? Finally, take the sentences, "Let's eat Mother"/"Let's eat, Mother."

The presence of word order is apparent in Youngster's own verbalization: "Here ball," "here daddy," "baby here," "dog here," or "more milk," "more up."

3. Counting. While at this age learning will be mainly by rote memory, he will learn to count from such rhymes as "One Little, Two Little, Three Little Indians."

4. Self-control. It is necessary to really listen and attend to what the song says in order to carry out the actions. When it says "clap," "jump," or "stop," he must translate what he has heard into a physical movement and clap, jump, or stop.

We urge you to make music a family affair. Before the days of television, families created their own entertainment, and singing together was very popular. Develop your own songbook from current rhythms, folk-rock, and old timers.■

The Feeling Game

Place three differently shaped toys under a blanket. They might be a small ball, a block, and a doll. Then find a fourth toy that is just like one of the hidden toys. Show her this toy and say, "There is a toy just like this under the blanket. Reach under the blanket and try to find it. But don't look, just feel."

While you hold the blanket so that Youngster's hands stay covered, encourage her to feel each toy in turn to decide which is the right one. Then she should pull out the chosen toy and see if it matches the one on top.

If she chooses correctly, you can tell her how successful she is at matching. Or give her a little reward if you are used to doing so. However, just making the match may be reward enough.

If she doesn't get the right toy, show her all three of the covered toys so she can see what a true match looks like. Then cover all three up again, mix them around and let her try again.

The Feeling Game has some advantages over matching by looking. The main advantage right now is that it slows Youngster and makes her concentrate. This is because it takes longer for hands to feel a shape than for the eyes to see it. Since the eyes can see a shape quickly, it is all too easy to take a quick look at something and then decide, even though that quick look could be wrong. But when Youngster runs her fingers over the toys, she must build up a picture of them in her mind over a period of time. She must concentrate a little longer than she would by just looking.

For another thing, the game is new and different. You can keep it fun by playing it only once or twice at a session or by changing the objects. It is best to stop with Youngster wanting more. That way she will ask you to play the game rather than vice versa.

Finally, the game encourages her to make a match between one of her senses (touch) and another (vision). This is the passing of information from one sense to another. It is a skill that helps to make human beings unique, and will be very important later in school learning.

Start with easy items so Youngster can be successful the very first time. Begin with toys that are familiar and that she can tell apart by feel. Then you can use your own judgment in varying the hidden toys in order to challenge her.

There are other variations of the game that will work as well. One is to use a single object whose name she doesn't know, but with two or three visible choices above the blanket. After feeling the covered object, she should point to the object on top that is just like the one she felt.

Another, more difficult variation is to use a single familiar object under the blanket and ask her to tell you what it is.

Since she feels only one thing in these variations she doesn't have to concentrate as long. If she answers too incorrectly, it may be better to go back to the form where three toys are hidden.■

Is Dressing Your Child Getting To Be a Real Hassle?

Dressing a 2 1/2-year-old child can be enough to try the patience of Job! His demands for independence alternate unpredictably with times of complete dependence when he goes limp like he's a doll and refuses to help.

Temper tantrums are common during dressing. A parent pushes against time and Youngster balks or dawdles.

Running away as soon as Mommy starts dressing him is a favorite game of children of this age. Two-and-a-half loves to be chased—and as soon as he is caught and brought back, he runs away again.

If caught, picked up and forcibly returned to the dressing spot he may throw a temper tantrum. Or he may pull, tug, squirm, and wiggle until his parent is totally exasperated.

Be smart and change his game by having him follow you. For example, as you move toward the bathroom, you might say: "Come to the bathroom when you are ready to get dressed." Then go to the bathroom. This usually brings Two-and-a-half running almost immediately, crying "I'm ready! I'm ready!"

When he finds you in the bathroom, quietly and calmly *close the door*—even lock it if Two-and-a-half is really fast moving.

Dressing may also be easier if he is placed on the lid of the toilet seat or on a clothes hamper. However, be prepared to return him to the floor if his activity makes it likely that he will fall.

As soon as he finds you are going to be firm with him, he is likely to be more cooperative so that he can go back to play as soon as dressing is over.■

"I Had It First"

Now that your child can talk, she will sometimes use language in order to get her own way.

When parents hear one child say to another, "I had it first," they know the statement is an open declaration of war.

Not surprisingly, parents are sometimes confused about what to do when their child quarrels with another child. If they seek advice from other parents, they probably will hear conflicting solutions that range from unbridled permissiveness to strict authoritarianism. And if they read what parenting "experts" have written about how to handle children's quarrels, they will find an equally bewildering array of opinions.

How then can you decide as a parent what you are going to do?

Three things will help you to decide what to do in resolving children's conflicts: (1) Knowledge of normal child development; (2) Knowledge about a variety of different strategies for dealing with behavioral problems; and (3) The ability to apply this knowledge to yourself, your child, and the specific situation with which you are dealing.

(1) One of the main reasons for *Growing Child* is to provide parents with the knowledge they need about typical child development. So our readers should be very much aware that conflicts and quarrels are a normal part of growing up.

Getting along with others and sharing one's possessions are skills that a 2 1/2-year-old child is just beginning to learn. Sometimes these skills can be learned by the child herself through everyday interaction with other children. At other times a parent's direct intervention is needed. Physical fighting and scratching or biting, for example, require immediate parental direction.

(2) When the time comes for direct intervention, it is helpful for the parent to have knowledge about a variety of different strategies for dealing with behavioral problems. Otherwise there will be an inclination to use the same strategy for every situation. Unfortunately a plan that works well in one circumstance may be too strong in a different situation or too weak to be effective in a third.

The books for parents listed below present different strategies for dealing with children's problems. Even though you may disagree with the opinions expressed in one or more of these books, we recommend that you at least become aware of alternatives that other parents have found helpful.

(3) A parent needs to consider how and when to apply the parenting knowledge acquired.

CONTINUED ON PAGE 185

Reading List

Growing Child seeks to provide helpful information for parents in a unique manner by following a child's development month by month. Parents sometimes ask advice about other reading materials that might also be helpful. This is a list of some good books about child rearing which should be available at a local bookstore or your public library.

Brazelton, T. Berry (1984), **To Listen to a Child**. Addison-Wesley.

Berends, Polly Berrien (1987), **Whole Child/Whole Parent**. Harper & Row.

Bush, Richard (1980), **A Parent's Guide to Child Therapy**. Delacorte Press.

Calladine, Carole and Andrew (1979), **Raising Brothers and Sisters Without Raising the Roof**. Winston Press.

Crary, Elizabeth (1979), **Without Spanking or Spoiling**. Parenting Press.

Elkind, David (1981), **The Hurried Child: Growing Up Too Fast Too Soon**. Addison-Wesley.

Ferber, Richard (1985), **Solve Your Child's Sleep Problems**. Simon & Schuster.

Kaban, Barb (1979), **Choosing Toys for Children from Birth to Age Five**. Shocken Books.

Lansky, Vicki (1980), **Best Practical Parenting Tips**. Meadowbrook Press.

Leach, Penelope (1985), **Your Baby and Child From Birth to Age Five**. Knopf.

LeShan, Eda (1985), **When Your Child Drives You Crazy**. St. Martin's Press.

Lickona, Thomas (1983), **Raising Good Children**. Bantam Books.

Miller, Karen (1984), **Things To Do With Toddlers and Twos**. Telshare.

Shelov, Stephen P., Editor (1991), **Caring For Your Baby and Young Child: Birth To Age 5.** Bantam Books.

Shiff, Eileen, Editor (1987), **Experts Advise Parents: A Guide To Raising Loving, Responsible Children**. Delacorte Press.

Smith, Helen Wheeler (1982), **A Survival Handbook for Preschool Mothers**. Cambridge.

White, Burton L. (1988), **Educating the Infant and Toddler**. Lexington Books. ∎

Hang On—But Don't Get Hung Up!

ost of us at *Growing Child* are parents, too. We know what it is to worry about how well our children are doing. We also know how good it is to enjoy and savor our children's growing experiences.

In every child's growing up there are ups and downs. One day you think he'll surely be President. The next day you think you'll be lucky if he manages to stay out of jail. These wild swings between good and bad feelings about your child are all part of the business of being a parent.

Being a parent is a truly great experience, but at times, it can cause you exasperation! May we assure you such wild swings in your feelings are perfectly normal. We know that you sometimes wonder if you're doing the right thing because we have wondered the same thing about ourselves.

What we're really trying to say is that we do not write for *Growing Child* in a vacuum. We are with you in your suffering and your delight because we have been where you are now. We know the joys of seeing our children and grandchildren grow and learn. We also know the agony of how many mistakes we have made as parents. These feelings, some good and some painful, are all part of being parents. It "goes with the territory."

Our practical advice to you is simply this:"Hang on, but don't get hung up." Hang on because: (1) You know that almost every parent has felt what you are feeling now; (2) There are so many good things about your child's growing and development which can give you pleasure; (3) One or two problems now are not going to affect your child forever.

Hang on by: (1) Living with your child's developmental problems from day to day; (2) Enjoying him, laughing with him, holding him close when the dark moments close in upon both of you; (3) Simply getting through the ordinary routines of each day. If you ever feel it's getting too difficult for you, talk to a close friend or other parents who can share their own experiences.

But, whatever you do, please do not get "hung up." Do not mentally bite your fingernails or waste your emotional energy in wondering if you are a "perfect parent," whatever that may mean.

Do not hover over your child. Do not constantly ask yourself, "Is he doing all right?"

Above all, do not pressure your child into performing at ever-higher levels. Do not make him feel that you love him *only* if he performs well. He should know that you love him because he is your child.

He belongs to you. He is important to you. The knowledge that he matters, that he is loved for himself alone, is the greatest gift you can give your child. But you cannot give your child this gift if you are hung up over how well he is doing.

Above all, let Youngster know in a hundred different ways that you love him. Show him that he matters and that he belongs. Show him that he is a vital part of your world. If you do this we think you will greatly improve his chances for success in school and also in the world beyond school.■

CONTINUED FROM PAGE 184

Should the parent immediately intervene as the all-knowing, all-powerful authority figure? Or should the parent get the child to assume responsibility for solving her own conflict problems?

Deciding which strategy to use will involve consideration of your own needs, those of your child, and the specific characteristics of each particular situation.

Too often parents don't realize that they have their own inner feelings and needs when trying to settle children's quarrels. Frequently these quarrels bother the parents more than they bother the children involved. Becoming aware of our own inner needs as parents is a first prerequisite to effective intervention in children's conflicts.

We must also be aware of the individual characteristics of each child involved. Conflicts in which one child is always the aggressor and the other child is always the victim will require more long-term interventions by the parent than a child's spur-of-the-moment outburst which is sometimes quickly resolved without any parental involvement. Knowing the unique characteristics of the children involved is therefore a prerequisite in dealing with their conflicts.

It is also important to consider any special characteristics of the situation. For example, some conflicts are more likely to arise before bedtime when children are tired. Being aware of the specific circumstances under which a conflict arises can be helpful not only in resolving it but also in preventing a similar recurrence in the future.

In short, there is no one solution that will resolve all children's conflicts in all circumstances. But parents who have some basic knowledge of child development and of different intervention strategies and who are aware of the factors involved in applying that knowledge are the ones best equipped to make a decision about what they will do when they hear their child scream, "I had it first!"■

CONTINUED FROM PAGE 182

IV. Producing rhythm

Youngster also likes to make music, particularly with home-made musical instruments. Some examples:

(1) Cymbals—use two flat pot lids.

(2) Razzle dazzle—use dried peas or macaroni placed in a flour shaker.

(3) Timpani—use wooden spoons for striking metal pie tins and containers from canned goods.

(4) Fife—use a paper towel cylinder into which you have punched five small holes in a row down the top of the cylinder. Next cover one end with wax paper which has been securely taped with cellophane.

Now when Youngster vocalizes into the tube, the sound will be amplified. Should he cover some of the holes on the cylinder with his fingers, he will discover that he can produce different tones.

(5) Maracas—Use an empty salt box into which you place small stones and tape it closed. The maracas can be thumped or shaken.

(6) Drums—Use an empty 46 oz. round juice can or gallon paint can. Remove both ends. From a sheet of flexible plastic material such as vinyl, cut out two identical large circles, large enough to cover the ends of the can.

Next, punch holes around the edges of the circles. Cover the ends of the can with the circles and lace them tightly to each other with a leather shoelace, lacing through the holes back and forth along the side of the container.

(7) Harmonica—Use a large clean comb covered with tissue paper which when blown with the mouth slightly open makes a real brassy sound.

(8) Guitar—Use the bottom of a shoe box with eight to 10 colored rubber bands of varying sizes stretched across it. It can be plucked with finger or teaspoon.∎

CONTINUED FROM PAGE 181

and screams to whispering or talking in a low monotone.

From loud demands of "me do it!" to dawdling.

These extremes of behavior are not necessarily mood swings. They are fluctuations due to Youngster's narrow base of experience. She must try both extremes to find out which one works best for her at any given moment. Only by trying out the extremes will she eventually find a "middle way."

Parental "management" of problems, rather than overly strict discipline techniques, will lead to better parent-child relationships during this period. Forcing her into a given course of behavior is apt to bring on a temper tantrum. With a better understanding of her present confusions and some wise anticipation of problems, she can be led to *want* to do what you desire.

So, love her, enjoy her unpredictability, and help her learn from experience during this complex developmental period.∎

www.growingchild.com

Contributing Authors

Phil Bach, O.D., Ph.D.
Miriam Bender, Ph.D.
Joseph Braga, Ed.D.
Laurie Braga, Ph.D.
George Early, Ph.D.
Liam Grimley, Ph.D.
Robert Hannemann, M.D., F.A.A.P.
Sylvia Kottler, M.S.
Bill Peterson, Ph.D.

Growing Child, Inc.
P.O. Box 620
Lafayette, Indiana 47902
Telephone: 1-800-927-7289
©2005 Growing Child, Inc.

Dear Growing Child:

"Each month I am grateful for your concern and efforts which help me understand my children and parenting better. I wish I'd had you when my oldest son was a baby!"

Sondra C.
Yamhill, OR

Next Month

- *Playing with Toy Guns*
- *A Special Time*

Growing Child®

A Special Time

Youngster's major incentive for language development right now is her need to communicate something to somebody. Parents should be a real audience, without pretending, even if the child produces only a few short sentences at a time. It is from these informal utterances that more formal language will eventually emerge.

Many parents think that because they are with the child most of the time, they, in fact, provide her an audience.

However, if one examines the routine of a typical home, Mom and Dad are involved with answering the door or telephone, washing clothes and dishes, making beds, or preparing dinner.

What is really needed is a "Special Time," however brief. This special time differs from the rest of the day because it belongs to Youngster exclusively. She isn't interrupting your work just to get attention.

Special Time is "special" because it is entirely devoted to listening and attending to the child. Of course, this means privacy—no answering phones or checking on food in the oven.

Special Time differs from the rest of the day because it belongs to Youngster exclusively. It is entirely devoted to listening and attending to her.

How much time is required? Only about fifteen minutes. That's about the maximum that parent and child can hold each other's attention at this age.

It is good to plan for Special Time:

(1) Explain simply what it is—you both will be together and she can tell you or show you what she wants to do.

It is very important that you do not direct the program. Otherwise you will defeat the objective.

When *she* must tell you what *she* wants to do, her mind is more active formulating and expressing her ideas and wishes.

(2) Help her to better understand the concept of "time."

If you have an alarm clock, set it to go off when the time limit is reached. Or show her the face of the clock and point to where Special Time begins and ends.

If during the day it appears that the child wants your attention and you are too busy, remind her about the approach-

ing Special Time. If it is a regular habit, she will learn to wait.

Because all good things end too soon, prepare her for the end of Special Time.

Even if she has no awareness of "five more minutes," continued daily use of such a warning will alert her to the fact that it is almost over.

Thus, in planning Special Time you are educating Youngster to a temporal (time) order: the anticipation of Special Time each day, the length of time she will have your undivided attention, and the reminder about when it will be over.

(3) It may be necessary to set limits on what can or cannot be done during Special Time, especially if the child is inclined to want to do the same thing, such as hearing the same story every day for two weeks. You may still allow her to choose and still set limits if you tell her honestly, "I'm tired of that book. Let's do something different in Special Time."

(4) As Youngster grows older, she will want to talk more—to express her feelings and to know that you are truly listening. Prepare yourself to be a good audience; this means active listening.

(5) Above all, make Special Time a good learning experience for your child by making it a fun time to be together. In that way, she will look forward to this Special Time. Children learn more easily and quickly when the learning experience is an enjoyable one.■

Playing with Toy Guns

hould I allow my child to play with toy guns? It's a question parents of young children frequently ask.

In the family where such forms of play are not tolerated, the troubling question still arises whenever the child visits a friend whose family has purchased toy rifles, revolvers, or laser guns.

In deciding what to do in such circumstances, parents need to consider three factors: The function of play in their child's development, the socially accepted aspects of aggressive play, and the "forbidden fruit" phenomenon.

Although many parents may think of their child's play as a time for "goofing off" rather than for learning, it is during play activities that some very important learning takes place.

Parents will have noted, for example, that during infancy it was mainly through enjoyable play activities that their infant learned to explore and eventually manipulate the objects in his environment.

Similarly, in the preschool years, eye-hand coordination and socialization skills are learned and developed during play activities.

In purchasing a toy, a most important question for parents to consider is what their child will learn from this new object. For example, with skill-building toys, the child will acquire and develop new skills or improve those already learned. It should be obvious that with aggressive-type toys, the child will learn aggressive-type behaviors.

Even though parents may teach their child to be peace-loving and respectful of other children, they are nevertheless faced with the reality that the environment in which their child is living is not always one of peace and harmony. That's why

Many parents have found that children can be endlessly inventive in devising ways to construct their own "guns" using a variety of materials and methods that vary from a simple stick to more complicated versions.

the socially accepted aspects of aggressive play need to be considered.

In our society some forms of aggressive behavior—such as assertiveness, competitiveness, and physical contact sports—are not only socially acceptable but are even encouraged and rewarded.

In teaching a child not to be unduly aggressive, parents should also consider teaching him necessary skills, including self-defense, for survival in the real world.

A word of caution to parents who may try to forbid their child from ever playing with an aggressive-type play object, such as a toy gun: Overzealous efforts may backfire. By dealing too harshly

with the problem, a child may become unduly attracted to the "forbidden fruit" which the parents have condemned.

Many parents have found that children can be endlessly inventive in devising ways to construct their own "guns" using a variety of materials and methods that vary from a simple stick to more complicated versions.

The most effective way for parents to deal with the problem is to approach it in a calm and reasonable manner. They must first decide what are the most important values they wish to transmit to their child. They must then explain these values in a manner that will be meaningful to him.

For example, many young children find it difficult to share their possessions with others. Parents can teach a child the value of sharing by pointing out the many ways in which he was made happy because others were willing to share with him. After all, children first learn about sharing by receiving rather than by giving.

Later, when children learn to treat others as they would want to be treated, they begin to express the value of sharing in their lives.

If parents find that their child has violated the values taught, they should wait, if possible, to discuss the matter in private rather than try to deal with it in public which would only humiliate the child.

Children are more likely to learn from what a parent *does* than from what a parent *says*. Parents who exhibit aggressive behavior in the home are likely to have an aggressive child. And parents who exhibit loving, caring, and peaceful behavior are likely to have a child who ultimately will exhibit those same behaviors. ■

Father Involvement

So much attention is naturally focused on the mother's role in child rearing that fathers may sometimes feel uncomfortable or out of place in this process. The role of a mother is obviously very special during pregnancy, giving birth, nursing the baby, and generally taking care of a young child's needs.

Nowadays, however, fathers are becoming more actively involved, not only in supporting the mother, but also in providing direct child care. At the same time, psychologists are discovering that fathers have a unique and very important role—different from that of the mother—in a child's development, especially during the toddler years.

A study of history can help to understand some changes in society that have had an impact on the role of fathers. Prior to the industrial revolution, many fathers were able to remain in close daily contact with their families as they worked on the land or had a home-based trade such as blacksmith, cobbler, or carpenter. In this way they were able to take an active part in day-to-day family affairs.

At the same time, children had more immediate access to their fathers during the day, sometimes working alongside Dad either in the fields or at his trade.

With the coming of the industrial revolution, however, fathers (and sometimes mothers) were required more and more to work away from home. From early morning until late in the evening, they were separated from daily family life. Mothers, who more frequently remained at home, became their children's primary caregivers. This eventually resulted in what sociologists have described as the "feminiza-

tion" of the parent's role.

Two recent changes in our society have had a significant impact on family life, namely, the women's movement and the age of computer technology.

With more mothers working outside the home in recent years, it is not surprising that many fathers are now taking a more active part in raising their children.

Examples of more active father involvement in family affairs can be found even before a baby is born. More and more fathers are now attending pre-birth classes with the mother. Also, the presence of fathers in the delivery room, either as coach or as supportive observer—a practice that was forbidden in most hospitals before the 1970s—is now clearly on the increase.

Studies have found that when a father is present during labor and delivery, the mother is likely to report lower levels of pain, receive less medication and is less likely to experience complications.

The coming of the computer age has also had an important impact on family life. Many parents—both fathers and mothers—can now perform at least part of their work at home where they can be in closer contact with

their children. Thus the potential for fathers to become more actively involved in child rearing is greater today than it was just a generation ago.

Recent studies indicate that when both fathers and mothers are together involved in child rearing, they both more often express positive feelings toward their children. Ultimately, children are the ones who benefit the most from these positive relationships.

Psychologists have also been interested in determining if there are differences in children's attachment to fathers and mothers. It has been found that from the age of 8 months—when strong attachments are first observed in children—they show greater attachment to both their fathers and mothers than to strangers.

Between 8 and 24 months an interesting difference emerges. In times of fear or stress, a child will more likely turn to the mother for comfort than to the father. In general, mothers are relied on in matters involving trust, sensitivity, and intimacy.

During the toddler years, however, a father's unique role becomes particularly important. At this age, as children strive for more autonomous behavior, they seek and receive more support from the father in striving for independence. They still rely on their mother when they are in need of comforting and nurturance.

Both of these types of experiences—the striving for independence and the continued need for nurturance—are important aspects of every child's development. The different roles of the father and mother thus complement one another in this developmental process.

Since it has been found that

——— CONTINUED ON PAGE 190 ———

———— CONTINUED FROM PAGE 189 ————

a child reacts differently to the father and mother, are there then differences in parenting styles between fathers and mothers?

It has been found that the differences are indeed sometimes quite substantial. Whereas mothers are more likely to engage in quiet, peaceful interactions such as smiling, talking or soothing, fathers are more likely to engage in more physical roughhousing with the child.

While the father is often perceived as the ultimate authority figure in the family, ("Wait until your father hears about this!") his interactions with the child are generally more playful. And 2-year-olds actively seek these playful interactions with the father. They particularly enjoy playing simple games such as hide-and-seek.

Through these playful activities, children will generally experience a broad range of emotions that they must learn to handle, laughing hysterically at one moment and being on the verge of tears at another.

During these playful experiences children not only learn better control of their emotions, but they also develop an important ability to "read" the non-verbal messages of others, as conveyed, for example, by Dad's facial expression or tone of voice. These lessons that are learned from interacting with Dad will prove most useful later when interacting with other adults or with peers.

There are, of course, variations in father-child relationships. It has been found, for example, that fathers with low self-esteem have a more negative impact on their children than mothers with low self-esteem.

A father's work environment can also influence father-child interactions. A father whose job provides a great deal of autonomy is more likely to encourage

independent behavior in his children. On the contrary, a father whose job is highly supervised with little or no autonomy will expect a high level of conformity in his children.

Sometimes fathers experience difficulty in interacting with their children at the end of the day's work. While Dad is ready and eager to read the child a story or play a game, he may find that Toddler is neither ready nor willing to engage in such interaction.

It may take the child some time to adjust from being with Mom or another caregiver throughout the day. It's wisest for Dad to let the child set the pace for their interaction, allowing it to unfold naturally rather than trying to create "organized joy." Under these

circumstances, children will usually give some indication when they are ready and eager for interaction with Dad.

If Mom has been with the child throughout the day, it may help the father-child interaction if she can find someplace else to go. This can be her time to enjoy a break while father and child spend some quality time together, giving one another their undivided, loving attention.

In summary, although the industrial revolution caused many fathers to be removed from the daily lives of their families, recent changes in our society have resulted in more active father involvement in the home. Father involvement in child rearing not only enriches a young child's life, it also enhances the lives of all members of a family.■

Single Parents

 note of clarification may be in order for single parents. While this article deals with father involvement in a child's development, it is recognized that, in today's world, there are many single parents engaged in child rearing without the support of a spouse.

Since it is not the purpose of this article to make single mothers feel guilty because of the absence of the child's father, the following points should be made clear:

1. A loving single-parent home is a preferable environment for a young child than one in which abusive relationships exist;

2. Single parents who raise a child alone under such circumstances deserve special recognition and encouragement;

3. It is often possible for a loving surrogate "father-figure" to fulfill a father's role in a child's life;

4. Children who grow up in a loving home environment can be extremely resilient in adapting to the conditions under which they live their lives. In their case, love seems to conquer all!■

Development of Sex-Role Concepts

Am I a boy or am I a girl? Will I always be the same? Why do boys and girls play differently?

What are some other differences between boys and girls?

These and other questions about children's development of gender and sex-role concepts have been studied extensively by researchers in recent years.

In order to understand the research findings, the reader will need to be familiar with some definitions that are commonly used. (See "Definitions" in box.)

Research studies have revealed that:

• Most children between 1 1/2 and 2 years of age are aware of their own "gender identity" as either a "boy" or "girl."

• Children between 2 1/2 and 3 years of age are also generally able to correctly label the gender of adults and other children.

This ability to accurately label "male" or "female" is of course only a first step in the child's development of gender concept. The child's response is frequently based on the type of toy another child is playing with, the type of clothing worn (pants or dress), or the length and style of the other person's hair.

As society changes, with some fathers having long hair, and with some mothers having short hair and wearing a shirt, tie, and pin-stripe suit, these cues to gender identity are becoming less clear for the young child.

Parents can easily test their child's ability to distinguish between the genders by pointing to pictures in a magazine and asking, "Which one is a woman/girl?" or "Which one is a man/boy?"

Once children have some initial grasp of gender identity, they begin to differentiate between the attitudes and behaviors associated with each gender, namely, the socially appropriate "sex-role stereotypes."

In each family, parents ultimately determine the values, attitudes, and behaviors they consider appropriate for their son or daughter. Being aware of important research findings will generally help parents provide well-informed guidance to their child.

Recent studies have found that:

• Between 2 and 3 years of age both boys and girls consider that girls like to cook, clean house, and play with dolls, whereas boys play with cars and trucks, use tools, and build things.

Some sex-role differences between boys and girls are, of course, biologically predetermined. Other differences are the result of cultural influences in the child's environment. Family, peers, and the media are three important influences which need to be considered.

(1) Recent research studies on *the family* have indicated that:

• During the preschool years parents generally provide both boys and girls with similar amounts of warmth and affection.

• Mothers did not appear to be concerned if their son or daughter played with a "masculine" or "feminine" toy, but fathers were found to disapprove strongly only when their sons played with girls' toys, even in homes where the parents expressed belief in gender equality.

• Among mothers, differences have been found between children of mothers who were homemakers and of those who worked outside the home. Both boys and girls of mothers who worked outside the home were found to have less rigidly stereotyped views of male and female roles. For example, these children considered it appropriate for women to be lawyers or doctors and for men to cook or clean house.

(2) Besides the family, the *peer group* has an important influence

——— CONTINUED ON PAGE 192 ———

Definitions

These are definitions for some of the terms most used in research studies dealing with sexual development:

Gender concept: The child's overall understanding of what it means to be either male or female—an understanding which progressively develops over many years.

Gender identity: The first step in the development of the gender concept by which the child can correctly label people, including him- or herself, as either male or female.

Gender constancy: Recognition that a person's gender will remain the same even if other aspects of the person may change (such as a man wearing a woman's wig and dress).

Sex-role concept: The child's overall understanding of differences in appropriate attitudes and behavior of a male or female in society.

Sex-role stereotypes: The attitudes and behaviors widely considered in society as appropriate or inappropriate for each gender.∎

————— CONTINUED FROM PAGE 191 —————

on the child's development of gender concept. It has been found that:

• Children as young as 2 1/2 years of age show a preference for same-sex playmates.

• They will also spend more time watching same-sex peers than opposite-sex peers.

• There are marked differences between boys and girls in their play activities even before 3 years of age. When boys play with other boys they generally engage in loud and vigorous physical games, whereas when girls play together they usually prefer quieter, more artistic activities.

(3) *Television and children's books* also influence a child's thinking about male and female roles. The U. S. Commission on Civil Rights has found that:

• Role models presented on television are strongly sex-typed. Men and boys are more often shown as strong, capable problem-solvers. Women and girls, on the other hand, are portrayed frequently as weak, dependent and conforming persons.

• Even cartoons convey a strong message to the child about sex-role stereotypes.

(4) Studies have also been done of *cross-sex preference*— boys who say they would rather be girls or girls who say they would rather be boys—a phenomenon that sometimes causes great concern to parents. These studies have found that:

• A child generally does not develop the concept of "gender constancy" until 5 years of age or older. Prior to that stage children do not have a clear notion that they will remain the same sex throughout life. Nor do they understand, for example, that wearing a dress does not necessarily make a person a woman.

• In our society there are more girls than boys who exhibit cross-sex preference.

This finding may not be too surprising in an age when women are seeking greater equality with men. Parents have also generally been more tolerant of "tomboy" behavior in girls than of "effeminate" qualities in boys. Parents are often particularly upset if their preschool son expresses a desire to be a girl. Yet at this age this may simply be a child's way of expressing a desire for more emotional warmth and affection.

As indicated earlier, parents ultimately determine the values, attitudes, and behaviors they consider appropriate for their son or daughter. In making that determination they need to take into account the child's own progressive development of gender and sex-role concepts.

They also need to be aware of important environmental influences such as family, peers, and the media. Helping a child to develop appropriate gender and sex-role concepts is a most important element in the overall development of your child's positive self-concept.■

www.growingchild.com

Contributing Authors

Phil Bach, O.D., Ph.D.
Miriam Bender, Ph.D.
Joseph Braga, Ed.D.
Laurie Braga, Ph.D.
George Early, Ph.D.
Liam Grimley, Ph.D.
Robert Hannemann, M.D., F.A.A.P.
Sylvia Kottler, M.S.
Bill Peterson, Ph.D.

Growing Child, Înc.
P.O. Box 620
Lafayette, Indiana 47902-0620
Telephone: 1-800-927-7289
©2005 Growing Child, Inc.

Next Month

■ *Why Children Misbehave*
■ *Looking, Listening, Learning*
■ *Needs and Wants*

Growing Child®

Dealing with Misbehavior

More than a few parents have expressed their feelings about their child by saying, "I wish I knew what to do about my child's behavior." It would be nice to have a simple solution—like a magic wand—for parents to use when they feel frustrated by their child's misbehavior.

Unfortunately, the reasons why children misbehave are too complicated for a simple solution. We become aware of this complexity when we try to change the way a parent and child interact. For example, most of us can appreciate how hard it is sometimes for a parent to control his or her temper after a child has misbehaved.

Even a simple analysis of such a negative interaction between parent and child would have to consider the characteristics of the parent, the child, and the specific situation in which the interaction occurred.

To make matters more complicated, each of these characteristics undergoes change from year to year, from week to week, and even from one time of day to another. It is also important to bear in mind that:

1) What works for one parent in disciplining a child may not work for another parent with the same child.

2) What proves to be an effective discipline strategy with one child may be ineffective or inappropriate for another child in the same family.

3) An approach that has worked well in one situation may not bring about the same desired result with the same child in a different situation.

How can *Growing Child* help you deal with misbehavior?

First, by reminding you that it is normal for young children to misbehave occasionally. It also is normal for parents to make mistakes and to lose their temper from time to time.

If you are thinking that you must be the only parent who can't handle misbehavior, then it is time to relax and realize you are not alone. Don't be too hard on yourself—try to take a good look at the situation. Parents who can laugh at themselves are more likely to have a child who is happy and well-adjusted.

If you feel an extreme sense of "aloneness" in dealing with your child's misbehavior problems, you might consider joining a parent support group or parent education class in your area. Sharing concerns with a good friend or listening to the problems other parents are having can help remove that sense of aloneness.

Second, we want to help by making you familiar with a number of different approaches for dealing with discipline problems. For example, in "Why Children Misbehave" on page 194, we present an approach developed by Rudolf Dreikurs which many parents have found helpful.

Future issues of *Growing Child* will include other approaches that have been widely acclaimed.

By becoming familiar with a variety of strategies for dealing with misbehavior, parents will be able to choose the approach best suited to the child, the parent, and the specific situation in which the misbehavior occurred.■

Needs and Wants

Now that Youngster is capable of expressing his requests verbally, it is important for parents to be able to differentiate their child's *needs* from his *wants.*

His *needs* are the things he must have for good physical or mental health. His *wants* refer to the things he would like to have but may not need.

Needs must be responded to in the interest of Youngster's development. *Wants* may be considered but they may also be rejected in the interest of health, safety, or family priorities.

Parents who feel obliged to satisfy all their child's *wants* may discover that they are harboring a little tyrant. Some parents are afraid of losing their child's love if they deny him all he wants—especially if their child becomes easily frustrated and angry when thwarted. But parents who feel secure in their love for their child will place appropriate limits on his wants as an expression of their love and concern for his well-being.■

Why Children Misbehave

Why does my child misbehave?" "What is she trying to accomplish by her misbehavior?"

"And why does she continue to misbehave even after I have told her that what she is doing is unacceptable?"

Some years ago, Rudolf Dreikurs, a noted child psychotherapist, identified four basic goals of children's misbehavior: (1) attention-getting, (2) power, (3) revenge, and (4) inadequacy or helplessness. These goals range from least serious psychological problems (attention-seeking behaviors) to most serious (feelings of inadequacy leading to discouragement).

It is not always easy to accurately identify these goals. One technique—which we discuss later in more detail—is for parents to identify their own feeling in response to the child's misbehavior. "How did I feel, how did I react when my child misbehaved?"

When parents have gained some insight and understanding of their child's goals, they are able to deal more effectively with the misbehavior. On the other hand, when parents don't understand the purpose behind the misbehavior, they may respond in an ineffective manner (for example, I don't know what to do with you). Sometimes the parent's response may lead to an increase in the child's misbehavior (for example, when the parent responds with negative attention to the child's attention-seeking goal).

The first goal of misbehavior identified by Dreikurs is *attention-getting*. The child who acts in this way thinks that to be important as a person she must constantly receive recognition from others.

Of course, we all love recognition at one time or another. Positive attention has many desirable aspects, such as enhancement of our own self-concept. Adults may seek atten-

tion by the clothes they wear or by the type of car they drive. Young children are less subtle. They shout, "Watch me, Mom. Watch me, Dad."

Some children receive attention by their good behavior. Other children misbehave as their only way to get attention. It is important to note that these children who misbehave to get attention would rather be corrected or even spanked than be ignored.

Consider the case of 2-year-old Monica who is playing quietly with her toys while Dad reads the newspaper. Suddenly there is a crash as Monica drops one of her toys which breaks on the floor. Dad jumps up and screams at Monica and she responds by running out of the room in tears.

The crisis in this home might have been avoided if Dad had paid more attention to Monica while she was playing so nicely. ("It looks like you are having fun with your dolls," or "You're doing a nice job building with those blocks").

Secondly, Dad would be a more effective parent if he reacted with greater self-control. Parents are role models, and children are apt to act the way they see their parents act. Since Dad jumped up and screamed, Monica is more likely to jump up and scream the next time she is upset.

What can you do if you find you are trapped into a negative response (for example, yelling, "Stop that. You're driving me crazy") whenever your child misbehaves (for example, by banging repeatedly on a drum with a big spoon)?

Here are some of the most effective ways for dealing with inappropriate attention-seeking: (1) First, as far as possible, try to ignore minor attention-seeking misbehaviors. This isn't always easy. It requires a lot of patience and self-control on the part of the parent. (2) Exercise self-control. The parent is the person who

decides when to give attention rather than being manipulated by the child. (3) Focus attention on the child's good behaviors rather than giving attention only to negative misbehaviors.

The second goal of misbehavior is *power*. This is exhibited by the child who wants to be the boss. She will not do what you want her to do. A parent's reaction may be anger ("I'll show you who is boss") or helplessness ("I don't know what to do with you"). Unfortunately, both of these reactions only strengthen the child's desire for power.

In the first case, by engaging in a power struggle with a parent, the child becomes more aware of the power she wields. Even if she loses an occasional battle she will still strive to win the war! In the second case, when the parent feels helpless the child assumes the role of boss, sometimes by crying loudly, screaming, or throwing a temper tantrum.

Consider the case of Joey, a 2-year-old who recently has been very uncooperative with his parents. When Mom tells Joey that it's time to go to bed, he responds that he is not going because he wants to play with his toys. Mom feels very upset because she considers her authority as a parent has not only been challenged but has been taken from her.

When the child's goal is power, it is best for the parent not to get embroiled in a power struggle. The issue of power can be removed altogether by changing the topic, ("Let me see if you washed behind your ears") or just by smiling, which can quickly disarm the child. Once the issue of power is removed the parent can calmly tell the child what she is to do without the child feeling humiliated by defeat.

CONTINUED ON PAGE 195

CONTINUED FROM PAGE 194

It is also a good idea for parents to give a power-seeking child opportunities to experience power in a way that is socially acceptable. This could be done, for example, by letting the child make some decisions about what clothes she might wear or what to serve for dinner.

In the case of the child whose goal is *revenge*, the parent is dealing with a more difficult problem. Such a child is aware of misbehaviors that are particularly irritating to parents.

Let us consider the case of Nancy, a 2-year-old who is angry because she has been told to stay in her room while her mother entertains some friends for morning coffee. Just before the guests arrive Nancy sneaks into the dining room, grabs a corner of the tablecloth and pulls all the dishes and place settings on to the floor.

Because the revengeful child acts in a vicious and sometimes brutal manner, it is likely that she is frequently punished and feels unloved by others. But it is the unloved child who needs love the most.

The first and often the most difficult step in dealing with a revengeful child is to avoid getting pulled into a revengeful relationship. Taking revenge on a child—for example, by hitting—only perpetuates the cycle of hatred, fear and revenge.

What a revengeful child needs most is positive unconditional love. This approach can be very difficult for parents whose feelings of anger are not under control. Parents need to be firm yet caring when dealing with such a child. ("I love you and I care about you. And because I love you, I can't let you hurt either yourself or someone else.") This caring approach—rather than an angry confrontational one—is ultimately the most effective way to deal with the revengeful child.

If the child's goal is to demonstrate *helplessness or inadequacy,* it is because she is so discouraged that she won't even attempt a task at which she might experience failure. Such a child is frequently described as "unmotivated."

Consider the case of Jimmy, a 3-year-old whose language development is delayed. When Jimmy was 2 he was very vocal. But like many 2-year-olds, he mispronounced many words, e.g. saying "college" instead of "cottage."

Jimmy's father decided he would insist on Jimmy pronouncing every word perfectly. After a few months Jimmy's parents noticed that he was no longer a vocal child. Now when Jimmy is asked to pronounce a new word, he usually won't even try. Instead, his face tightens and his eyes convey a helpless look. He uses helplessness as his way to avoid the risk of failure.

In working with the helpless child, choose experiences in which the child is capable of enjoying some success. If necessary modify the activity, such as a game, so that the child can participate successfully. Encourage positive efforts, no matter how imperfect they initially may be.

Above all, a parent must try to avoid despair (e.g. giving up on the child) which would only discourage the child even more.

In order to decide which approach will work best with your child it is important to understand the specific goal of your child's misbehavior. How can a parent identify these different goals?

The first step is to try to observe your child's behavior as though you were an objective third party. ("She just insulted her mother," rather than "She just insulted ME!")

The second step is to determine the emotional and behavioral reaction you had because of your child's misbehavior. This will provide a most important clue in determining which of the four goals is involved:

(1) Do I feel my child is trying to occupy too much of my time and is getting a lot of negative attention from me? (Attention-getting.)

(2) Do I feel that my authority is being challenged or threatened? (Power.)

(3) Do I feel hurt, angry, outraged, or revengeful toward my child? (Revenge.)

(4) Do I feel helpless—just not knowing what to do—about an apparently hopeless situation? (Inadequacy.)

Your own reactions as a parent are one of the best indicators of your child's goals of misbehavior. Awareness of your own feelings helps you to decide the most effective strategy for dealing with such misbehavior. This awareness also helps you to keep your own feelings under control so that you can guide your child more effectively toward socially appropriate positive behaviors.

Parents who wish to read more about this approach for handling misbehavior should consult the following books:

Dinkmeyer, D. & McKay, G. (1973). **Raising A Responsible Child.** New York: Simon & Schuster.

Dreikurs, R. & Soltz, V. (1974). **Children: The Challenge.** New York: Hawthorn.■

On Novelty

Young children respond to new events in their lives in ways that can't always be predicted.

One city child may eagerly explore everything in sight on his visit to a farm. Another may find the animals strange and frightening, the sounds and smells unpleasant. Or the same child may dislike the visit to one stranger's house but enjoy a visit to another's.

Much of this has to do with the feeling of security the child has in a particular situation. This in turn depends a great deal on how the new situation differs from what he knows and is used to.

If we could always see the world the way Youngster does, it would be much easier to explain his behavior. An understanding of how most children behave at a given age will generally help provide clues to your child's feelings, perceptions, and needs.

Youngster seems to do best with a combination of sameness and variety.

First of all, there are some activities where he demands a highly structured routine. He wants to do things the same way each time and he gets upset if the routine is changed even a little bit. This is most evident in the bedtime ritual.

He also shows a desire for routine at meals and in his style of using the potty. These activities are the ones that satisfy his most basic physical needs.

Adults have long since taken these foundations for granted, but not so with Youngster. He feels very keenly that they have to do with his well being and his dependent-on-others existence. As a result, they arouse strong emotional feelings for him.

When eating, sleeping, and eliminating he is sensitive to his parents' love and concern. Predictability means security to him. If his basic needs are consistently met in the same way, he is able to face the rest of the world with much more confidence.

In the world of ideas, a little more variety is preferred by Youngster. But even so he starts out with the security of some fixed ideas.

After discovering that a toy car has wheels and can roll, he spends some time strengthening this idea by rolling it back and forth under his hand or giving it short pushes. Only later does he begin the inevitable variations, like rolling it on all kinds of new surfaces or letting it coast down an incline.

We all like new ideas which relate to what we already know. If something is too unfamiliar, we can't handle it.

Once the basic idea is down pat, variations are interesting and a challenge for him. But just so much change and not too much.

In Month 5, we noted that Baby is most interested in new faces that are slightly different from those he is used to. If he is shown a face or a picture that is too much different, he loses interest.

The same principle applies for Youngster and even for adults. We all like new ideas which relate to what we already know. If something is too unfamiliar, we can't handle it. For instance, we rarely find it pleasant to read an article about a subject with which we are completely unfamiliar.

For Youngster, a completely new toy may not be appreciated during the period he is still trying out the possibilities of an old one. It is best to give new toys to him one at a time, at least a day or two apart, even though you may have bought him two or more toys on the same shopping trip.

Sometimes Youngster may not be ready for the advanced ideas a new toy entails. If so, he will use it in a manner that is consistent with his present level of development. A father who bought his not-yet-3-year-old a fancy battery-powered electric car was dismayed to see his son continue to push the car around by hand. The child was operating at an earlier level and was not ready for the novelty of such a completely new idea.

There are few times when novelty is so great as when you take Youngster on a trip away from home. The only familiar things may be his parents and the car. Even these seem different as new scenery rushes by and the conversation focuses on unfamiliar trip-related topics. It will help to take along a few of his favorite toys and picture books to keep him entertained while riding in the car.

A most difficult situation for many Youngsters is sleeping in a strange place, whether in a motel or at someone's house.

At such a time, his feeling of security will be greatly increased if you surround him with some things brought from home, especially from his own bedroom. The strangeness of a new bed can be lessened by substituting his own pillow and giving him whatever he normally takes to bed with him, such as a teddy bear.

Throughout the trip, the softness of a familiar fabric like a small blanket or an afghan can be enormously comforting.

Of course, the most comforting thing of all in a strange place is your own presence. Stay within range of his voice whenever possible. Then he can be assured that no matter what else changes, one thing stays the same: His parent is near when needed.■

Thinking of Teeth

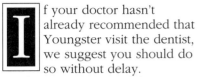

If your doctor hasn't already recommended that Youngster visit the dentist, we suggest you should do so without delay.

About 50 percent of the population seeks dental care only in emergency situations. Yet the major causes for dental disease begin in early childhood, even before the arrival of the second teeth.

Promoting care of teeth is in the interest of good health, articulate speech, and attractive appearance.

There have been reports about an alarming increase in the number of children under 5 years of age who have a condition of decaying teeth commonly known as "milk mouth" or "apple juice mouth." This arises when children are permitted to suck on bottles long past the age of weaning or when they are given the wrong kinds of drinks.

Parents have been known to give young children large quantities of fruit juice or soda pop, both of which are sugar fluids. Bacteria, which are always present in the mouth, then utilize this material to grow and eventually cause tooth decay.

Toothbrushing is necessary to remove these bacteria (plaque), but young children often are not able to brush their teeth properly. We might add that since toothbrushing is a motor skill, once learned, it is not forgotten. But it must be learned correctly.

It may be necessary for a parent to accomplish the daily toothbrushing, permitting the child to participate in whatever way he can, until the skill is learned. The addition of fluoride to toothpastes and the water supply has been recommended by the American Dental Association as another means of decay prevention.

Obviously parents can't always say "no" to sweets. Such a blanket rule usually makes children more desirous of what is forbidden. Rather, parents should encourage good eating habits by making available the kinds of goodies which are both nutritious and less likely to cause tooth decay.■

Looking, Listening, Learning

One of the main ideas behind *Growing Child* is to tell you about effective child development practices so you can help your child to grow and learn. In that way you are also helping your child get ready for school.

During the preschool years, your child is building the foundations for later school learning. Many research studies indicate that children who develop more slowly than normal frequently have trouble later in learning to read, write, spell, and "do" math.

So proper development now is most important for your child. If she develops well now, she should learn well later. We are trying to inform you about child development and at the same time present ideas to stimulate good development in your child.

Here are some everyday things you can do to encourage normal development:

1. **At the supermarket:** Let Youngster participate in your shopping. Let her share in getting some items and in making some simple decisions.

Talk to her about what you and she are doing there. For example, you may be getting things which are needed for breakfast, lunch, and dinner. She can get some items from the shelf and put them into the cart, with your help of course.

She can learn to identify certain items, such as her favorite cereal, and learn where they are located in the supermarket. Ask her to help you find where other items are located. Then let her go to their places, find the items, and place them in the cart.

All this is far superior to being wheeled passively through the supermarket where she only looks but does not do anything.

When she only looks, she is like a sponge that soaks up sights, sounds, and smells. This is one form of learning. But when she also does things she is developing and learning—and this is the name of the game. She develops best when she is actively involved in doing.

2. **In the car:** You can even use a trip in your car to promote normal development.

As you drive through your neighborhood, talk to her about the major landmarks which she can see. "Billy lives here and Susie lives there." Try to determine if she really has the idea about where Billy and Susie live.

There are other landmarks which should be important to her: the toy store, the bank, the service station, the post office, the supermarket.

Later let her tell you how to get to all those places from your house, including where her friends' houses are located.

The main idea is that you talk to her at times such as these so that she gets the basic connection between language—what she

CONTINUED ON PAGE 198

CONTINUED FROM PAGE 197

hears and says—and the places she sees as you drive.

3. **At home:** In any home there are many happenings which can be turned into good learning experiences. For instance, the laundry.

Laundry activities can provide great learning experiences. As you put clothes in the washer, let her help you.

As you pour detergent into a measuring cup, let her learn to do this.

As you take the clothes out of the washer, let her open the dryer door, help you to put the clothes in, and then close the door.

In helping you to do the laundry, she develops a sense of order. Her thinking is stimulated as she does her part. She begins to understand how all these activities take place in sequence.

The best part of laundry learning comes after the dryer has stopped. Then the clothes must be removed, folded, sorted, and finally put away.

At this point much good learning can take place once you know the secret for making it happen.

The biggest secret is to let her do as many of the activities as she can.

Let her take the clothes from the dryer. Help her sort them into appropriate piles because sorting is an extremely important ability. When she learns to sort, she is actually learning about categories.

When she learns about categories, she is beginning to develop her first tentative abilities to do abstract thinking.

Here are the sheets, here are the towels, here are Dad's socks, here are Sister's socks, etc. If you help her learn to sort the clothes in the laundry, you also are helping her begin to learn to do the abstract thinking she'll need later in school.

There are even more good learning experiences from the home laundry. After the clothes are sorted, she can help to fold them and put them away.

Help her learn where things go. Teach her to place the various objects in the correct places. Dad's socks go in this drawer. The towels go here in the linen closet. The sheets go over there. Her undershirts go in this drawer, etc.

As she learns that the different items of laundry go in particular places, she is really learning about the location of objects in space.

4. **In the outdoors:** There are probably many activities in your backyard in which she can participate. For example, if the flowers or the grass need to be watered, she can probably help with this activity.

If you take her to your local park, there are many things she will experience—the different trees, the flowers, the birds—all of which can become sources of new learning.■

www.growingchild.com

Contributing Authors

Phil Bach, O.D., Ph.D.
Miriam Bender, Ph.D.
Joseph Braga, Ed.D.
Laurie Braga, Ph.D.
George Early, Ph.D.
Liam Grimley, Ph.D.
Robert Hannemann, M.D., F.A.A.P.
Sylvia Kottler, M.S.
Bill Peterson, Ph.D.

Growing Child, Inc.
P.O. Box 620
Lafayette, Indiana 47902-0620
Telephone: 1-800-927-7289
©2005 Growing Child, Inc.

Next Month

- *Thumbsucking*
- *More About Toilet Training and Night Dryness*
- *Effective Parenting*

Growing Child.

Making Friends

lthough 3-year-olds can learn many social skills from interacting with parents and siblings, the forming of same-age friendships is an important aspect of growing up.

Same-age friends learn social skills from one another in a unique manner because they can perceive the world from a similar age-related perspective.

One of the ways in which young children learn from one another is by imitation. For example, if one child has developed a particular skill, he can help his friend develop the same skill. Friendships encourage exploration and learning in a variety of new environments.

Having a close friend can also help a child feel more secure in new situations with other children, such as in a daycare center or park playground.

Because 3-year-olds are by nature egocentric, it's not easy for them to perceive the world from another's perspective. Having a close friend makes it easier to develop perspective-taking skills—and thus become less egocentric—by learning, for example, to share with one another and to take turns. In the process, children get the rewarding feeling of being better accepted and liked by other children.

Some children make friends easily. If they are extroverts or outgoing by temperament, they quickly learn the social skills needed to make friends. This social skills might include

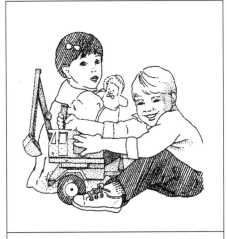

smiling at others making eye contact, showing an interest in others and being willing to listen to them, as well as learning to share and take turns.

Other children who are shy and slow to warm up have greater difficulty acquiring these social skills, especially if they prefer to play alone most of the time. Although all children need to eventually develop these skills, it is important for parents not to push too hard. For parents who are themselves outgoing with a large circle of friends, this can be particularly difficult.

A good way for parents to help a shy, introverted child is to invite just one other friendly playmate to their home and then give the children plenty of time and opportunity for their friendship to develop.

For some shy children, playing with either a younger or older child is easier than

playing with a same-age playmate. Playing with a younger child can provide an opportunity to be a leader in the relationship and thereby gain self-confidence. Playing with an older, friendly playmate can provide a nurturing environment more similar to the security of being with one's parents or other caring adults.

At three years of age, it doesn't much matter if a child prefers to have only one close friend rather than a whole group of friends. Friendship social skills can be learned from interacting with just one other playmate.

There is a big difference, however, between having at least one friend and having no friends at all. When a 3-year-old doesn't want to play with any other child, there is a problem which parents need to address.

What parents can do: Here are some suggestions to help a 3-year-old child make friends:

• Become more aware of your child's particular temperament, whether outgoing, warm and friendly or shy and introverted.

• Before your child interacts with another playmate, discuss the social skills needed for friendly interaction, such as the importance of sharing and taking turns.

• When getting to know a new playmate, a neutral site, such as a park or playground, will help to prevent squabbles over prized possessions.

• Before inviting your child's

CONTINUED ON PAGE 200

CONTINUED FROM PAGE 199

playmate to your home, it's wise to put away your own child's favorite teddy bear or playthings. If possible, provide duplicates of the same toy so as to avoid conflicts.

• Avoid games and activities which promote competition rather than cooperation.

• If the playmates begin to have a dispute, pa attention to what is happening, but don't immediately rush to intervene—unless, of course, one child is about to physically hurt the other. After all, it is from such disputes—unpleasant as they may be—that young children must learn the social skills of compromise and getting along with one another.

• When playmates begin to show signs of being tired or cranky, it is best to end the interactive playing and provide a quieter activity, such as listening to a story which you read to them.

• If your child is consistently rejected by other children, try to determine what your child may be doing that irritates others. For example, does he interact with other children in an over-aggressive or hyperactive manner? Does he know how to enter a game which other children are already playing? Are the other children appropriate playmates?
By determining the reason for rejection, parents are better able

to help their child make new friends.

In summary, making friends requires the development f social skills which, like academic and athletic skills, must be learned and repeatedly practiced. Some children acquire these skills easily and rapidly. Others experience greater difficulty.

Parents can help their child develop these social skills more easily when they are sensitive to the child's temperament and personality. The time and effort spent in helping a child develop the social skills needed for making friends will ultimately enable the child to be lead a richer and happier life.■

A Positive Attitude

 positive attitude can lead to better parenting. In life, two people can look at the same glass: while one sees it as "half full" the other sees it as "help empty." It's just a matter of positive versus negative attitude.

An attitude is something we can work on changing. If I perceive that my attitudes on life are more negative than positive, I can deliberately make a greater effort to focus on the positive (versus negative) aspects of each situation.

Here are three good reasons for seeking to develop and maintain a more positive attitude as a parent:

1. *My attitude helps to determine how I perceive my child's behavior.* For example, if my two-year-old has recently developed the habit of saying "No!" I can perceive that as either (a) "My child is develop-

ing a healthy sense of autonomy and independence" (a positive attitude) or (b) "My kid is becoming a little monster" (a negative attitude).

2. *My attitude helps to determine how I will react.* If I perceive my child's behavior in a positive manner ("He's learning to develop a sense of autonomy and independence"), I'm more likely to react to his behavior in a positive way. (For example, by showing him more love and affection to reassure him that it's natural and okay for him to want to demonstrate greater independence as he gets older.)

On the other hand, if I perceive the same behavior in a negative manner, I'm more likely to respond in a negative way ("You'll get a good spanking from me if you keep saying that!")

3. *My attitude will affect how my child will respond.* When a parent can exhibit a positive attitude

toward a child's behavior, the child will more likely develop a positive attitude toward life. Giving him the reassurance that he is loved unconditionally will help him to be more in tune with his world and, therefore, behave more positively.

On the contrary, when a child feels threatened and unloved because of a parent's negative attitude, he is more likely to develop negative feelings toward himself, which ultimately will lead to worse misbehavior.

It's important to note, however that having a positive attitude toward a child's behavior ("I think my child is terrific") is not the same as spoiling a child ("My child can do no wrong"). Whereas a spoiled child will eventually exhibit misbehavior increasingly more demanding of parents, the child who is treated by parents with a positive—yet realistic—attitude will more likely develop a similar, more positive outlook on life.■

More About Toilet Training and Night Dryness

All normal children sooner or later become toilet trained. Bowel control is easier to accomplish than bladder control. It is often established by 2 years of age.

Bladder control is developed in two stages: first while the child is awake and then when the child is asleep. Girls usually accomplish bladder control while awake by about 2 years of age, whereas boys are a few months later.

It should be emphasized, however, that bladder control develops at different rates in different children. About 50 percent of 2-year-olds (boys and girls) can stay dry at night, 75 percent of 3-year-olds, and about 90 percent of 5-year-olds. In other words, bedwetting by a 3-year-old is within normal limits. Bedwetting that occurs past the age of 5 may be abnormal and should be reported to a physician who can determine if there are physical reasons.

Under no circumstances should a 3-year-old be blamed or punished for bedwetting. Heightened anxiety may even increase the likelihood that it will occur again. Parents should try not to express concern unless the child himself considers his bedwetting to be a problem.

There are a number of measures that may be taken to decrease the likelihood of bedwetting:

(1) Check on drinking habits before bedtime. This does not mean depriving the child of liquids, but rather seeing that he practices reasonable moderation.

(2) It is important that the child makes a visit to the toilet and tries to completely empty his bladder just before going to bed. Even if he does not think he needs to go, it is wise to establish this practice as a part of bedtime routine.

(3) Some parents have experienced success by taking a sleeping child to the toilet to urinate at the time the parents are getting ready for bed.

There are a number of other measures, such as medication or an electric alarm apparatus, which may be used for those older children for whom bedwetting continues to be a problem.

Because there are a number of organic causes for bedwetting such as diabetes, kidney disease, or abnormalities of the urinary tract, it is wise to consult a physician if the problem persists.■

Receptive and Expressive Language

In trying to understand how a child's language develops, it is important to be aware of the difference between receptive language and expressive language.

Receptive language refers to the ability to understand words that are heard, whereas **expressive** language refers to the ability to use words to speak.

Children's receptive language exceeds their expressive language. In other words, at any age, a child can understand more than she can say.

Here are some characteristics of a 3-year-old's **receptive** language.

• Indicates through her activity that she can associate words with one another. For example, she can react appropriately if asked, "May I have a bite of your apple?"

• Knows size differences and can select "small" or "big" cookie when presented with a selection.

• Demonstrates an understanding of most commonly used verbs and adjectives.

• Understands some long and complicated sentences.

• Enjoys stories read from books with pictures and recognizes small details in the pictures.

• Loves a tape or CD player. She may even adjust the sound level, indicating that her hearing is very acute.

• Mimics adult social behavior when asked to show feelings of anger, exasperation, sympathy.

• Identifies geometric forms when asked to point to a square, cross, or circle.

• Comprehends simple cause-and-effect relationships, such as turning a switch when told to turn off the light.

Here are some characteristics of a 3-year-old's **expressive** language:

• Refers to herself by using "I" rather than her proper name.

• Employs the pronouns, "I," "me," "you" in speech.

• Says a few nursery rhymes.

• Names at least one color correctly.

• Repeats two or more numbers correctly.

• Tells gender when asked, "Are you a girl or boy?"

• Can give both first and last name upon request.

• Uses three to four word sentences.

• Chatters sensibly to herself as she plays alone.

• Stammers sometimes in her eagerness to talk.

• Displaces inflections such as "He pick it ups," or "I ran homed."

• Mixes up word opposites: hot/cold, open/close, on/off, up/down.

• Asks questions that begin with "what," "why," "where."■

Different Kinds of Attention

Have you had the experience of reading a simple sentence or paragraph and afterwards not having the slightest idea of what you just read? You looked at all the words but you didn't really focus your attention on them. In other words, your attention was at a low level.

There are different levels of attention. The first level, which may be called *unfocused attention,* is very common in young children.

At this level, although your child may appear to be listening to what you say, her mind is in another world. She may be just daydreaming or she may be distracted by something that truly interests her such as a large cat outside the window. She may show some interest in a very simple jigsaw puzzle for a while. But after looking at all the pieces, she quickly becomes disinterested or bored with the task.

The second level may be called *focused impulsive attention.* At this level Youngster will attend to a task but will act in an impulsive manner.

In trying to solve the puzzle, for example, she may pick up one likely-looking piece and repeatedly try to make it fit in a space where it doesn't belong. Or she may blurt out her answer before you have finished asking her a question. On another occasion she may charge toward her bedroom before you have had time to tell her what you want her to get there. These are all examples of focused impulsive attention.

At the third level Youngster exhibits *active attention.* In working with the puzzle, for example, she will use trial-and-error. If one piece doesn't fit, she will immediately try another. The key to attaining this level is developing the ability to try different solutions to a problem.

The fourth and highest level of attention is *reflective attention.* At

this level the child will give some thought to possible solutions to a problem before taking any action. In solving the puzzle, for example, she would probably examine carefully the shape of the piece that is needed, then look at some similar pieces before choosing the most likely one.

Youngster may operate at different levels of attention at different times of the day, depending on her interest in a task or how tired she may be. This is not too surprising since adults also may operate at any of the four levels of attention, sometimes daydreaming, sometimes acting impulsively, sometimes using trial-and-error and sometimes being reflective.

Since good attentional skills are important for learning, here are some hints on how to improve your child's attention:

• Select tasks and activities that have a high interest value for your child. She will exhibit the lowest level of attention on tasks that she finds boring or monotonous.

• Be sure that the task is at an appropriate level of difficulty for her. In order to maintain her interest, the task must be somewhat challenging. But if she begins to show signs of frustration or engages in repetitive unproductive behavior, the task is probably too difficult. Either select a less difficult task or offer your help.

• Be sensitive to your child's

feelings. A child's level of attention will drop and she will become frustrated if she is tired or if she has stayed too long with one task.

With young children it is better to arrange for several short periods of attending than to strive for a longer period that exceeds their attention span.

• Act as a role model for the behavior you want in your child. In solving a puzzle, for example, offer some suggestions for possible solutions, if your child is having difficulty.

• Use the "think-aloud" method so that your child will know what you are thinking before you act.

For example: "I'm going to try this piece here because it appears to have the right shape to fit in this space." By using this type of verbal self-instruction you are teaching your child to reflect on the solution rather than using an impulsive or trial-and-error method.

• Encourage your child to attempt to do what you just did, namely, to talk aloud about the solution before taking any action.

Don't try to correct her grammar or pronunciation at this time as this may keep her from talking freely.

• Let your child work at her own pace. It will take her some time to develop the skills for higher levels of attention. As far as possible, resist the temptation to "jump in" with the correct solution.

• Praise your child for effort as well as for success. Above all, don't get angry when she fails. Your anger will only increase the likelihood of failure in the future.

• Make sure to have lots of fun as you engage in these activities with your child so that she will develop these important attentional skills in a highly favorable learning environment.■

Insect Bites and Stings

Insect bites and stings are a part of everyday life, especially when a family lives or visits in a rural, wooded area. In recent years, as the use of insecticides has decreased, insects have been moving closer and closer to densely populated areas.

Many kinds of insects bite—horseflies, deerflies, sandflies, chiggers, mosquitoes, fleas, bedbugs, lice.

Other insects, such as bees, yellow jackets, hornets and wasps, sting. Some insects, such as the fire ant, simultaneously bite and sting.

Most insect bites cause discomfort but are not dangerous. Many, particularly those caused by mosquitoes, deerflies, fleas, and chiggers, can be prevented by the use of an insect repellent that can be sprayed or rubbed on the skin. Many of these repellents are so mild that they can be used even on a very young baby as long as one takes care to keep them away from eyes, nose and mouth.

One must also take care to keep them away from the hands of children who are prone to suck on their fingers. Some care should also be taken not to get the repellents on toys or other objects that children might put in their mouths.

Venomous stings (bee, yellow jacket, hornet, wasp) are much more difficult to prevent. They are also more painful and dangerous when they occur.

Children should be warned against going barefoot in clover-loaded grass since stings will likely occur on the feet when the warning is ignored. Also, eating sweet-smelling foods (oranges, apples, popsicles, etc.) in areas where bees are present, will tend to attract them.

Wasps generally do not bother people unless they are disturbed. They particularly like to nest near doors and windows, in summer cottages or garages. They can be removed only by someone skilled at doing this.

Dangerous spider bites are rare in the United States. They can be prevented by checking the bedroom and basement areas of the home and using insecticides when necessary.

Also, children should be warned against playing on or near wood piles or in old barns since this is where the two significant biting spiders (the black widow and the brown recluse) are likely to be found.

Should a bite occur in these surroundings, and the spider tentatively be identified as black widow (approximately 1/2 inch in length and having light yellow or red markings on its underside) or a brown recluse (approximately the same size but with a dark fiddle-shaped marking on its back) medical help should be sought as soon as possible.

Specific treatments are available for these bites. It is important that they be started as soon as possible after the bite occurs.

Much less dangerous, but still very irritating, are bites by chiggers. These occur most often during the summer months. They are frequently found after an outing in the woods, particularly after one has been sitting in a grassy or leafy picnic area. They are more prevalent in isolated, wooded areas than in those that are heavily trafficked. Good insect repellents will usually prevent chigger bites. But should they occur and cause a great deal of discomfort, antihistamines prescribed by your doctor will help relieve the symptoms.

Scabies is a troublesome itch which is caused by the female itch mite. It spreads from person to person in much the same manner as lice. Although it causes a great deal of itching, it can be treated by specific medicines prescribed by your doctor.

In general, insect bites, regardless of their cause, respond to a few simple remedies: (1) Cool compresses relieve the itching and decrease the area of inflammation; (2) Antihistamines, orally, or in special lotions or sprays (your doctor can tell you which one to use), will help relieve the symptoms for longer periods of time.

If there is any question about a severe reaction (dizziness, fainting, nausea, fast heart rate, breathing difficulty, itching all over the body, or difficulty with urinating) continue the compresses and take your child to the nearest emergency medical help that is available (doctor, emergency room, nurse, police or fire department).

Once it is known that a child reacts severely to a certain insect bite, emergency medications must be kept on hand. In some cases, your physician may recommend desensitization injections.

Parents need to warn their children that insects, such as bees, do not like to be disturbed, particularly when they are gathering nectar on bright, warm days. They are especially irritable, and hence more likely to sting, after a shower of rain has washed the nectar from the flowers.

If a child accidentally upsets a nest of insects, it is possible that she may receive numerous stings over her whole body. In this case it is wise to administer an antihistamine, if available, and to place the child in a bath of cool water. Then seek immediate medical assistance.

Bee stings and mosquito bites may become more swollen on the second or third day. But most insect bites begin to disappear within 24 hours. ∎

Thumbsucking

humbsucking is a subject of concern to many parents. Infants are born with a natural instinct for sucking. It is this sucking reflex that enables a baby to obtain nourishment from either the breast or bottle during the first few months of life.

Besides satisfying the baby's physiological needs, sucking also produces feelings of comfort, security and pleasure. Infants like to suck anything within their reach such as a toy or blanket or—most commonly of all—their thumb or finger.

Sucking usually produces feelings of contentment because of its association with being held and fed. It has been noted that children who regularly suck their thumbs often have a relaxed, serene approach to life.

It has also been noted that thumbsucking is a normal tension-reducing act in young children. When a child is tired or anxious, he is more likely to engage in thumbsucking.

Most children outgrow this practice by the age of 3 1/2 years. A few persist long past the age of 4. They may suck so vigorously and for such a long period that the upper front baby teeth are pushed forward and the lower teeth backward.

Dentists point out that this tilting of the baby teeth will most likely have little or no effect on the permanent teeth unless the thumbsucking persists past the age of 4. Parents who are concerned about the effect of thumbsucking on their child's permanent teeth should discuss this matter with their dentist.

For children over 4, dentists will sometimes fit a dental appliance that not only corrects any distortion of the teeth but also serves to discourage thumbsucking.

What about the use of other devices to discourage thumbsucking, such as elbow splints, mittens or bitter-tasting substances? In general, these methods have not been effective because as soon as they are discontinued, the thumbsucking begins again.

If the child's thumbsucking occurs at times of anxiety or tiredness, it is more important to try to change these underlying causal factors than to try to terminate the habit.

When the child is old enough to want to stop sucking his thumb, he often does so quite suddenly and spontaneously. Warm words of encouragement, either from the dentist or from a parent—without any undue pressure—may sometimes speed up the process.

Some parents prefer the use of a pacifier to thumbsucking because children, generally, can more easily give up the pacifier than the thumb.

The age at which children should be encouraged to give up thumbsucking or pacifier varies. Many pediatricians feel it should be before these behaviors become embarrassing to the child or before they begin to harm his teeth, which is usually by age 4.■

---

www.growingchild.com

Contributing Authors

Phil Bach, O.D., Ph.D.
Miriam Bender, Ph.D.
Joseph Braga, Ed.D.
Laurie Braga, Ph.D.
George Early, Ph.D.
Liam Grimley, Ph.D.
Robert Hannemann, M.D., F.A.A.P.
Sylvia Kottler, M.S.
Bill Peterson, Ph.D.

Growing Child, Inc.
P.O. Box 620
Lafayette, Indiana 47902
Telephone: 1-800-927-7289
©2005 Growing Child, Inc.

Dear Growing Child:

"I'd like to take this opportunity to tell you how much I enjoy Growing Child. It's a comfort to know that my child is right on target as far as development is concerned.

"Your issues are truly a blessing in informing me on what to expect."

Mary C.
Rosedale, NY

Next Month

- *Teasing*
- *A Tricycle Is a Learning Machine*
- *Animal Bites*

Growing Child®

Your Child as Scientist, Sculptor, Artist

For the child who is almost 3 years of age, there are many wonderful learning experiences in and around your home.

All you have to do as a parent is be aware of Youngster's curiosity and involve her in some simple and exciting learning activities. We encourage you to be creative in developing your own activities around the home.

To get you started we offer some suggested ways for your child to assume the roles of scientist, sculptor, and artist!

1. **The Scientist**. When you take the ice tray out of the freezer, let Youngster see the ice cubes in the tray. If you turn the tray upside down, she will be amazed that the cubes don't fall out.

When you put the ice cubes in a bowl, let her feel one of them in her hand. Let her put a cube in a cup of hot water to watch it dissolve. When you refill the ice tray with water, let her feel the water before you put the tray back in the freezer to make more ice cubes.

As you and Youngster engage in this activity together, talk with her about what you are doing and about what is happening. (For example, "What happened to the ice cube?") Obviously she won't understand everything you say. But she is learning new words and new concepts: solid, liquid, ice, freezing, melting.

Ask her some simple questions to test her understanding about what is happening. And be prepared to answer her questions as simply as you can.

A good learning environment for young children does not require expensive, sophisticated equipment. Everyday household items can be a young child's best learning tools.

2. **The Sculptor.** Junk modeling can be fun. Start by collecting household junk—paper towel rolls, reels from sticky tape, spools from thread, scraps of material, gift wrap, kitchen foil, paper sacks, ribbons, elastic, candy wrappers, tea bag envelopes, shells, pebbles, etc.

As Youngster assembles and sorts the junk, ask "Where do you think this came from?" Questions like this encourage your child to organize her ideas and to think creatively.

Obviously she will offer many incorrect and absurd answers. Here's your chance to provide new information without discrediting what she has said: "Well, that's interesting. Do you want to know something else?"

It is also an opportunity to talk about ecology. By collecting junk you are helping to reuse waste rather than discard it.

With some strong glue, cardboard or construction paper and the "treasures" she's accumulated, Youngster is now ready to create some wonderful sculptures which you can display in the kitchen.

3. **The Artist.** At about age 3, Youngster can make a simple drawing of a person. Don't worry if the drawing is somewhat crude such as a large head with two leg stumps beneath it. Encourage her to talk about what she has drawn.

Sometimes she may just want to scribble to experience the visual effect of her strenuous arm movements. For this purpose a blackboard and chalk are very useful.

You can make your own blackboard by painting a piece of pressed wood with two or three coats of chalkboard paint.

If the pressed wood measures at least 18" x 24", it will also serve as a painting easel when a large pad of newsprint is clipped to it.

As Youngster draws, you can talk about the shapes she makes—"circle," "cross," "square," —or the colors she is using— "red," "green," "blue." Little children like new words, especially when they can relate the new words directly to what they are doing.

A good learning environment for young children does not require expensive and highly sophisticated equipment. Everyday household items, especially when used in a creative manner, can be a young child's best learning tools.■

Animal Bites

Taking care of a pet can teach a child valuable lessons about kindness and responsibility. But, sooner or later, a child must also learn that animals may bite.

Fortunately most animal bites are not serious and can be treated by thoroughly washing the injured area with soap and water and by applying an antibiotic cream or ointment. If the bite wound is deep, cover it with a sterile dressing and bandage. A physician's advice should always be sought if the bite is deep or occurs on any part of the child's head or neck.

Rabies is a major concern for children bitten by animals. It is a fatal disease which is usually transmitted by the saliva of an infected animal. Rabies is extremely rare in pets unless they have been in contact with wild animals.

Children are bitten more often by healthy animals than by infected ones. If your child is bitten by a rodent (rabbit, squirrel, hamster, guinea pig, gerbil, chipmunk, rat, or mouse) it is very unlikely that he will get rabies. In most cases rabies vaccine is not given.

Bites by carnivorous animals (skunks, foxes, coyotes, raccoons, dogs, cats, and bats) are much more dangerous and, in many cases, rabies vaccine is given. An animal that behaves peculiarly or attacks without provocation may have rabies. Here are some general instructions for handling animal bites. For the child:

(1) Wash the wound thoroughly with soap and water.

(2) If the wound is extensive or through the full thickness of skin, contact your physician. Suturing animal bites can be done after careful cleansing and trimming of the injured tissue; however, the wound frequently becomes infected.

(3) Check on the child's tetanus immunization status.

For the animal:

(1) Try to capture the animal alive—provided it is safe to do so—and keep it confined for two weeks. An animal that is healthy for at least five days is probably not contagious at the time of the bite or scratch. If it is healthy for two weeks, it can be judged to be non-rabid.

If the animal is killed, save its head or carcass, if possible, because examination can determine if it was rabid at the time of its death. A veterinarian or emergency room personnel can tell you where to find the nearest examining center.

(2) Check on the animal's rabies vaccine if it is a pet and has been seen by a veterinarian.∎

How to Remove a Stinger

In the case of insect stings, if the stinger can be seen and is not too deeply embedded, it may be easily removed. Gently scrape it loose rather than trying to pull it out. Pinching the stinger between the fingers may force irritating poison from the venom sac into the skin.

Do not attempt to remove the stinger from a honeybee bite since it has a barb at the end which embeds itself into the skin.

The area should be washed well and left alone.∎

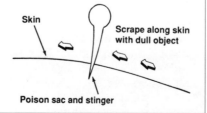

Skin

Scrape along skin with dull object

Poison sac and stinger

Tick Bites and Disease

Ticks are found in wooded areas and attach themselves to the skin in a painless fashion. Once attached, they suck the blood from the victim and, in some cases, discharge disease-causing organisms into the surrounding tissue and bloodstream. Most tick bites do not cause much reaction except for minor skin irritation; however, they can be related to two serious generalized illnesses—Rocky Mountain spotted fever and Lyme disease.

Rocky Mountain spotted fever is associated with only a minimal bite reaction but later with a rash, particularly over the knees and elbows, accompanied by a high fever. It can also involve the brain and spinal cord and can be life-threatening. However, early appropriate antibiotic treatment can prevent these serious complications.

Lyme disease is named for the Connecticut city where it was first reported. It is carried by a small tick and is associated with a severe reaction at the bite site. The disease itself is characterized by a low grade fever and prolonged feelings of tiredness and aching in the joints and muscles. It too can be successfully treated with antibiotics, especially if they are used early in the illness.

The best way to prevent these diseases is to avoid exposure to ticks. Insect repellents are helpful, but the most effective preventive is protective clothing that covers exposed areas.

A tick can be removed by grasping its head with a tweezer and gently pulling it free from the skin. Care should be taken not to squeeze the body since this may force additional infecting material into the skin. If the tick cannot be easily removed in this fashion, a physician should be consulted.∎

Preschooler's Learning Processes Are Different

For centuries young children were thought of as miniature adults. During the past 100 years, however, more has been learned about the significant differences in the ways in which adults and young children perceive the world than in all previous centuries combined. Being aware of those differences can enable parents to better understand and stimulate their own child's learning.

Here are six ways in which adults and young children perceive the world differently:

1. *While adults lose much of their sense of curiosity, a preschooler is curious about everything in his world.*

He wants to know how come he can hear grandmother's voice on the telephone even though she lives over 200 miles away!

Questions seem to be never-ending. What will happen if he mixes the yellow and blue paints? Where does the sun go in the evening? Are those cartoon characters really singing inside the TV set?

Parents can rekindle their own sense of curiosity by telling their child honestly, "I don't know the answer to your question, but we can try to find out the answer together."

Nothing stifles a young child's curiosity as much as a parent's negative rebuke or scolding for asking a question. On the other hand, the more parents seek to answer questions in a simple and honest manner, the more their child's curiosity and learning will flourish and develop.

2. *While adults generally find constant repetition to be boring, preschoolers love repetition and*

The more parents seek to answer questions in a simple and honest manner, the more their child's curiosity and learning will flourish and develop.

their learning thrives on it.

After reading an enjoyable book, adults are usually ready to begin another one. Not so with a preschooler. He wants you to read to him "Goodnight Moon"—or whatever his favorite bedtime book may be—tonight, tomorrow night, and the night after! Again and again and again!

Why do young children crave the kind of repetition that can bore adults? Young children have to deal with so much newness in their daily lives that it's a relief for them to be able at times to experience sameness and predictability. Amid so many new experiences, it's reassuring that their favorite storybook always has the same predictable ending.

Predictability gives a young child a sense of some control over the events in his life. The more you repeat the same

routine in his daily activities, for example, the more at ease he will be. If you forget some detail in the bedtime routine—such as forgetting to kiss his teddy bear good night—you will promptly be reminded of the proper sequence of events!

Repetition also helps young children deal with feelings of fear or anxiety. For example, your preschooler may ask you to repeat over and over the story of Humpty Dumpty who had a great fall. Fearing that he may experience a similar consequence if he were to fall, he can gradually come to terms with his feelings of fear by having you repeat the story in a calm voice—while he is nestled safely and comfortably in your lap!

3. *While adults are clock-watchers, conscious of time, a preschooler has not yet developed a similar sense of time.*

There can sometimes be a conflict when parents are focused on the time of day whereas the child is focused on the *sequence,* but not the *timing* of events.

For example, if by 3:30 p.m. a preschooler has not yet had his 3 o'clock nap, it's more important to him that you maintain the sequence of reading a story to him before nap time than to be concerned about the time on the clock. It's best to adjust to his world in which the focus is on *sequence* rather than *time* of day.

A good way to avoid hassles when getting ready for a new activity, such as a ride in the car, is to allow twice as much time as you think it will take. In that way, you will feel more

CONTINUED ON PAGE 208

CONTINUED FROM PAGE 207

relaxed and your child will feel less pressured.

Young children also need a transition period between one activity and another. Whereas an adult may look at the clock and think, "I must leave immediately," young children need some buffer time between finishing one activity and beginning another. Before leaving the playground in the park, for example, the parent might announce, "There's time for just three more rides down the slide."

Although a preschooler can't yet tell time, if the parent says, "Just five more minutes," those words will also convey the message that it's time to adjust mentally to the end of one activity and the beginning of another. It's also a good way to introduce your child gradually to the concept of measuring time.

4. *While adults can focus on just one thing over a period of time, preschoolers tend to be multifocused.*

While carrying a book for you to read to him, for example, your preschooler may spot a piece of red wool on the floor that attracts his full attention. He becomes totally absorbed by his newfound interest and will quickly forget what he set out to do.

It's as though one new distraction after another demands his immediate interest and attention. Because adults don't normally behave in this manner, some parents may find this type of behavior to be very irritating.

They would do well to overcome their initial irritation and use the child's signal of interest as a "teachable moment" during which the child's mind is receptive to new learning—rather than try to impose on the child a rigidly planned schedule of learning activities.

Children learn best when they demonstrate a desire to acquire new knowledge related to what interests them—even when those interests shift from one moment to another.

5. *While adults are often more preoccupied with the end product (such as being neatly dressed), preschoolers are more concerned about being involved in and even mastering the process.*

Young children have a built-in desire to develop competence. A 12-month-old, for example, may spill half his food on his clothes or on the floor in his determination to get the spoon to his mouth by himself, without any help.

You know—and probably he knows too—that his feeding could be accomplished much more efficiently if he would just let an adult do all the work for him!

Fortunately his desire to master this skill is more important to him right now than his desire for food.

Throughout their young lives, children continue to develop self-mastery of new skills: brushing teeth, dressing themselves, learning to ride a bike ... and eventually, as teenagers, learning to drive.

A child's desire to master self-care skills can be difficult for parents for a number of reasons. First, it demands a lot of patience on the part of parents. It usually means abandoning one's own standards—such as seeing the child neatly dressed—in the interest of letting him be involved in the process, even though the end result may look far from perfect.

If you tell your child that he is too young to help you, or that he won't do it the right way, he will have missed a very important learning experience.

Another reason that a child's desire to develop self-mastery of new skills may be difficult for some parents is because it makes them feel that their "little baby" is growing up too fast. They enjoyed taking care of all their child's needs and find it difficult to adjust to a new stage of development.

6. *Children learn best when they are involved as active rather than passive learners.*

That's why it's important for parents to find ways to involve their child actively in what they are doing. When preparing dinner, for example, you might invite your preschooler to help you stir whatever ingredients you are mixing. It may make things a little more messy in the kitchen! Just don't be too surprised to hear him proudly tell someone later that he and Mom or Daddy were the ones who prepared the dinner.

He will feel so proud of his accomplishment that he will want to help you in other ways as well. If you are changing his baby sister's diaper, for example, you could ask him to hold the clean diaper for you and hand it to you when you need it. In that way, you help him become actively involved in this activity rather than being a passive observer who feels excluded from what you are doing. Children who consistently feel excluded by adults are most likely to exhibit misbehavior problems.

By involving your child in as many of your daily activities—even at the expense of neatness and efficiency—you are not only providing great real-life learning experiences, but you are also helping him develop a positive self-concept. ∎

A Tricycle Is a Learning Machine

If you have not bought your child a tricycle yet, it's time you thought about getting one. A tricycle is an excellent tool for good development. A tricycle helps your child develop some very important skills. As he pedals his tricycle he learns how to shift from his left side to his right side. He pushes first with one foot and then with the other. In this way he learns that he has two different sides. Here's why this type learning is so important:

As teachers and consultants, we frequently deal with school-aged children who experience reading problems. Some of these children have difficulty distinguishing between letters like "b" and "d" or "p" and "q."

The difference between "b" and "d" is, of course, determined by the vertical line being on the left ("b") or the right ("d") side of the letter.

As your child learns to ride his tricycle, he is learning the difference between left and right within his own body. This is a skill which should help him later in school to distinguish between the letters "b" and "d," "p" and "q."

Don't try to teach him at this stage the difference between the concepts of "left" and "right." This cognitive concept learning will come later. All he needs right now is the experience of his left foot and right foot as he synchronizes his leg movements.

The tricycle also helps him learn about timing. In order to ride a tricycle well, he must shift from side-to-side at the proper time. He cannot shift at just any old time. He must make the shift at precisely the right time.

Time will also be very important in school learning. To spell correctly he must learn to get the letters in a word in the proper time and spatial sequence. Some school children who have spelling problems may spell "first" as "frist" or "girl" as "gril." These errors are examples of general problems in organizing time and space.

If Youngster learns to ride his trike smoothly, rhythmically, and efficiently, he is also learning to organize his movements in time. This basic learning should help him with later school learning.

Many parents ask what kind of tricycle they should buy. There are many different varieties on the market so it is wise to shop around in order to find the one that is best for your child.

Three general considerations are important in the selection: (1) your child's safety; (2) your child's learning experiences; and (3) the trike's durability.

Here are some more specific recommendations:

• Choose an upright model—the old-fashioned kind—rather than the plastic "big wheels" type for all of the three reasons listed above. The upright model is easier for a young child to control and provides him with a clear and unobstructed view of where he's going.

• Select a tricycle that is the correct size for your child right now. Learning to ride a tricycle can be dangerous if the child's feet can just barely reach the pedals. Some tricycles are manufactured with adjustable seats and handlebars so that your child can safely ride the same tricycle now and, with proper adjustments, at a later age.

• Choose a tricycle with a wide wheel base. Such a tricycle is less likely to tip over if your child suddenly tries to turn a sharp corner.

• Look for a tricycle without spokes. Spokes can cause serious injuries especially to hands and feet. A child's belt or loose clothing may also get caught in the spokes, resulting in an accident.

• Make sure that the handlebars don't turn too freely or too far. Many good tricycles have stops that prevent this from happening.

• The tricycle should be made so that the seat doesn't extend over the back axle. In this way, if your child ever rides in reverse or is hit from behind, the shock will be absorbed by the trike's frame rather than by the child's back or kidneys.

•Protect your child from injury by making surehe is wearing an approved bicycle helmet. Look for a "Snell Approved" or "Meets ANSI Z 90.4 Standard" sticker inside or on the box.

Once you have purchased a suitable tricycle, your child will be ready for the fun to begin. If he doesn't immediately understand how to make the tricycle go, you may push him gently along. When you push him make sure that his feet are on the pedals so that he will feel his feet moving as the pedals rotate. Taking his feet off the pedals could result in being hit by a rotating pedal.

It is wise to check your child's tricycle periodically to make sure that it is in good working order. A loose screw or protruding bolt could result in an accident that was easily avoidable.

Teach your child to use the tricycle in the way it was designed to be used. You should not permit your child to try acrobatic stunts such as standing on the pedals or riding with no hands on the handlebars. You should also discourage your child from "colliding" for fun both for his own safety and for good maintenance of the tricycle.

With a little care and precaution your child can use his tricycle as a wonderful learning machine while enjoying many hours of accident-free, fun-filled riding.■

Teasing

Parents frequently ask how to help their child combat teasing from peers or older youngsters. Children who engage in a cruel kind of teasing of other children usually come from homes where sarcasm and hostility—sometimes fashioned in joke form—are used constantly.

Most parents are able to control their anger and do not physically harm their child. Yet some parents do not stop to consider that regular teasing sometimes constitutes a form of emotional abuse. While these parents cannot be accused of physically abusing their child, the effects of emotional abuse may sometimes be more damaging to the child.

Even though some adults engage in gentle teasing with other adults, it is inappropriate to engage in this practice with a preschool child. The adult may consider it funny or well-intentioned. But the young child has not developed the sophistication needed to handle this practice. Hence it becomes a form of emotional cruelty.

What can parents do to help their child deal with teasing from peers or older youngsters? A parent's presence is an effective way to keep older children in line. When trouble appears to be developing, the parent may redirect the play or introduce a new activity.

Children usually take their cues from their parents' behavior. If parents do not appear to be upset themselves, the child will more likely remain calm. However, if parents become indignant in front of Youngster or retell teasing or bullying incidents, these experiences may become magnified in the child's mind. This tends to reinforce his timidity and fearful feelings.

When parents are overprotective, they intervene to "rescue" their child too soon or too often. This teaches the child that the only defense is the parent's presence. Overprotective parents may inhibit their child's development of self-confidence and positive self-esteem. It is important for parents to maintain a balance between watchful concern and unnecessary intrusion.

In summary, what can you do to help your child combat teasing and its effects?

(1) Eliminate teasing from your own behavior.

(2) Be present, unobtrusively, when your child is playing with other children.

(3) Let your child deal with problems he is capable of handling without your immediate intervention.

(4) Keep cool and don't become agitated when your child tells you stories about how he was tormented. Listen to his story, comfort him for a minute and then observe more carefully how the children are playing together.

(5) Avoid discussing the episode with others in Youngster's presence.

(6) Maintain a good sense of humor which is good both for you and for your child.■

---

www.growingchild.com

Contributing Authors

Phil Bach, O.D., Ph.D.
Miriam Bender, Ph.D.
Joseph Braga, Ed.D.
Laurie Braga, Ph.D.
George Early, Ph.D.
Liam Grimley, Ph.D.
Robert Hannemann, M.D., F.A.A.P.
Sylvia Kottler, M.S.
Bill Peterson, Ph.D.

Growing Child, Inc.
P.O. Box 620
Lafayette, Indiana 47902-0620
Telephone: 1-800-927-7289
©2005 Growing Child, Inc.

Next Month

- *Almost 3 Years Old*
- *Fibs and Obscenities*
- *A Start on Telling Time*

Growing Child®

Almost 3 Years Old

s Youngster approaches her third birthday, it is good to review briefly some of the important changes that have taken place during the past three years.

In general, there has been a gradual shift from a totally dependent baby to a more independent child.

This shift has occurred because of a number of important changes which we will discuss. These include the effects of her physical growth and development, increased receptive and expressive language, more cognitive abilities, and more varied social experiences.

Because of her physical growth and development, Youngster now enjoys greater mobility, especially around the house and outdoors.

Her newly acquired gross and fine motor skills enable her to enjoy drawing with crayons, or doing projects that involve cutting with scissors and pasting with glue.

Now that she is better able to entertain herself with these and other activities, she is usually easier to take care of and less demanding of a parent's time and attention.

She has also become more skillful in dressing and undressing herself. She can put on or take off socks, shirts, slacks and coats. But she still needs help with buttons, zippers and tying shoelaces.

At mealtimes she can use her own cup or glass and can handle a fork and spoon.

She is also capable of helping with simple chores in the kitchen and yard.

Her efforts don't equal those of an adult, but her active involvement in the world of work is an important part of her developmental growth.

Parents can encourage this involvement, for example, by assigning simple tasks such as "Please hand me that roll of paper towels" and praising her efforts.

By now her vocabulary has begun to catch up with her drive to communicate her needs and desires. The use of three- and four-word sentences enables her to express herself more clearly.

She can be very conversational at times, wanting to talk to anyone and everyone. She talks to herself and to her doll, teddy bear, and toys. In this way she tries out new words and experiments with their meanings.

Her increased cognitive abilities enable her to classify things by function, such as her clothes, books, or toys.

Later will come the ability to classify by size, color, or shape. But she is learning that everything has its own place. She is more organized in her activities and more orderly in putting away her toys.

She has developed a better understanding of time. Yesterday, today, and tomorrow begin to have meaning. While she will still exhibit impatience with delay in meeting her needs, there is a greater willingness on her part to wait.

She is ready to make simple choices. For example, letting her make some of the decisions about what she will wear today will help her develop decision-making skills.

At first, having to make choices will complicate her world and slow her down. But with practice she will become more expert at making these choices.

The major breakthroughs in her language and cognitive development that have occurred in the past few months have opened a whole new world of social experiences.

She can now use her imagination to play "house," "shop," "doctor," "nurse," "firefighter," "bus driver," or anything else she chooses.

She will sometimes use these imaginary roles to act out some inner feelings. For example, she might make her doll sit in the corner because she was "naughty" or "misbehaved."

Her games and play will now more often involve interaction with other children.

Whereas one year ago she preferred solitary play even when she was in the company of other children, she now enjoys playing with others. She may at times be bossy and demanding as she tries out newly acquired social skills and roles.

Even conflict and disagreement during play are an important part of social development. When children disagree about something, they learn that there is another perspective that is different from their own self-centered viewpoint.

The time that Youngster

CONTINUED ON PAGE 212

CONTINUED FROM PAGE 211

spends playing with other children is much more than social interaction—it becomes a key element in her development of new language and cognitive skills.

When children play with one another, they expand each other's experiences in vocabulary, pretend play, and creative thinking.

As Youngster interacts with other children, she also learns to share. She begins to exhibit altruistic behavior and to show empathy for the feelings of others. She reaches out to other children. She shows tenderness and compassion especially toward a younger child.

If another child is crying, for example, because her "tower" of blocks just fell down, Youngster probably won't try to rebuild the "tower." She will most likely put her arm around her crying friend's shoulder.

At about this age, children begin to show awareness of their own gender identity and prefer playing with same-sex peers. This is related to their developing cognitive skills of classification and organization which we discussed earlier.

Just as she has learned to classify things by function, such as clothes, books, or toys, so too she has now begun to classify people as either male or female and to observe some of the ways in which males and females differ.

In general, Youngster is happy that she is now able to do so many things on her own. Her demands on her parents become less as she achieves a greater degree of independence in self-care.

She appears to be more sociable and agreeable. She is easier to live with as she learns to achieve a greater sense of balance in her life.■

Fibs and Obscenities

bout this time most children tell lies or fibs that can be real whoppers! Parents frequently become concerned and wonder what to do.

Before you do anything, we suggest you decide whether the child (1) is deliberately creating fantasy, (2) is telling fibs to avoid possible punishment, or (3) is simply unable to distinguish between reality and fantasy.

A child is deliberately creating fantasy, for example, when he applies colored chalk to his lips and plays "Mother." Or he may develop an imaginary playmate such as an invisible child or animal.

At this age, a child's intellectual horizons are expanding. As long as you and the child know when it's time to stop, you can enjoy his tall stories. Or you can create your own just to see how absurd they may become.

Second, for some children their first lie is often due to a fear of punishment. Parents can sometimes prevent this form of lying if they first ask themselves some questions:

a.) Is it possible that the punishments may be so severe as to make the child very nervous?

b.) Did the parents already know the truth about what happened before they questioned their child?

If so, why did they ask their child a question for which they already knew the answer?

In general, it is more effective for parents to confront their child with what they know to be the truth about a situation. Then they can follow that up with the consequences. These consequences should be moderate so as not to induce more lying.

Third, some children lie because they are consistently unable to distinguish between fantasy and reality. Those in this group are frequently unaware that they have told a lie. These children, especially the more severe cases, usually require professional help rather than punishment.

What about the child who more than occasionally fibs?

First check yourself out to be certain that your own quota of tall tales is low. Children will imitate their parents' behavior.

Next, let the child know that there is a payoff for being truthful. You can do this by immediately rewarding the child for "fessing up" and sparing the punishment.

Youngster's vocabulary by now may include a variety of swear words or obscenities. It is important to be aware that making a big fuss over these words will most likely only increase Youngster's fascination with them.

The most successful treatment is to tell your child quickly and calmly that you don't approve of those words. In this way you communicate your values to your child.

If your child lives in an environment where he constantly hears these words being used by others—playmates or sometimes even their parents— it is important for you to explain that your values are different from those of other people.

Use this opportunity to express your own values to your child. You can say, for example, "In our family, we don't use words like that."

How parents handle a young child's fibs and obscenities can have an important effect on his personality and character.■

A Start on Telling Time

A preschool child can be given a start toward learning almost anything, as long as the material is presented at his own level.

This does not mean that simple arithmetic or word problems can be learned at this age.

What it means is that every task is made up of a number of simpler tasks. In turn these tasks are composed of still simpler tasks, and so on.

A child can be given a head start if he is allowed to experience those tasks that he can do at his stage of development.

The trick is to break a higher level activity down into its simpler parts. Then let the child do the parts that he is capable of doing, and help him with the parts that he cannot do.

We used this idea in an earlier article, "Dressing As Partnership." This article explained that Youngster could be encouraged to make the simple movements that he could make. The parent would direct the movements in the right order and continue any movement which Youngster could not complete by himself.

Another example of giving a child a head start is the matter of telling time. We have previously discussed Youngster's developing sense of past, present, and future.

We have suggested fostering his appreciation of time by calling his attention to the order in which different events occur.

The importance of consistency and predictability in his regular

A preschool child can be given a start toward learning almost anything, as long as the material is presented at the child's own level.

daily schedule was also emphasized.

As Youngster's awareness of time grows, time words like "when" begin to appear in his vocabulary, often in the form of questions. Thus he will begin to ask, "When can I play with Ricky?"

To indicate a short period of time, the usual answer to this kind of question is "Pretty soon."

For a longer period of time, it will help to provide a familiar event as a marker such as, "After we eat supper." Youngster will soon learn the meaning of such answers.

In keeping with this idea of introducing an important skill simply and early, there is another answer to Youngster's "when" questions that you can use part of the time.

When Youngster is hungry in the evening and impatient with the speed of the dinner preparations, point to the large hand of the clock and say to him, "We will have dinner when this big hand gets to the bottom (or the top) of the clock."

Point to where the hand will be as you say this. Then make every effort to meet that prediction accurately.

If he is not familiar with the

clock, you will have to explain that the hand does move even though it moves too slowly for him to see it.

Don't try to teach him hours and minutes. This is difficult even for some kindergartners to understand.

If Youngster asks you what the little hand is for, just tell him that it moves even more slowly than the big hand and he doesn't have to watch it.

We suggest you use only the hour and half-hour positions of the minute hand. Youngster is familiar with top and bottom but will have trouble with the side positions like 3 and 9 o'clock.

Of course, for this method to work, you will have to be no more than an hour away from the predicted event. But that is the longest time Youngster can be expected to check the clock's progress.

You can also use these clock positions for other important happenings. For example, you can indicate the time you will leave for the store, or show when you will be coming home.

In the same way, the clock can be used to signal the approach of bedtime.

If you suddenly make an announcement about bedtime, Youngster will most likely be upset because your timing appears to him to be arbitrary.

But if you provide a five-minute or 10-minute warning, you are better preparing him for this future event.

He still may not like the final announcement but he has had more time to prepare for it and to adjust to this new reality.

Then when bedtime has arrived it will seem less abrupt to him and he will feel better about making the change.

Importantly, he will be learning, at his level, the practical activity of telling time. ■

Transactional Analysis

It is not unusual for parents of a preschool child to sometimes feel helpless in dealing with discipline problems. We may occasionally hear a parent say: "I've tried every form of discipline with my child, from being very nice to being very stern, and nothing seems to work."

When a child's behavior is particularly troublesome, parents often say or do things which they later regret. They don't know what else they could have said or done under the same circumstances. That's when some knowledge of transactional analysis (called TA for short) can be most helpful.

According to TA, our words and our behaviors can be categorized into three different aspects of our personality. They are the "Parent," the "Adult," and the "Child." These states continue to exist in each of us throughout our whole lives.

Let's consider an example: It's Saturday evening in the Wilson's home. They've worked hard all day preparing for the special friends they have invited for dinner. The guests are due to arrive at any moment. Suddenly there is a crash in the dining room. Mrs. Wilson rushes in to find her 3-year-old daughter, Jane, sheepishly getting up off the floor.

Jane, it appears, had climbed on a chair to get a better look at the beautifully festive dinner table. Unfortunately, her foot slipped. As she fell, she grabbed a corner of the tablecloth. She did not realize that in doing so she would bring all those lovely dishes crashing to the floor.

In that moment, Mrs. Wilson is torn between two extreme emotions: she is very angry with Jane for what she has just done; at the same time, she feels sorry for her daughter who may have hurt herself.

Most parents can probably think of other situations similar to the one we have just described in which they felt torn between the different options of what to say and do. Transactional analysis is a system developed by Dr. Eric Berne to help people deal with such problem situations.

According to Berne, each individual's personality is made up of three parts, which he called *ego states*, namely, the "Parent," the "Adult," and the "Child." These three ego states have developed by the time a person is 2 years old. Whenever two people interact, their communication will involve one of the three ego states in one person interacting with one of the three in the other person.

Mrs. Wilson could have reacted in any one of the three ego states by asking her daughter Jane any one of these questions:

- Why did you have to make that mess, Jane? (Mrs. Wilson as "Parent").
- Will you help me, Jane, to clean up this mess? (Mrs. Wilson as "Adult").
- Why does this always happen to me whenever we invite company? (Mrs. Wilson as "Child").

Similarly, Jane could have responded with any one of these statements:

- I shouldn't have climbed on the chair. (Jane as "Parent").
- Mom, I'll help you pick up the pieces. (Jane as "Adult").
- It wasn't my fault that I slipped. (Jane as "Child").

The "Parent" in each person is made up of the "tapes" we have stored of all the parental comments and corrections we have received over the years from those in authority. Children also have a "Parent" state which imitates what they have observed in their parents.

The "Child" consists of the "tapes" of our experiences in childhood. We can relate to positive feelings in our "Child" state, such as carefree fun on a sunny afternoon. We can also relate to negative feelings in our "Child" state, such as feeling helpless or like a "no good" person after we have been harshly corrected.

The point of TA is that we don't have to respond to a situation in either our "Parent" state or our "Child" state. When we think about the situation rationally and objectively, there really is a third option, namely, the "Adult" state.

The "Adult" state is the one in which we gather necessary information before we react. The "Adult" is capable of remaining calm and objective while processing this information in a rational manner.

In our earlier scenario, Mrs. Wilson may have experienced her own "Child" state ("I can't take this any longer") or her "Parent" state ("My daughter Jane deserves a good spank on the behind"). But if she was able to remain sufficiently calm and rational, her "Adult" state would have been able to function ("Let's all help to get this mess cleaned up before our guests arrive").

Parents who act in their "Adult" state are more likely to get an "Adult" state response from their child. For example, Jane's "Adult" state response to her Mom might be to help pick up the dishes on the floor rather than feeling mad at herself (her "Parent" state) or feeling sorry for herself (her "Child" state). When the child's "Adult" state is given the opportunity to develop—as a result of interaction with the parent's "Adult" state—the child is likely to become a more rational and mature human being.

It should be emphasized, however, that it is not always necessary or appropriate for the

——— CONTINUED ON PAGE 215 ———

CONTINUED FROM PAGE 214

parent to act in the "Adult" state. There are occasions when children need correction by the "Parent." An example would be if they disobey the rules of the road. ("You should never run across the road without looking each way.")

Similarly, there are other occasions when the parent's "Child" state is definitely most appropriate. For example, this works when both parent and child are having fun playing a game together.

How then does TA help to foster better parent-child interactions? TA helps by providing a framework in which to analyze and understand parent-child interactions. On the basis of that analysis and understanding parents can decide whether the parent-child interaction is appropriate or in need of change.

The methods of TA are particularly suited to the parent who says: "I've tried everything to change my child's behavior, but nothing works for me." Frequently underlying this statement is the misguided assumption that the "Parent" state is the only state for parents to use in changing a child's behavior.

By changing the questions asked and the statements made by the parent to the child, it is possible to change a "Parent"-to-"Child" interaction into an "Adult"-to-"Adult" interaction, thereby helping to bring out the best in you and in your child.

Parents who wish to know more about transactional analysis can read:

Games People Play by Eric Berne.

TA For Tots by Erie Berne.

I'm OK—You're OK by Thomas A. Harris.

Transactional Analysis by Muriel James.

The Total Handbook of Transactional Analysis by S. Woolams and M. Brown.∎

Improving Listening Skills

In an earlier article, we noted that feeling objects, one at a time, encouraged better concentration and longer attention span than simply looking at several objects all at once. The principle of considering things one at a time in sequence can also be used in building better listening skills. Here are three games that can help improve listening skills.

(1) **"I spy."** Pick an object in the room that is visible to Youngster and to you. Describe several of its attributes so that he can guess what it is. Thus for a chair you might say, "I see something that is made of wood and has a back and four legs. What do I spy?" Or for scissors, "I see something that is small and shiny and made of metal, and you use it with paper."

The idea is to have Youngster listen to all the clues, remember them and try to put them together.

Be careful about action phrases like "you sit on it" or "you can cut with it," for they may give so big a hint that they detract from the other clues, unless the action phrase also applies to other objects in the room. Of course, Youngster should get his turn to describe something if he has successfully identified your object.

Naturally his descriptions are apt to be ambiguous and heavily loaded with size and color words ("it's big and red"). But if you choose a "wrong" object that still matches his description, that is part of the educational value of the game, for it shows him that he must be more exact and use words that uniquely describe the object.

(2) **"Which one sounds like mine?"** Save four identical boxes, the kind whose tops can be closed securely. Place one box in front of yourself and the other three in front of Youngster. Select four pairs of objects small enough

to fit into the boxes.

Place one of a pair in your box and the other one of the pair in one of Youngster's boxes. Place a different object in each of the other two of Youngster's boxes. Then close the lids on all the boxes.

Have him shake your box to hear the sound of the object rattling inside it. After that he should shake each of "his" boxes in turn to try to find the box containing the same object as the one in your box.

Usually each object will have its own unique rattle or thud. It is best to use objects that weigh about the same to eliminate weight clues. You can change the object in your box four times before you are back to the one you started with. As in the first game, Youngster must pay close attention and consider each thing in a sequence over a period of time. So concentration is developed as well as listening skills.

(3) **"Whisper game."** Another useful principle in encouraging careful listening—and concentration in general—is to reduce the intensity of the stimulus. You can do this with the "whisper game."

Place in front of Youngster five objects whose names he knows. Then sit behind him and whisper, ever so quietly, the name of one of them.

Ask him to tell you which one you named. Here you can easily vary the difficulty of the game according to the loudness of your whisper and the amount of background noise present.

Youngster will be very anxious to whisper to you, too. That is something he doesn't get much practice in doing during the course of his everyday play! You can reverse roles so that you have to pick out the object whose name he whispers.

All of these activities can help to improve your child's listening skills.∎

Teaching Opposites and Associations

Youngster is beginning to understand the concept of opposites. At first he may not understand the relationship, so you may have to spend some time explaining what "opposite" means.

A good way to teach some simple opposites is by means of a picture storybook. Make your own book by clipping from magazines, catalogs, and newspapers those pictures which will help teach the following concepts:

(1) Big/little. An elephant and a mouse. You can even make a rhyme about the elephant as *big* as a house beside the *little* gray mouse.

(2) Indoors/outdoors. A picture of children eating at the kitchen table, and another where they are having a picnic on the grass.

(3) Wet/dry. A picture of a child with raincoat, boots, and umbrella walking through a puddle and another of a youngster sitting in front of a warm fire.

(4) Fast/slow. A picture of someone riding a motorcycle and another of someone pushing a baby buggy.

(5) Hard/soft. A picture of two children lying down; one on the hard ground, the other on a soft pillow or mattress.

Eventually you can test Youngster's understanding of opposites by just saying the stimulus word (e.g. big, indoors, wet, fast, hard) without showing him any picture and asking him to say the opposite of that word (e.g. little, outdoors, dry, slow, soft).

You can use the picture book you made to teach opposites to also teach Youngster about associations.

Start out by placing three pictures in front of him. Now ask an association question. For example, "Which one says meow?"

Youngster must make the association between the sound "meow" and the cat in the picture.

Here are some more examples of association questions:

"Which one flies in the air?"
"Which one feels cold?"
"Which one tastes sweet?"

If he has difficulty with the task, you can help him by saying, "Here's one that says meow. It's a cat!" Put the picture down, and allow Youngster a turn. If he missed one earlier, go back to that one to make sure he has learned it.

Should a wrong choice be made, point out something specific about that card to help him recognize it the next time.

Eventually Youngster will probably want to ask the questions for you to answer as he becomes more familiar with the associations. ∎

www.growingchild.com

Contributing Authors

Phil Bach, O.D., Ph.D.
Miriam Bender, Ph.D.
Joseph Braga, Ed.D.
Laurie Braga, Ph.D.
George Early, Ph.D.
Liam Grimley, Ph.D.
Robert Hannemann, M.D., F.A.A.P.
Sylvia Kottler, M.S.
Bill Peterson, Ph.D.

Growing Child, Inc.
P.O. Box 620
Lafayette, Indiana 47902-0620
Telephone: 1-800-927-7289
©2005 Growing Child, Inc.

Next Month

- *Three Years Old*
- *Developmental Milestones*
- *Preschool Education Programs*

Growing Child®

Three Years Old

hree years old—magic words which mark the end of babyhood and the beginning of early childhood!

Most parents would like to raise a child who is self-confident, as well as being mature, self-reliant, and socially responsible.

Recent studies have shown that parents who combine loving warmth with clear standards and expectations for their child's behavior are more likely to succeed than parents who are either too strict or too permissive. By giving your child some work reponsibilities within a loving home environment, you are helping to promote your child's self-confidence.

Where does a child learn self-discipline and responsibility? At home, in what Maria Montessori called "practical life experiences."

At 3 years of age your child is capable of performing many tasks around the house. Instead of fabricating "busy work" for him, invite him to share in everyday family chores and responsibilities.

He can help set the table and wipe up spills. He can dust furniture and help polish silver or shoes. He can arrange flowers and water them. He can clean floors with a mop or broom.

By giving your child some work responsibilities within a loving home environment, you are helping to promote his self-confidence.

In the kitchen, he can help prepare food. He can pour cereal and milk in a bowl. He can stir foods that need mixing.

After dinner he can be assigned to dry or sort the flatware.

When you are cleaning the living room give him a cloth moistened with furniture polish.

He can help empty wastebaskets.

In the bathroom he can help clean the bathtub and basin. When doing the laundry, he can help sort the clothes.

Be patient with any mistakes he makes. And don't expect perfection the first time he tries to do something. It won't be long before he exhibits a sense of self-confidence and competency as he masters different skills.

There are many good reasons for involving your child in practical experiences in the home. Learning to pay attention, sorting and counting items, making decisions, and solving problems are all school-readiness skills that are essential for cognitive development.

Most importantly, by working in a loving environment your child learns self-reliance, independence, and self-control, all of which promote greater self-confidence and self-esteem.■

The Beginning of Early Childhood

our young learner has made tremendous strides in these first 36 months. In that period of time she has developed physically, intellectually, emotionally, and socially. She has learned to walk, run, jump, and throw. She can now take care of many of her own needs.

Having learned the basics of speech and language, she has gained much knowledge. She has learned to express her feelings and to relate to adults and other children. At the same time she has been absorbing the customs and values of your home. And she has been learning to adapt to the demands of her environment.

Your young learner has reached this watershed between babyhood and early childhood. So, on the next page of this issue we will review what a "typical" 3-year-old child can do.

When we discuss a "typical child," it is important to be aware that if we looked at a large number of 3-year-olds, we would find that a majority of them will have achieved or surpassed these skills, while some others will not yet have attained them. So you will probably find that your child is less advanced in some areas, more advanced in others, and "just typical" in the remainder.■

Developmental Milestones –3 Years

Language

- Recognizes own name in written form and can identify two or more letters in name.
- Gives information about self when asked, including name, age, and sex.
- Asks questions frequently which begin with "What?" "Who?" and "Where?"
- Knows several simple nursery rhymes, can recite a few, and even sings some on occasion.
- Talks to self, usually about recent events or favorite make-believe characters.
- Carries on a conversation with adults and peers and can be understood even by a stranger.
- Enjoys talking on the telephone to a familiar person.
- Uses grammar in unconventional manner and speech contains some sound substitutions.
- Uses personal pronouns ("I" "me" "mine") as well as some plurals and prepositions.
- Counts by rote up to 10 but has no awareness of quantity beyond two or three.

Motor (Gross)

- Walks smoothly forward, backward, or side ways, sometimes swinging arms in adult fashion.
- Runs with better control and can now change speed or direction.
- Jumps upward or forward, clearing floor by a few inches.
- Climbs up and down stairs independently by putting both feet on each step. Can climb stairs with alternating feet if someone holds his hand.
- Hops forward on preferred foot two or more times but can stand still on one foot only momentarily.
- Walks on a straight line without falling off line.
- Pedals a tricycle and steers it around corners and obstacles.
- Climbs up the ladder of a slide or other play equipment but may still want a helping hand at the bottom of a high slide.
- Kicks a rolling ball, making contact successfully only about three out of five times.
- Throws a ball in a specific direction with one hand and may step forward onto the foot on throwing side.
- Catches a large ball with both arms if thrown from less than 6 feet.

Fine Motor Development

- Holds pencil with fingers in proper position near the point between the first two fingers and thumb.
- Copies at least two simple geometric figures, such as a circle or cross.
- Draws a person though the legs may protrude downward directly from the head or the arms may be drawn in place of the ears.
- Paints with a crayon or brush, usually covering a whole page, but the picture may not be named until after completion.
- Cuts paper with a scissors but may not yet be able to cut along a straight line.
- Strings beads on a shoelace.
- Completes simple puzzles which have five or six pieces.
- Builds a tower with six or more blocks.
- Opens a door by turning the doorknob.

Self-help Skills

- Can dress and undress self, especially with shirt or coat that opens in front and with pants and underpants—but still needs help with sweaters, small buttons, or other fasteners.
- Washes and dries hands and face.
- Brushes teeth but needs help putting toothpaste on brush.
- Puts shoes on correct feet but needs help with shoelaces.
- Wipes own running nose with a tissue.
- Eats at table with fork and spoon.
- Uses napkin to wipe mouth or hands during mealtime.
- Shows awareness of danger by staying away from hot stove or electrical outlet.
- Shows some awareness of the meaning of money.

Social Relationships

- Starting to have special friends.
- Enjoys having another child at home to play with.
- Learning to take turns in games.
- Learning to share and cooperate, even asking permission to play with a toy being used by another child.
- Says "please" and "thank you" at appropriate times.
- Plays make-believe games with other children.
- Shows greater awareness of people's names.
- Repeats phrases other people have used.
- Demonstrates affection appropriately toward adults and other children.
- Recognizes feelings of others such as joy, sadness, or anger.
- Chooses a favorite television show by operating television controls independently.■

These milestones are guidelines only. All children do not develop at the same speed, nor do they spend the same amount of time at each stage of their development. Usually a child is ahead in some areas, behind in others, and "typical" in still other areas. The concept of the "typical" child describes the general characteristics of children at a given age.

Preschool Education Programs

ow that your child is 3 years old, you may be considering enrolling her in a good preschool education program.

Two wage-earner families are now more common in our society. So, it is no surprise that in recent years more attention has been devoted to quality preschool education.

Even in families where a parent can be a full-time caregiver, the educational and social benefits of a good preschool program deserve some consideration.

It should be noted, however, that not all preschool programs would be good for your child.

Some programs have such a rigid academic curriculum that they resemble a first or second grade classroom.

Other programs are structured so loosely that they could more correctly be called "play groups."

Somewhere between these two extremes lies the "ideal" preschool education program.

How then does one select a good preschool education program?

There are some general considerations that need to be taken into account such as location, hours of operation, and cost.

There are also some specific aspects—including (1) the program's children, (2) staff, (3) parent participation, (4) facilities, and (5) resources—which need to be evaluated during a visit to the program.

In a good preschool education program, the children are happy, the staff gives attention to planning each day's activities, parents are actively involved, and there are good facilities and resources available.

• Children

Do the children in the program appear to be happy?

Do they interact appropriately with one another? Are they encouraged, for example, to learn to take turns?

Are the children encouraged to talk to one another and to the adults in the room?

Are the children engaged in activities that have high interest level as well as social and educational value?

• Staff

Do the adults in charge of the program appear to be warm and friendly? Have they acquired the knowledge needed about preschool education and child development as evidenced by their training and qualifications?

Are there at least two adults for every 15 children in the program?

Are the adults aware of the individual needs of each child? Do they vary their expectations accordingly? Do they maintain good records of each child's strengths and weaknesses?

• Parent Participation

Are parents encouraged to participate in the program and to visit their child's classroom in order to observe the various activities?

Are the opinions of parents regularly sought and listened to?

Does the program have a parents' advisory committee?

Are parents well informed about their child's specific strengths and weaknesses?

Is there a parent's handbook with policies on absences, holidays, illness, and accidents?

• Facilities

Is the building safe for children?

Are there smoke detectors and adequate exits in case of fire? Are fire drills conducted periodically?

If food is served, are proper standards of hygiene observed? Are the meals and snacks nutritious?

Is there adequate ventilation in the building?

Is the indoor play area adequate with at least 35-40 square feet of floor space per child?

• Resources

Is there adequate equipment for both outdoor and indoor activities?

Are the outdoor play areas in a safe location? Is the outdoor equipment—swings, slides, climbers—in good condition?

Indoors, is there an adequate supply of hands-on materials—sand, clay, paints, etc.—for the children to engage in creative activities?

Are there other resources available—picture books, blocks, puzzles—for the children to use?

Are VCRs, recorders and phonographs available with records and tapes suitable for young people?

In summary, in a good preschool education program, the children are happy, the staff gives attention to planning each day's activities, parents are actively involved, and there are good facilities and resources available.

In an environment where learning is fun, all children are encouraged to develop their own creative abilities.■

The Sounds of Music

ow is a good time for parents to give some thought to music's place in their 3-year-old's life.

Every child is born with some musical aptitude and abilities which need to be developed. Musical talent is not just something that emerges full-blown at about 9 or 10 years of age. It is something that needs to be carefully nourished throughout the preschool years.

Young children appear to develop their musical abilities best through casual learning, such as providing musical background for their play activities, rather than through highly structured music lessons.

It is important to remember that, even in later life, most people who learn music don't become professional musicians. But they generally develop a lifelong interest that brings a lot of joy into their lives.

Focusing on music in your child's life is not just an investment for future happiness. It pays immediate dividends in the following ways:

• **Play activities**. Children show a natural responsiveness to music—singing, dancing, or listening to nursery rhymes—during their play. A great benefit of music is that it enhances the learning that takes place in play by providing repetition and heightened interest in the activities.

• **Movement songs.** It is important for later school learning that young children develop good perceptual-motor coordination, for example, connecting what they hear with what they do. Movement songs help develop coordination, for example, by improving timing, accuracy, and smoothness of muscle movements.

• **Emotional expression.** Children like to create their own music, sometimes in the form of songs with meaningless words. These songs help them to express their inner emotional states. Their own original songs also help them to express their independence, identity, and unique personality.

• **Relaxation and stress reduction.** For centuries parents have used lullabies to sing a child to sleep. Soothing music can also be used at other times to calm a child who experiences stress or who appears tense. For example, a child who becomes restless and irritable on a long journey may quietly drift into sleep with the sound of soft music.

• **Educational dividends.** Apart from the benefits already listed, music has many other educational dividends. For example, through music many mental disciplines, such as attention, concentration, and memory, are learned and enhanced.

In focusing attention on the place of music in child development, it is important for parents to work within their child's frame of reference rather than impose their own adult requirements. Most 3-year-old children will not respond well to structured music lessons.

Likewise, if a child is upset or tired, it is not a good time to introduce musical movement activities.

By being sensitive to a child's appropriate stage of development and inner emotional state, parents can enjoy much fun with their child while engaged in musical activities.

Favorable exposure to musical experiences during the early childhood years also helps develop a deeper appreciation of good music in later life. ∎

How 3-Year-Olds Think

ometimes your 3-year-old child may behave in ways that you find hard to understand. Such behavior may even upset you. At times like that it is important to be aware that 3-year-olds don't think in the same way adults think.

How then do young children think? A great deal of insight into young children's thinking has been gained by the work of a famous Swiss scientist, Jean Piaget. He found, for example, that young children are often unable to cooperate with adults and with peers because their thinking is *egocentric*. This means that they tend to see a situation only from their own point of view. They are not yet capable of seeing it from another's point of view.

Even adults may sometimes have difficulty seeing things from another person's perspective. As an exercise in perspective taking, write the word "WAS". Now, below that word, write how the word would appear to someone sitting across the table from you. To see if what you wrote down is correct just turn the page around to see how the word "WAS" appears when it is upside down!

You can test your child's egocentricity in a number of different ways. For example, one parent asked her 3-year-old son: "Do you have a brother?" He said: "Yes." "What's his name?"

——— **CONTINUED ON PAGE 221** ———

CONTINUED FROM PAGE 220

"Billy." "Does Billy have a brother?" "No." This 3-year-old was simply incapable of seeing the world from Billy's perspective.

Another way to demonstrate egocentricity is to seat Youngster across the table from another child, Jimmy. Use two identical toy animals or pictures. Place one animal in front of Youngster. Then say, "Jimmy sees the animal from the other side of the table. With this second animal, show me what Jimmy sees."

After he has tried—and failed—you can let him go over to the other side of the table to see what Jimmy actually sees.

Most children of this age will think that the other person will see the same view that they do. They are apparently not yet able to understand that a scene will look different to a person who sees it from a different perspective.

From a social standpoint as well as from an intellectual one, taking another person's point of view is an important skill which Youngster gradually acquires through repeated encounters with other children and adults. This is one reason why social interaction with other children becomes very important at this age.

An egocentric child, when playing a game that involves taking turns in rolling the dice, may show no consideration for another child's point of view. He wants to continue rolling the dice until he gets a "six" as though he was the only person playing the game!

In attempting to control the behavior of a 3-year-old, it is generally useless to explain how his behavior will affect another child's feelings. Saying to him, "You will hurt Joe's feelings if you don't share your toys" will be ineffective. But he will understand the personal conse-

quence: "You won't be allowed to visit Joe unless you share your toys with him."

On the other hand, a young child who puts his arm around another child who is crying shows that he is growing out of egocentrism by learning to relate to another person's perspective.

At this stage of development your child is also learning to use and manipulate symbols. Language is an important part of *symbolic representation*, i.e. representing an object or event by a symbol. As a child begins to understand the meaning of words, which are symbols, they begin to take on very concrete or personal characteristics.

The word "tricycle," for example, may refer to "*my* tricycle which is *red*" but not to Susie's because it is *pink*. Eventually, of course, the child must learn the abstract concept "tricycle" which may be applied to all tricycles irrespective of specific shape, color, or size.

A 3-year-old will also demonstrate symbolic thought in play. He can pretend that he is "Mom" or that the large cardboard box is a "house." Young children often deal with their feelings of anxiety or frustration by engaging in symbolic play. These symbolic games are important therefore not only for a young child's intellectual development but also for his emotional development.

Another characteristic of a young child's thinking is what Piaget called *transductive reasoning*. As adults we are familiar with deductive reasoning and inductive reasoning. In deductive reasoning we move from what is general to the specific. For example, if I know that all Irish setters are red, then if someone promises to give me an Irish setter, I can conclude it will be red.

In inductive reasoning, on the other hand, we move from the

specific to what is general. For example, if I note that a Labrador retriever which I have seen is black, I reason inductively that all Labrador retrievers are black.

In transductive reasoning, the young child moves from one particular to another particular. Sometimes the conclusion is correct. But often it is not only wrong but also amusing.

Let's consider some examples of transductive reasoning. If Jimmy is accustomed to going to the playground every afternoon, on the day you can't take him to the playground, he is likely to say, "Today didn't have an afternoon." In other words, for him the concepts of "playground" and "afternoon" are interrelated—you can't have one without the other!

Another example of transductive reasoning is when a 3-year-old has noticed that his Daddy wears a certain coat every day he goes to work. He begins to associate the absence of the coat from the closet with Daddy being at work. But if Daddy leaves the coat at home one day because the weather is warm, Youngster simply concludes that Daddy cannot be at work. Work and the coat are linked inseparably in his mind.

Transductive reasoning can also lead to *animistic reasoning*, which is the belief that inanimate objects are alive. If a child hears that the sun will *rise* tomorrow at 6 a.m., he will attribute life to the sun. If asked: "Is the sun alive?" he may answer: "Of course, because it will rise."

Yet another characteristic of a preschooler's thinking is *irreversibility*. With reversible thinking a person can think about going from one point to another and then return to the starting point. For example, if I know that 3 + 5 = 8, then with reversible thinking, I will also know that 8 - 5 = 3. A child won't be expected to have this ability until the first grade.

CONTINUED ON PAGE 222

CONTINUED FROM PAGE 221

Until they develop reversibility, young children are at a considerable disadvantage with only irreversible thinking.

Consider, for example, the child who rides his tricycle a long way down a sloping street. As he rapidly turns the pedals he is thinking only of the good feelings he enjoys. He is unable to weigh the consequences in reverse order, namely, that in order to return he will have to pedal a long way uphill. He can't yet play backward in his head the actions that will be needed to return.

Even after repeating these actions many times, he will still consider it someone else's responsibility—usually Mom's or Dad's—to come get him at the bottom of the hill.

You can check your child's present state of irreversibility using Piaget's classic example with two identical balls of clay. Let your child see you roll one ball into a long thin shape. Then ask the child if there is more clay in the round piece or in the long thin piece. Children are usually about 7 or 8 years of age before they consistently answer this question correctly. To answer the problem correctly a child has to be able to visualize mentally the long thin strip being rolled back into a ball of clay.

While the errors and fallacies of Youngster's reasoning seem obvious to adults, it is important to be aware that at 3 years of age Youngster is not yet capable of such reasoning. Hence allowances must frequently be made for faulty reasoning—even when it means going to the bottom of the hill to retrieve both him and his tricycle!

This brings us to another point about Youngster's thinking. He does not suddenly change from one form of thinking to another. The change takes place gradually. It happens first for simple problems, then later for harder problems of the same type. Thus we can't say that at a certain age

Youngster will show one, and only one, kind of thinking.

With problem solving, the kind of thinking Youngster does depends upon the difficulty of the problem. This in turn is related to several other factors, such as the amount of memory required, the number of items that he must attend to, as well as his general familiarity with the different aspects of the problem.

In discussing egocentricity, for example, we chose a simple situation with toy animals or pictures. But long after Youngster is able to position the second animal correctly, he will have trouble with a more difficult problem of the same type, like how the word "WAS" would appear from the other side of the table.

Being aware of Youngster's level of development—what he can and cannot do—can help parents to gently inspire him to more advanced levels of thinking. This awareness, as well as the opportunity to explore and interact with other preschool children are key ingredients of early childhood education.■

www.growingchild.com

Contributing Authors

Phil Bach, O.D., Ph.D.
Miriam Bender, Ph.D.
Joseph Braga, Ed.D.
Laurie Braga, Ph.D.
George Early, Ph.D.
Liam Grimley, Ph.D.
Robert Hannemann, M.D., F.A.A.P.
Sylvia Kottler, M.S.
Bill Peterson, Ph.D.

Growing Child, Inc.
P.O. Box 620
Lafayette, Indiana 47902
Telephone: 1-800-388-2624
©2005 Growing Child, Inc3

Dear Growing Child:

"I am writing to say thank you for putting out such an informative and exciting newsletter. I look forward to reading my newsletter and finding out answers to my many questions about my little girl's growth and development.

"Being first-time parents, my husband and I really enjoy reading about our baby and what to expect from month to month. Thank you!"

Eric and Debra S.
Stayton, OR

Next Month

- *Social Skills at Three*
- *Learning and Talking*
- *The Importance of Laughter*

Growing Child®

Social Skills at Three

Many 3-year-olds are outgoing, full of talk, and willing to make friendly overtures to other children. But in a strange social situation even the most outgoing child may suddenly become anxious, fearful and shy. This is particularly true of an only child or a child who is adjusting to a new baby in the family.

Pushing a child forward and insisting that she make a place for herself in a group of unfamiliar children who are already involved in play is *not* the answer. Such parental efforts may only add to the child's anxiety and tension and may even delay her development of social independence.

Some parents seem to expect socially mature behaviors of children which they do not expect of themselves! We may forget the sinking feeling *we* have experienced upon finding ourselves all alone in a group of strangers.

If we expect a socially inexperienced 3-year-old to feel comfortable under the same circumstances, we fail to recognize that by her behavior, she is pleading, "I'm scared! What if they don't want me? Don't make me go alone!" Instead of helping the child, we punish her by our disapproval.

Let's look at some of the ways parents can make social experiences more comfortable and enjoyable for their child.

One way is by role-playing or rehearsal. Dad, knowing that the children whom his daughter Jane will meet at her friend's home would be strangers to her, might talk with Jane about her friend and about each of the children whom she will meet. If Jane knows even one child in the group, Dad would refresh Jane's memory of that child. For example, "You remember Elizabeth. She was the girl who let you play with her doll."

Dad could initiate a game of "How to meet someone new" and have Jane learn to say "Hello! I'm Jane. What's your name?"

Dad could arrange to be the first to arrive at a party so that Jane would have to meet and adapt to only the host child. Then as the other children arrive Jane would be an "insider," not an "outsider." Dad could also explain to Jane that some of the other children might be shy or afraid, then have Jane practice bringing the shy child into the group. For example, "Would you like to help me take this doll for a walk in her stroller?"

Another way of providing Jane with security would be for Daddy to suggest that Jane play quietly near him. In that way she could watch the other children playing for a while if she didn't want to join them right away.

Upon arrival Dad could take the time to introduce Jane to the other children. This introduction should be more than just exchanging first names.

A good host or hostess, or even a courteous friend, will take the time to make an introduction meaningful by noting common interests or by engaging both persons in a short conversation until each feels at ease with the other. In this case, engaging the two children in a mutual activity, such as rolling a ball to one another, might be sufficient.

If Jane becomes engaged in play, Dad can show her and tell her where he will be if she needs him. Even an older child will feel more secure if she knows where to find her father or mother.

Play is often more fun when shared. An occasional wave of the hand or smile from Dad will help the sharing. Or Jane may choose to rest for a few minutes by Mom's side before rejoining the group of children.

Should *you* be the hostess, you can be helpful to the shy child. At the same time you can teach your own child social skills and consideration for others. Call your child to you. Introduce the new child. Suggest something like, "Jane, will you show Mary the swings and the sand pile? Ask her if she would like to play with you in the yard for a while."

A 3-year-old is capable of cooperative play. She enjoys it. But she is not yet very experienced in social interaction. An only child or one whose younger brother or sister is still a baby often has little experience in playing with other children her age. It takes time and experience to learn to play together in a group, to share toys comfortably, to take turns, and to role play.

She needs the support and reassurance that only her parents can give her as she attempts to strike out into the social world of her peers. ■

Training to Get Ready

The normal 3-year-old should by now be part of the everyday structure of family life. He should not be shunted aside or pampered, but should do his part, even if it is only a very small part of what the family is doing.

He should be permitted to do his part even when it slows down or frustrates other members of the family. It is in doing things for himself that he learns and develops good organizational skills.

Let's face it. There is a very real problem in having a pre-school child assume a meaningful part in today's family life. Our society is so complicated and rushed that young children tend to have most things done for them instead of doing them for themselves.

Life for the young child was not always like this. Fifty or 60 years ago the young child was needed in a very real way as a part of his family. He was required to do many things which the family needed to have done. He did things like "fetch and carry." This usually consisted of some fairly simple requests: "Hand me the sugar bowl.

"Now I need one cup of flour. Here is the cup. Fill it to the top.

"Now, pour out one cup of milk. Try not to spill any.

"Now bring me the baking soda from the pantry shelf—it's in the yellow box. Thank you! You've been a great help!"

In these and countless other ways the child of yesterday was exposed to the order and sequence of everyday life.

In doing these small tasks he discovered how his activities were part of an everyday systematic, orderly, structured pattern of family life. Daily routine experiences made him a vital part of organized family life. In the process he learned how his world was organized.

Unfortunately, in the rush of today's world, a child sometimes is not provided those important experiences.

We strongly recommend that you include your 3-year-old child in as many household tasks as possible. In doing so, you are providing him with important learning experiences—training to get ready.

Although this may take time and patience on your part, your child's increased involvement in the life and activities of your family will more than repay all your efforts. ∎

Learning and Talking

It is in the course of daily living—dressing, eating, walking, playing, or riding in the car—that new concepts are learned. This is because knowledge comes naturally when the learning involves action.

Let's consider, for example, the concept "together." There are many opportunities each day to teach this concept. When washing you might say, "Bring your hands *together*" as you show Youngster how to lather up with soap.

A few minutes later you might again introduce the concept of "together" as you demonstrate the action when dressing: "Bring the snaps *together* so that they will close."

You can also illustrate the concept of "together" as you gather toys like popbeads, nesting eggs and building blocks saying: "Let's gather *together* all the toys that look like this one."

The outdoors—backyard, park, curbstone garden—provide occasions for parents to point out the way trees, grass, flowers, shrubs, or fences look. Talk about their location, shape, size, and color.

When practical, encourage Youngster to experiment—"Can you close your arms around this tree trunk? Is it possible to do the same thing to other trees, to larger trees?"

Such an experiment will demonstrate comparatives, that one tree is "thicker" or "skinnier" than another. Comparative words like "more," "less," "lighter," "darker," "shorter," "longer," are essential to learn so that later he can arrange objects in some kind of order.

It is good to use the arms and eyes together when making comparisons.

With experiences of this sort, Youngster will become competent to make the same comparisons, and be equally accurate, using only his eyes.

Little words like "under," "in," "on," "over" convey a precise meaning which is often lost on a young child. Provoke curiosity and ask questions that require the use of these prepositions. "Can you see the bug *on* the flower?"

With an incorrect answer you can casually provide the proper information. "Look hard, see the bug? It is *on* the flower. We wouldn't see it if it was *in* the flower. And we couldn't see it if it was *under* the flower." ∎

The Importance of Laughter

By 3 years of age, children have generally developed a good sense of humor. They enjoy having fun either alone or with others. Laughter is part of their everyday lives.

For both children and adults, humor generally stems from the unexpected—the surprise element. But a young child's sense of humor is different in many ways from that of an adult.

If parents try to understand their child's humor, laughter can become a shared experience within the family.

Humor then becomes a powerful bond that is enjoyed and appreciated by both parent and child.

What are some of the characteristics of a 3-year-old's humor? How does it differ from that of adults?

Young children's humor is, in general, simple, open, spontaneous and unsophisticated. For example, seeing a tall set of blocks fall may be considered very amusing by a young child.

Children's humor is also likely to be visual in orientation (laughing at a funny face), whereas adult humor is often more auditory (sharing a funny joke).

Likewise, young children laugh about concrete situations (slapstick comedy), whereas adult humor is more likely to be abstract (a play upon words, a pun, or an "inside" subtle joke).

In recent years, researchers have been studying the effects of laughter on the human body. They have postulated a wide array of benefits from laughter, such as increased oxygen in the blood stream, enhanced respiration, increased heart rate, and improved blood pressure.

They have also been studying the relationship between

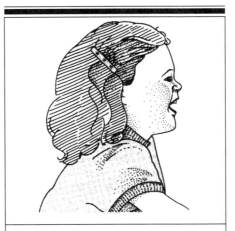

laughter and the production and release of endorphins, the body's own pain-reducing substance.

It is important therefore for parents to be aware of the role that humor can play in overall medical and psychological wellness.

Young children's humor is simple, open, spontaneous, and unsophisticated.

Besides these positive aspects, there are some negative aspects that need to be avoided, namely, tickling, teasing, and making fun of a young child.

Although tickling may initially cause a child to laugh, if it persists it can become a subtle form of child abuse.

Likewise, although teasing a young child may initially seem attractive because of the increased attention received, a 3-year-old generally does not have the cognitive sophistication needed to perceive humor in teasing remarks.

Parents who make fun of their child inflict emotional hurt—sometimes unconsciously—on the child.

A wise rule of thumb for parents to follow is that it is healthy and fun to laugh *with* your child (for example, by watching a funny cartoon together). But it is generally unhealthy and harmful to laugh *at* your child by making fun of his shortcomings or failures.

It is, of course, healthy for us as parents to develop the ability to laugh at ourselves.

Laughter helps us avoid taking ourselves too seriously. It helps us keep stress under control, keep problems in perspective, and generally maintain a healthy psychological balance in our lives.

If parents find that there is little time for laughter in their home, they should try to improve the quality of humor in their family life.

There are a number of ways in which to integrate humor into your family life.

• Read books to your child by authors whom your child considers funny. Just be sure he can also see the funny pictures in the book.

• Watch some funny movies together.

• Share some funny greeting cards—especially personalized handmade ones—on birthdays and other special celebrations.

Other ways in which parents can improve the level of humor in the home is by keeping a "Laugh Journal," "Funny Pictures" photo album, or videotapes in which are recorded some of life's funniest and most precious moments.

If we fail to record these fun experiences, we unfortunately tend to forget them. But the longer we keep these records, the funnier they appear.

Sharing a laugh together is not only an effective buffer against depression and stress. It also helps both parents and children to develop and maintain a healthy positive outlook on life.∎

Building Blocks of Your Child's Self-esteem

All children need to feel (1) loved, (2) challenged, and (3) competent. These are the essential building blocks of self-esteem.

(1) **Loved.** Children need to feel loved just for being themselves. Here are some ways in which parents can enhance their child's self-esteem by their love:

• Set aside a special time of the day or a special day of the week when you and your child can spend uninterrupted time together. (This may include, for example, going together to the mall to select shoes or some item of clothing for your child.)

• Keep records of your child's development. This may include keeping a scrapbook with samples of your child's artwork, or a special photo album or a home videotape of your child's favorite activities.

• Keep anecdotal records. Write down some fun things that happened along the way with the dates. In later years these will become treasured memories.

• On your child's birthday or on some other special occasions, write a letter to your child in which you indicate some of the ways in which your child is special to you. Be sure to keep these letters for your child's future reading.

(2) **Challenged.** In order to build self-esteem, a child needs to have challenging experiences which are developmentally appropriate, such as the ones we indicate regularly in *Growing Child*.

• If the activities are too easy, your child will be disinterested and will soon become bored.

• On the other hand, if the activities are too difficult, frustration will result, followed by feelings of inferiority.

• Activities that are develop-mentally appropriate provide your child with a sense of challenge leading to success. By experiencing such growth and achievement, children learn to take pride in their accomplishments and in themselves.

(3) **Competent.** All children need to have a sense of competence, a measure of their own individual strengths and weaknesses.

• Helping children develop self-help skills gives them feelings of autonomy and independence which enhance their self-esteem.

• Children need to be praised for effort, not just for success.

• They also need to learn how to profit from mistakes and cope with weaknesses.

What to avoid. It's also important for parents to know what can harm a child's self-esteem. Here are some things to avoid:

• Avoid stereotyping children, such as by saying, "All girls must be ladylike." "Boys don't cry." Such stereotypes destroy a child's sense of uniqueness.

• Avoid negative labels such as dummy, lazy, slow-poke, or fatty.

• Avoid comparisons such as, "You didn't do as good a job as your brother." Such comparisons foster feelings of inadequacy in a child and ultimately lower self-esteem.

Research studies indicate that the parents of children with high self-esteem try to provide a positive "can do" atmosphere in the home.

Furthermore, enhancement of a child's self-esteem doesn't just happen by itself. It requires a conscious effort by parents to provide positive experiences through which their child feels more loved, challenged, and competent.

These are the essential building blocks for enhancement of your child's self-esteem.■

Going for a Walk

A walk in the outdoors with Youngster can serve many useful purposes. Walking provides good exercise, particularly if it involves climbing up and down hills. It is also a great way to relax and to have fun with Youngster.

When you take Youngster for a walk, make it a "curiosity walk." Help her explore casually with the senses of touch, smell, taste, hearing, and vision.

In the woods or in the park, stop to examine a rock, a plant, or a tree.

Such questions as "What does it feel like? " "How does it smell?" "Can it make a sound?" "Do you know something it looks like?" will provoke Youngster's interest. Your answers will allow you to supply new and descriptive words such as "mushy," "squeaky," "lumpy," "bumpy," "squishy," "enormous," etc.

A walk in the outdoors can also be enjoyed by treating it as an obstacle course game.

Movements "between," "around," "across," "inside of," "under," and "on top of" objects increase your child's awareness of herself. How can she can use her body and limbs? Where are her arms and legs when she climbs on a gate or crosses a shallow stream in bare feet? What are the different ways she must use her body in order to succeed, namely to bend, stretch, pull, push, twist, turn, wiggle, creep, shake, squeeze, stoop?

As you play and explore together, Youngster gets lot of practice in using not only her body but also her mind to tackle the obstacles.■

Turning Trash Into Treasures

ome years ago an architect in Denmark gained an important insight into young children's play. He observed—to his dismay—that young children preferred to play with discarded material from an abandoned construction site rather than with the elaborate, sophisticated equipment he had designed for a city playground. From that insight a new idea, the "Junk Playground," was born.

Every parent can create a "junk playground" for his or her child. It means saving some items that would otherwise become trash and converting them into treasures for a young child's play.

Here are some considerations in selecting these recycled treasures.

Young children like the outcome of their play to be open-ended. They also prefer play materials which allow them to be creative and interactive. Some examples will help clarify what we mean.

Young children enjoy playing with simple blocks of wood, for example, because this form of play is open-ended. The blocks of wood can become anything they want them to be: a house, a truck, a wall, etc. Playing with blocks enables a child to be both creative and interactive, rather than intellectually stagnant and passive.

On the other hand, play with some commercial toys, such as an electric train, is not open-ended. An electric train is always just an electric train. For the most part it is meant to be passively observed.

Play materials do not have to be expensive in order to provide a child with good learning experiences. There are many items in your home that could be recycled as playthings rather than discarded.

Look for items that will challenge your child's creative abilities. Young children like to experiment, act on hunches, test and re-test simple hypotheses.

Here are some examples of how to turn trash into treasures:

(1) Boxes come in all sizes and shapes: flat, round, tall, square, or rectangle. A packing box may become a spaceship or a submarine. By laying it flat and opening the ends, it can become a tunnel or a train.

Boxes can also be used for interactive group games such as putting a doll to sleep in its "bed," playing "store," or pretending the box is a "classroom."

What privacy children can have when they retreat into a box! They can create a world of their own as extensive as the boundaries of their imaginations.

And if bad weather should happen to destroy your child's outdoor "spaceship," there is no cause for worry. A trip to the nearest appliance store will provide a replacement—perhaps even a bigger and better "space-ship"—free of charge!

Smaller boxes may be used for storing objects such as baseball cards or toy cars. These boxes can be stacked on top of one another or laid end to end. They can be pushed or pulled depending on the function they have in a young child's imagination.

In the process your child learns to discriminate size, shape, weight, and texture of each box, making practical trial-and-error judgments based on these discriminations.

(2) Old tires can be used for play in a variety of ways. A large tractor tire will make an excellent sandbox. A car tire can be used as a swing either vertically suspended from one rope or horizontally suspended by two ropes (see diagram).

All these activities can help your child's perceptual motor development.

(3) Other recyclable items:

Egg cartons: The sections are useful for matching colors and shapes, or for sorting items such as buttons, coins, and bottle caps.

Old magazines: Cut out pictures to make into a collage with scissors and paste. Or paste a magazine picture on a sheet of cardboard and cut into simple puzzle pieces.

Paper bags: Make a mask by cutting out a place for the eyes, ears, nose, and mouth.

Old sock or old glove: Save that single sock or glove whose mate has been lost. Use it to create a fun puppet character.

Clothespins: Color each one a different color (red, green, blue, etc.). Match the color of a clothespin with the color of an assorted array of similarly colored papers or other objects.

Carpet samples: These can be used to teach color, shapes, textures, etc. With a group of young children they can also be used as stepping stones for a stand-up version of the game "musical chairs." Each time the music stops remove a carpet sample until there is only one piece left.

From these examples it should be obvious why play materials do not have to be expensive in order to provide a child with good learning experiences.

By recycling—turning trash into treasures—you are providing your child with great playful learning experiences. You are also helping to save the planet.■

A Study of Communication

It is important for parents to make learning as enjoyable as possible. It is also important for parents to communicate with their child in terms that are simple, clear and precise.

In a study involving mothers and children, an investigator asked each mother to teach the same lesson to her child.

The task involved sorting objects and explaining the "rules." It was left to each mother to explain the task in her own words.

The investigator then analyzed the differences in the ways in which the mothers communicated with their children and found they could be divided into two groups.

Group I

Group I were the mothers who were successful in communicating simply, clearly, and precisely. These mothers also made the task seem like fun with comments like:.

1. "I've got another game to teach you that you will like."

2. "That's a big one, John. Remember we're going to keep the big ones separate from the little ones. Now, you do it."

3. "Mrs. Smith wants me to show you how to do this. If you pay close attention, you can learn how to do it. Then you'll have time to play later."

Group II

In contrast, the mothers in Group II were more impersonal and authoritarian in dealing with their child. These mothers often hindered their child's learning.

1. "There's another thing you have to learn here. So sit down and pay attention."

2. "No, no, that's not what I showed you! Put that with the big ones where it belongs."

3. "Now you're playing around. You don't even know how to do this. You want me to call Mrs.

Smith? Quit playing around or I'm going to call the lady in on you. See how you'll like that."

Summary

We may note that the Group I mothers were precise and clear in their instructions. Yet they communicated with their children in a warm and loving manner.

In contrast, the Group II mothers were more blunt, threatening, and authoritarian in their approach. This type of approach is likely to frighten a child and thereby inhibit learning.■

www.growingchild.com

Contributing Authors

Phil Bach, O.D., Ph.D.
Miriam Bender, Ph.D.
Joseph Braga, Ed.D.
Laurie Braga, Ph.D.
George Early, Ph.D.
Liam Grimley, Ph.D.
Robert Hannemann, M.D., F.A.A.P.
Sylvia Kottler, M.S.
Bill Peterson, Ph.D.

Growing Child, Inc.
P.O. Box 620
Lafayette, Indiana 47902
Telephone: 1-800-927-72894
©2005 Growing Child, Inc.

Next Month

- **The Scribblers**
- **Seeing, Hearing, Speaking**
- **Some Characteristics of Good Parenting**

Growing Child®

Seeing, Hearing, Speaking

ge 3 is a magic time for children. Once they have reached that milestone, they can tell you what they see and hear so that these two vital senses can be accurately evaluated.

It is also possible to evaluate their ability to speak. This doesn't mean that children don't speak before age 3. On the contrary, many of them, particularly girls, speak very well at 2 or 2 1/2. Many boys, however, although they understand and follow directions, do not speak in sentences until age 3.

Many doctors who care for children test vision, hearing, and speech as early as the child is able to cooperate. Those who don't provide this testing can refer parents to organizations and clinics that can do it at a reasonable cost. Parents should not hesitate to request this important testing for their children.

Vision testing can be done using an eye test chart that uses the letter E in different sizes or positions which the child is asked to identify or imitate.

Hearing is tested with a set of earphones through which instructions are given to point at objects such as horses, birds, and dogs, on a chart.

Speech screening can be done by having the child identify objects or tell what is happening in pictures, and repeating what the examiner says, such as: "The horse is running." "The dog says bow-wow."

State and federal laws, such as Public Law 99-457, now require that assessment and treatment services be made available to infants and young children who are developmentally delayed or considered "at risk" of substantial developmental delay.

For more information on these laws, contact your local member of Congress, or your local school corporation, or the Department of Education in your state.∎

Language Development at Three Years of Age

uring the preschool years, a young child's vocabulary is developing very rapidly. Just think that whereas your child knew only about 300 words one year ago, he will most likely know about 1,500 words by age 4. And by age 6 his vocabulary will have typically increased to between 8,000 and 14,000 words.

Parents play an important role in this amazing change by talking to, listening to, and reading to their child, as well as asking and answering questions.

Besides learning new words, a 3-year-old is also starting to use past tense, auxiliary verbs, prepositions, superlatives and so on.

During this period of development many children exhibit articulation errors (such as saying "wettuce" instead of "lettuce").

They also exhibit many grammatical errors (saying "I goed" instead of "I went," "worser" instead of "worse"). Often these errors conform to some rule in the child's mind (a past tense always ends in "ed," or comparatives end in "er").

What should parents do—or not do—about these errors? In general, it is not helpful to focus attention on the child's errors. Correcting a child will most likely cause the child embarrassment and annoyance. Frequent or harsh correction may inhibit the child from speaking.

There are other methods that are more appropriate. If, for example, you have frequently heard your child say correctly, "I went," it is probably best to ignore the rare occasion on which she says, "I goed."

If a child consistently uses a wrong form ("I goed there"), the parent can continue the conversation, inserting the correct form ("Yes, I *went* there too")—even sometimes with some stress on the corrected word.

Parents can also expand on their child's utterances. For example, if a child says, "Me want to go store," the parent might respond, "I hear you saying 'I want to go to the store.' Yes, we'll leave in about fifteen minutes." In this way, the child is helped to learn the correct expression without humiliation or embarrassment.∎

Songs: A Way to Develop Space Awareness and Speech Improvement

Now is a good time to introduce new vocabulary. An enjoyable way to teach a child new words, with their correct forms and sounds, is by using songs.

When you accompany the words of the song with gestures, you'll have even more fun. And you will provide a better learning experience for your child.

Parents can even adapt the words of a song in order to teach a specific sound that is deficient.

Here are some examples of some popular childhood songs:

(1) The Bus Song (tune: The Mulberry Bush)

The people in the bus go up and down;
Up and down, up and down;
The people in the bus go up and down, all around the town.

(Don't forget the gestures as you sing)

Other verses (or make up your own):

The wipers on the bus go swish, swish, swish, etc.
The brakes on the bus go roomp, roomp, roomp, etc.
The money on the bus goes clink, clink, clink, etc.
The baby on the bus goes wah, wah, wah, etc.
The tires on the bus go eek, eek, eek, etc.

(2) Old MacDonald's Farm

Children love to imitate animal sounds in this old favorite.

Old MacDonald had a farm,
Ee-i-ee-i-o.
And on his farm he had a (cow) (or any animal),
Ee-i-ee-i-o.
With a (moo), (moo) here,
And a (moo), (moo) there,
Here a (moo), there a (moo)
Everywhere a (moo-moo),
Old MacDonald had a farm,
Ee-i-ee-i-o.

Other animals and their sounds: duck *(quack)*, pig *(oink)*, horse *(neigh)*, chicken *(cluck)*, rooster *(cock-a-doodle-doo)*, cat *(meow)*, bird *(tweet)*.

Stuffed animals and their make-believe sounds can be created to add to Youngster's enjoyment.

(3) The Hokie Pokie

This song helps to teach the different parts of the body.

Since 3-year-olds cannot yet easily discriminate "right" from "left," it is best not to make an issue if they make this error.

It is best to stand in a circle so that everyone can participate in this song.

Here's how it goes:

You put your head in (place head forward into circle).
You take your head out (place head away from circle).
You put your head in, and you shake it all about (shake head back away from circle).
You do the Hokie-Pokie (raise arms above head)
And you turn yourself around (turn around in place).
That's what it's all about (clap hands three times).

Variations of body parts: *left leg, right leg, left arm, right arm, left hand, right hand, left elbow, right elbow, left knee, right knee, left foot, right foot.*

(4) Loobie-Loo

Again each of the body parts must do the same thing, "shake," "put in," "take out," "turn."

I put my right foot in,
I take my right foot out,
I give my right foot a shake, shake, shake,
And turn myself about.
Chorus:
Here we go Loobie-Lee,
Here we go Loobie-Lie,
Here we go Loobie-Loo,
All on a Saturday night.

Again the variations of body parts may be used: *left foot, right foot, left hand, right hand, left elbow, right elbow,* etc.

At this age children cannot usually distinguish accurately between left and right. So don't worry about correcting left/right errors at this stage. Just enjoy singing and acting out the song.

(5) One Little Duckling

This song can teach simple number concepts, matching the number of fingers to the number word.

***One** little duckling, yellow and new* (hold up one finger),
*Had a fuzzy brother and that made **two*** (hold up two fingers).
***Two** little ducklings and now you can see,*
*They had a little sister and that made **three*** (hold up three fingers).
***Three** little ducklings watched the river flow,*
*Along came another and that made **four*** (hold up four fingers).
***Four** little ducklings went to swim and dive,*
*They met a little neighbor and that made **five*** (hold up five fingers).
***Five** little ducklings, watch them grow,*
*They turn into **five** big ducks, you know.* ■

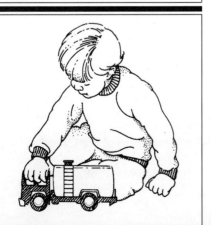

Observing, Thinking, and Speaking

Here are some specific suggestions for activities to help a young child learn to observe more accurately, to think more clearly, and to speak more effectively.

(1) **Activities which encourage accuracy in observation**. "What will happen if we drop this ball on the floor?" "What will happen if we set the little truck on the top of this slope?"

(2) **Activities which require organization**. "How many things can you name that fly? Things that walk? Things that are green?"

(3) **Activities which encourage sensitivity to the environment**. "Can you make yourself act like one of these—a dog? A bunny? A lion?" "Pretend you're a bus driver (doctor, farmer, etc.). What should you be doing?"

(4) **Activities which demand the making of theories**. "What would happen if we mixed this green paint with this yellow paint?" "If we let all the water out of this bathtub, where would this little sailboat go?"

(5) **Activities which provoke creative imagination**. Begin a story and invite Youngster to make up an ending. Or ask: "What are some of the things we could make with this ball of clay?"

(6) **Activities to promote flexibility.** Give Youngster some shapes (triangles, rectangles, semicircles, etc.) that you have cut out in paper and ask her to make as many things as she can out of them. Give her some wooden blocks to make a road, a tower, a bridge, etc. Help her cut up different pictures from magazines and paste them into designs.■

Your Child's Nutritional Needs

Although, as a nation, we appear to know more about health-related issues than any previous generation, the United States is often described as a nation with poor health habits. Many children are being raised today on fast-food diets that are too high in fat, protein, and sugar.

The development of good eating habits in children is particularly important during the preschool years. Their energy needs greatly increase as they move through the early childhood period.

The food children eat affects not only their energy level but also their physical growth and general health, including their immunity to diseases.

Unfortunately it is not possible to prescribe a simple nutritional formula that would apply equally to all children of the same age, size, and sex. This is because the rate of physical growth, energy level, and basal metabolism will differ from one child to another.

In spite of individual differences, all preschool children need a well-balanced proportion of fats, carbo-

hydrates, proteins, vitamins, and minerals in their everyday diet.

The easiest way for parents to plan adequate nutrition for their child is to follow the basic food groups in the Food Guide Pyramid.

The meat, poultry, fish, dry beans, eggs, and nuts group. This group includes poultry, fish, and eggs, as well as meats such as beef, pork, and lamb. Legumes (dry beans and peas) and nuts are also included in this group. All of these foods provide a good source of protein, vitamins, and iron. Two to three servings are recommended daily.

The milk, yogurt, and cheese group. Included in this group are whole milk, buttermilk, skim milk and cottage cheese. Hard cheeses and ice cream are alternatives. These products provide calcium, protein, and vitamins. Two to three servings are recommended daily.

The vegetable and fruit group. Children get vitamins, fiber, minerals, and carbohydrates from this group. Three to five servings of vegetables and two to four servings of fruit are recommended daily.

The bread, cereal, rice, and pasta group. These foods provide important sources of protein, iron, and carbohydrates. Six to 11 daily servings are recommended.

For the final group—**fats, oils, and sweets**—spare usage is recommended.

A young child needs good nutrients for proper bone formation and muscle development. A balanced diet provides the body with needed energy. It also helps prevent some illnesses such as colds or flu and conditions such as obesity.■

Order and Structure: Youngster's Room

Last month we talked about how important it is for your child to feel that he is a real part of what happens every day in his family. Now we want to deal with some specific ways that you can help to make this happen.

Let's begin with his room. There should be a certain time of day when (with a little help from mother and father) he gets his room in order.

What particular time of day is not all that important. The specific time will depend upon your family's routine and schedule.

What is important is that the time for ordering his room be the same each day. For most families the few minutes before bedtime works best for these activities.

What do we mean when we say he should "get his room in order?"

In general we mean that there should be a particular place for each of his possessions (toys, clothing, prized collections, etc.) and that he should learn the place where each object belongs.

Each toy should have its particular place, and he should learn where the place is for that toy. The teddy bear goes here, the doll goes there, the ball goes over there, and so on.

As he learns about individual objects and the place where each object goes, he is learning basic lessons about space and how objects are organized in space.

Later in school he will have to learn spelling (which involves the sequential order of letters in a word) and reading (which involves the sequential order of words in a sentence).

Another way of teaching him about space is to have him help you put away his own clothing from the laundry. "The socks go in this drawer, the underwear goes in that drawer, the shirts go here, and the trousers go there." Let him put clothing items in their proper places to the extent that he is able to cooperate. As he solves these problems he is solving problems in space.

Our message at this point should be quite clear—we are suggesting that you help your child get his room organized.

This should help him cope with the organization of space, a skill that will be required later for school learning. It is as simple and as profound as that.■

Scratches and Cuts

Scratches are an almost everyday occurrence with young children. Although it is often painful, a minor scratch can generally be taken care of by washing with soap and water and by applying an antibiotic cream.

Cuts or deep scratches usually go through the first layer of skin. They are sometimes deep enough to require some type of procedure such as a suture to bring the skin edges together.

This is necessary to prevent infection and excessive scarring. Not all cuts need to be sutured, however.

A minor scratch can generally be taken care of by washing with soap and water and by applying an antibiotic cream.

If the cut is clean and one inch or less in length with the skin edges only 1/8" or less apart, a butterfly closure can be used to close the wound.

These closures are available at the drug store and look like this:

This is what you do:
(1) Cleanse the injury and apply one end of the butterfly.
(2) Pull the skin edges together and apply the other end of the butterfly.

Sometimes two or three butterflies are necessary.

The butterflies must be left on for at least five days. They should be covered with an adhesive bandage or other sterile bandage.

The cut should be checked daily for signs of infection (redness, swelling, drainage, etc.). Call your doctor if these occur or if you cannot maintain the closure of the wound following the instructions given above.

Your child's tetanus immunization status also should be checked in case a tetanus booster is needed.

As a general rule, if a child has had the basic baby immunizations (DTP) and the wound is not unusually dirty, no booster is needed.

In the case of an older child, if the wound is dirty and/or more than five years has elapsed since the last tetanus booster, a physician should be contacted for advice.■

Some Characteristics of Good Parenting

ome research studies have been conducted to determine the characteristics of parents whose children exhibited appropriate developmental progress. The parents in these studies represented a cross-section of backgrounds and income levels. They were observed in their own homes by professional observers. What did the observers report?

Children who exhibited good social, emotional, and intellectual development were found to have parents who enjoyed child-rearing. These parents also had confidence in their own parenting skills.

The *quality* of parent-child interactions was found to be more important than the *quantity* of time spent with a child.

The most successful parents exhibited these characteristics:

• They talked to their children a lot and encouraged them to express or act out their own ideas.

• Discipline was consistent

and reasonable, without yelling or spanking.

• Many opportunities to learn were offered—stopping to answer a question or read a book, allowing the children a chance to manipulate or explore with their hands in order to discover answers to their questions.

• Encouragement and praise were high on the list, yet the parents were not so absorbed in their children that they could not enjoy them.

• Finally, regardless of age, the child was well-liked by the parent.■

The Scribblers

ost 3-year-olds like to scribble. They've just got to close their fist around that fat black crayon and scribble around and around, in huge arcs, angular zig-zags, blurs, blobs—sometimes even on a bedroom wall!

Scribbling may look like useless nonsense. But there is some sense to it. Scribbling gives birth to drawing—and to writing, too—some day.

A big circle will eventually become a face. Tight round scribbles make eyes, looser ones make curly hair. Short lines make

arms, fingers, mouth, spiky hair.

What do you say when Youngster comes home from the babysitter's or from pre-school class with a proud collection of scribbled pages?

A parent's first reaction should be one of encouragement, like "Good work, Johnny!"

If possible, hang these scribbles on a bulletin board or on the refrigerator door. In your child's eyes, they aren't meaningless scribbles, but creative works of art.

Even the great artist Picasso was once an ardent scribbler!■

It's for the Birds

herever you live—in the city, in the suburbs or on a farm—there's one kind of wildlife that's always around: birds. There's something about birds that can delight and intrigue almost everybody.

Birds, with their different colors, sounds, shapes, and sizes, bedazzle toddlers. Three-year-olds are delighted by their chirping, tweeting, and hopping around.

If you sprinkle birdseed on your windowsill or hang a feeder in your yard, sparrows will certainly spy their breakfast. If you go out with bread every day to the same spot, birds will learn your schedule. Some, like pigeons, will cluster at your feet for a treat. What a thrill for Youngster!

In winter, for hungry winged visitors, you can tie a piece of suet to a string. Hang it outside your window. Or use a big pine cone with bacon fat or peanut butter smeared into its crevices.

At first the birds will just be little shapes to your child, moving almost too fast for him to follow. Gradually he'll notice their colors and the sounds they make. He'll begin to recognize the same colors, sounds, shapes, and sizes as they keep returning.

Keep a simple bird book handy, one with clear, colorful pictures. Help your child rediscover the birds he sees among the pictures in the bird book and learn their names: the sparrow, the pigeon, and the bluejay are common and easy to identify.

After a while, he will have his own favorite birds. He will know where to find their pictures in the bird book. And he will also be able to identify them outdoors. You will thus enrich your child's enjoyment and appreciation of nature.■

In Case of Emergency

hen older children participate in school sports, scout camp, or other sponsored activities, it is customary for parents to be asked to sign a Prior Consent Form.

Prior consent may be needed in case an accident occurs and the parent cannot be reached immediately.

It authorizes a physician or other medical personnel to provide medical treatment for the child, such as anesthesia, surgery, or even hospitalization.

Now that many 3-year-olds participate in childcare, nursery or preschool programs, it is important to consider giving prior consent for medical treatment for your child.

What would happen if your child needed immediate medical treatment while being cared for by a babysitter, friend, or relative? If you could not be reached, would the physician or hospital have the authority to treat your child? Who would have authority in your absence to decide what medical treatment should be provided?

Some hospitals have a Prior Consent Form for medical treatment which, when signed, is kept on file to be used in case of emergency. These forms are usually available at the hospital's Emergency Room. Be aware, however, that the Prior Consent Form that is available at some hospitals may only provide for treatment by the staff of that particular hospital.

Some physicians and hospitals may have more specific requirements for prior consent for medical treatment which are usually related to the terms of their insurance policies.

Some hospitals and medical providers also require that the consent be notarized.

Here is an example of a very simple Prior Consent Form.

Prior Consent Form

I hereby give my permission for (Adult's Name) to follow whatever procedures are deemed suitable to secure medical attention for my child (Child's Name) should he/she become ill or sustain an injury. My permission is also granted to transport my child (Child's Name) to the doctor or hospital in order to receive whatever medical treatment is deemed necessary. I assume responsibility for whatever expenses will be involved. Signed by:

Parent/Guardian_____

Date_____

For the sake of your child's health and for your own peace of mind, we recommend that you provide written authorization for a responsible adult to approve emergency medical treatment for your child whenever it may be difficult or impossible to reach you. It is wise to discuss these matters with an attorney who is familiar with the federal, state, and local laws for emergency medical treatment of minor children which apply in your area.■

---

www.growingchild.com

Contributing Authors

Phil Bach, O.D., Ph.D.
Miriam Bender, Ph.D.
Joseph Braga, Ed.D.
Laurie Braga, Ph.D.
George Early, Ph.D.
Liam Grimley, Ph.D.
Robert Hannemann, M.D., F.A.A.P.
Sylvia Kottler, M.S.
Bill Peterson, Ph.D.

Growing Child, Inc.
P.O. Box 620
Lafayette, Indiana 47902
Telephone: 1-800-927-7289
©2005 Growing Child, Inc.

Next Month

- *A Word About Handedness*
- *Emotional Roller Coasters*
- *How Labels Affect Your Child*

Growing Child.

Emotional Roller Coasters

hree-year-olds generally experience great fluctuations in their self-esteem and self-confidence.

At times they act as though they could conquer the world. At other times, they appear to want to creep back into the safe and protective environment of babyhood.

These fluctuations are a normal part of growing up. For example, as you watch your 3-year-old venture into a world of new social experiences—whether in daycare, nursery school or with other playmates at home—it is sometimes difficult to let go of her. But she is determined to demonstrate to the world that she can do things on her own. She wants Mom or Dad to "Let me do this by myself."

Within minutes, however, she may quickly panic if she thinks she has been left alone. She comes running to your side for the comfort, reassurance, or encouragement that she needs.

These emotional ups and downs—emotional roller coasters—may test a parent's patience to the limit. As adults, we prefer emotional stability in our interactions with others. Toddler, on the other hand, is more accustomed to emotional ups and downs as she learns to deal with her feelings.

Coping with Toddler's emo-

A realistic goal is to strive to be a good parent most— or, at least, part—of the time.

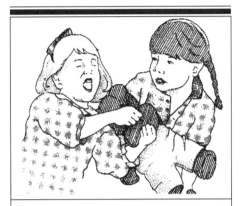

tional swings demands great patience and self-control on the part of parents. If they feel that their patience has reached its limit, it is good, if possible, to withdraw from the situation, even for a few moments.

Parents occasionally need a "two minute time-out" to gather their composure. When they return they generally can deal more effectively with a troublesome situation.

It is often reassuring for parents simply to be aware that their child's emotional roller coasters are a normal part of growing up.

It is also reassuring to know that all parents, at one time or another, have difficulty in dealing with these situations. A warm dependable relationship is the best stabilizer a child can have at times of emotional turbulence.

Beyond satisfying Toddler's basic physical needs such as good nutrition and providing a healthy, safe environment, her most important need at this age is for a dependable affectionate relationship with at least one significant adult in her life.

This relationship provides her

with the essential element of stability she needs as she moves onward toward higher stages of intellectual, emotional and social development. It is the secure anchor she needs as she experiences waves of sometimes baffling new experiences.

When Toddler can count on the faithful love of someone special—whether in success or in failure, in accomplishment or in adversity—her feelings of trust and positive self-esteem are nourished and developed.

On the other hand, children who fail to develop this important bond become apprehensive and mistrustful of themselves and of others.

One of the great challenges of good parenting is in letting your child know she is loved without being either overly protective of her or overly intrusive into her own private world. It involves being sensitive and responsive to her inner emotional needs, rather than imposing affection on her in ways she does not want.

That demands insight, flexibility, and self-control on the part of the parent and, at times, may seem almost impossible to accomplish.

Let's face it: It's impossible to be a perfect parent all the time. A more realistic goal is just to strive to be a good parent most—or, at least, part—of the time!

Striving to be a good parent involves trying to find a balance—a happy medium—between letting your child go in order to experience independence and holding on to her with affection whenever she needs your emotional support.∎

A Word about Handedness

As you watch Youngster throw a beanbag or draw a figure, you may begin to notice a preference for one hand over the other.

Many preschoolers, however, use either their left or right hand without a clear preference showing up until later in their development.

Although we refer to this preference as "handedness," it may also be observed in the child's choosing to kick with either the left or right foot.

For many years parents and teachers assumed it was their duty to force left-handed children to write with their right hand. Some recent research studies have indicated that this was not a good idea.

The viewpoint currently advocated is that the choice of whether to use left or right should be made by the child. The reason is that there is evidence to indicate that hand preference is not determined solely by environmental factors, but also is influenced by genetic factors.

In a recent study of the handedness of adopted children, for example, it was found that their hand preference was not related to the handedness of their adoptive parents, but was related to that of their biological parents.

Although it is usually during the preschool years that parents first begin to notice their child's handedness, even infants have been found to show a preference for one side of their body over the other.

In a study of newborns, it was found that some infants preferred to turn their heads to the left, while others preferred the right. This preference was found to be related to their hand preference at a later age.

Infants have also been found to favor one side more than the other when grasping a toy or other object. These findings indicate important genetic and environmental influences.

Parents frequently ask if a child will be disadvantaged in any way because of being left-handed.

With right-handers outnumbering left-handers in the ratio of about 9:1, it is not too surprising that left-handers may frequently experience the discrimination of living in a "right-handed" world.

Fortunately, in recent years, there has been a growing awareness of the needs of left-handers—with scissors, golf clubs, classroom desks, etc., now designed specifically for left-handers. Where these conditions don't prevail, "lefties" and their parents should speak out for their "rights"! (No pun intended!)

If your child is left-handed, he is very fortunate to have some excellent role models. These include artists such as Leonardo da Vinci and Pablo Picasso, as well as political leaders such as Benjamin Franklin and Presidents Gerald Ford, George Bush, and Bill Clinton.

In sports, "lefties" have demonstrated outstanding success, notably in tennis, baseball and soccer.

In one study of the Scholastic Aptitude Test (SAT) involving more than 100,000 students, it was found that 20 percent of the

> *Even infants have been found to show a preference for one side of their body over the other.*

highest scoring group were left-handed—even though "lefties" comprise only 10 percent of the general population.

All of this evidence would seem to indicate that, while left-handedness may sometimes be a nuisance in a "right-handed" world, it is not a handicap in terms of intellectual, artistic, social, or political abilities.

Even though Youngster may not yet manifest a clear preference for left or right, there are some things you can do now to help the development of your child's handedness:

1. Make a practice of presenting objects to the middle of his body. For example, if you hand him a toy, place it midway between his two hands.

2. Likewise, when rolling a ball to be kicked by him, try not to pre-judge which foot he will use to kick. Just roll it straight toward him and let him choose left or right.

3. Let your child establish his own dominant handedness. If you, or later his classroom teacher, try to force him to become either right-handed or left-handed, he may manifest "mixed handedness" (i.e. choosing either hand indiscriminately) which, in some school-aged children, has been found to be related to learning problems.

4. After years of trying unsuccessfully to make all children right-handed, educators and psychologists today want children to use their own dominant hand or foot.

Parents who help their child develop his own dominant hand or foot are helping to prepare him for later success in school. ■

How Labels Affect Your Child

J "Jimmy, you're *klutzy*."
"Nancy, you're the *bright* one in the family."
"Jenny is always very *shy*."
"Jimmy is a really *dumb, stupid* kid."

As parents we use labels all the time to describe our children. No matter how much we try to avoid comparing one child with another, we invariably end up labeling them in some way.

Why do we use these labels? One reason is that labels enable us to categorize, that is to simplify, our world. Unfortunately, the real world—especially the world of young children—is far more complex than the categories we use.

In using labels, it is important to ask how these labels may affect a child. While there is no simple answer to this question, there are a number of important factors to be considered. These include: (1) the type of label, positive or negative, that is used; (2) the overall quality of the parent-child relationship; (3) the emotional tone with which a label is expressed; (4) the frequency with which the label is used; and (5) the apparent effect the label has on the child.

Obviously, negative labels—such as repeatedly calling a child "dumb," "stupid," or "ugly"—are the ones most likely to be harmful. Many adults can attest to the long-lasting effects—even into adulthood—of negative labels acquired in childhood.

It should be noted that even positive labels, when used inappropriately, can also be harmful to a child.

For example, some adults may try to live out their own unfulfilled dreams in their children's lives: "I know Johnny is going to be a star quarterback some day." "Mary is going to be the brightest student in her class." In this way, young children are sometimes overburdened with trying to live up to a

parent's positive but unrealistic expectations.

The second important factor is the overall quality of the parent-child relationship in the home. If a child lives in a relaxed, trustful, loving environment, she will most likely interpret any label within the context of the family's secure loving environment. However, where there is repeated conflict and tension between parent and child, labels are more likely to be perceived in a negative manner by the child.

The third factor to be considered is the emotional tone with which a label is expressed. Telling a child "You're just like your grandfather" may be either a compliment or an insult depending on the tone of voice.

Even when a child is too young to understand fully the meaning of a label ("You're a nerd"), he will generally be aware of the adult's emotional state. And the emotional context will usually determine whether the child perceives the label as conveying approval or disapproval.

Another important factor is the frequency with which a label is used. A label, such as "You're klutzy," that is used frequently and consistently is much more likely to have a long-lasting effect on a child than one that is used only rarely or intermit-

tently.

A fifth factor to consider is how a particular label appears to affect the child. A child who is repeatedly told she is "lazy," for example, may learn to tune out this message. She has heard the label used so often that she is now convinced this is a permanent characteristic about which she can do little or nothing—except, of course, to be patient with those nagging parents who continue to remind her she is "lazy." The negative label serves, in effect, as a self-fulfilling prophecy.

Furthermore, by meeting a parent's worst expectations, a child has found a sure way to get her parent's attention, even though it is negative attention.

What then can parents do about the use of labels—so that they are helpful rather than harmful to a child? Here are some suggestions:

• Develop greater awareness of the labels you use most frequently to describe your child.

• Remember that positive nurturing labels, when used wisely, can truly enhance a child's self-esteem and boost self-confidence.

• When using positive labels, don't overdo it as your child may feel pressured to live up to unrealistic expectations.

• If you get in the habit of negatively labeling a child, you're not alone if you find it difficult to break this pattern. Just keep trying.

• Rather than using an all-encompassing negative label, ("You're an *impossible* child"), try to focus on the behavior you desire ("Pick up your toys when you have finished playing with them").

• Also, instead of using a negative label, ("You're a very messy child"), reframe it in terms of its opposite positive quality.

——— **CONTINUED ON PAGE 240** ———

Some Changes in Language

During the past few months, you may have noticed some changes in Youngster's language. As preschoolers progress beyond the two-word utterances which are characteristic of 2-year-olds ("Jimmy bath"), a number of important changes may now be noted, including:

- More use of plurals ("cats")
- More use of possessives ("dog's")
- More use of past tense with "ed" ("played")
- More use of prepositions ("at," "in," "on")
- More use of indefinite and definite articles ("a," "an," "the")
- More use of the verb "to be"
- More use of wh-questions ("when," "what," "where")

As Youngster learns to experiment with these new forms of language, you will hear much overgeneralization of rules ("My two foots," "I wented"). Even though these expressions may sound very amusing to you, it is important to focus on Youngster's meaning rather than laugh at her efforts. Laughter may inhibit her desire to learn.

A good way to deal with language errors is to repeat what she just said—using the correct form in your own sentence—to indicate you understood her message. In this way, she will learn the correct form without the humiliation of laughter or constant correction.

One of the best ways children learn language is by having an adult read stories to them. Often they will ask for a favorite story over and over again. While the repetition may seem boring to an adult, Youngster enjoys the opportunity to verify the sound and the meaning of new words.

It has been estimated that by the time a child reaches 6 years of age, she will have acquired a vocabulary of over 8,000 words. Right now, she can be learning, on average, four to eight new words a day. So, she needs an audience of at least one person with whom to utilize her newly learned words.■

The Importance of Perceptual-motor Development

You have probably found that your 3-year-old child loves to run and jump and hop and throw. Even though she is not yet ready to qualify for the Olympic Games, she wants your attention, ("Watch me! Watch me!") and your applause ("Well done!") after completing a 3-inch high jump or a 6-inch long jump! These activities are an important part of her developing perceptual-motor skills.

When we speak of perception and perceptual development we are referring to the brain's ability to interpret information received through the senses (hearing, vision, taste, smell, touch).

In many different activities a child's muscles must work in conjunction with perception (eye-hand coordination, for example). The ability to combine motor activity with perception is referred to as perceptual-motor skill.

Perceptual-motor skills play an important part in later school-related activities such as in the 3 Rs and in sports. The foundations for perceptual-motor development are laid during the early childhood years. That is why we want to focus attention now on your child's development of fine motor skills (finger dexterity, for example) and gross motor skills (activities involving the larger muscles).

You have probably noticed over the past few months that Youngster has been developing better fine motor skills. For example, she can now pick up very small objects with her fingers.

But she is still somewhat clumsy at times. When doing a simple puzzle, for example, she may see a piece that clearly belongs in a certain space. But her fingers somehow cannot get it to fit right. She may even pound the piece with her fist to try to make it fit!

Three-year-olds also love to stack objects on top of one another. They can sometimes build remarkably tall towers. In building these towers, they are improving their visual and fine motor skills. But since they haven't yet learned that the largest objects must go on the bottom, the whole tower may come crashing down when they try to put a large object on top.

There is also dramatic improvement in Youngster's gross motor skills, such as walking, running, jumping, throwing. It probably won't surprise you that researchers have found that 3-year-olds have a higher activity level than at any other age in their life cycle. They run, they fall, they roll, they get up and, then, they try to run some more.

In the next section we will suggest how parents can help Toddler develop and enjoy perceptual-motor skills. These skills will be useful later in life for other learning activities.■

Activities for Improving Perceptual-motor Skills

ecause of Youngster's increased muscle development and high activity level, he needs a lot of daily exercise. The more variety you can provide, the more fun you and your child will have—and the better will be the learning environment.

Most of the activities we have in mind for developing perceptual-motor skills can be enjoyed in your own backyard. If you don't have a backyard, you can take him to the nearest neighborhood park or playground. Or you might be able to construct a play area in the basement of your home.

By now, your child is probably already familiar with conventional playground equipment: swings, slides, jungle gyms, and teeter-totters. These items will continue to be favorites for many years to come.

There are many other things that you can easily make which will help your child's gross motor development. Besides, they will provide many hours of fun and enjoyment. And they are relatively inexpensive to make. Here are some suggestions:

Balancing Game: On the ground draw a 10-foot-long line that is about 4 inches wide. The objective is for Youngster to walk from one end to the other without stepping off the line. As he becomes more proficient, you can make the line both longer and narrower. When he is even more proficient, you can use a beam that is raised one inch above the ground to continue to challenge his balancing abilities.

Counting Game: Instead of discarding that old mattress, cover it with a plastic slipcover so that you can lay it on the ground. Children love to jump on a mattress. Just make sure nothing protrudes from it that might cut or hurt your child. Count aloud how many times he jumps: "One, two, three ..." Eventually, from practice, he will be counting with you.

Jumping Game: Cut some round logs that are at least 18 inches in diameter and about 12 inches tall. Youngster will love jumping to the ground, or from one to the other if they are spaced closely enough together. Another variation is to have him jump into a sand pile from an upturned wood box.

Throwing Game: Cut some holes about 6 to 9 inches in diameter in a piece of 3/4 inch plywood or particle board. Then fill different size throwing bags with beans or sand. The object is for Youngster to throw a bag through a hole while standing behind a line. Instead of bean bags, you could also use tennis balls. As he gets better at this game, you can move the line farther back to provide a new challenge.

Shooting Baskets: A variation of the Throwing Game is to use wastebaskets instead of a board. The baskets can be placed on the ground at different lengths from the throwing line. You can even assign different points, if you wish, such as one point for shooting the beanbag into the nearest basket, two points for the next farthest away, etc.

Ladders: Youngster will enjoy climbing small ladders. They can be made of rope or wood or metal. Make sure that the base of the ladder is secured firmly, that the steps are close enough together for him to mount or descend one step at a time, and that he can get a firm grip of the ladder with both his hands.

Boxes: Don't throw away those large cardboard boxes that appliances come in. With Youngster's creative imagination, a large box can be transformed into a spaceship, a house, a truck, a train, or anything else he and his friends want it to be.

Seat Swing: A sturdy seat swing can be made very easily by attaching two pieces of strong rope or chain to the ends of a flat piece of wood that serves as a seat. The swing can be suspended between two trees or from a bar.

Stepping Stones: Old auto tires can be partially buried upright in the ground to form a series of "stepping stones" (see diagram). Youngster can carefully balance and step from "stone" to "stone."

As you watch Youngster enjoying these activities, you will probably think of other games to invent. These suggestions will help to get you started on activities which serve to develop perceptual-motor skills.

It is good to start with activities that are well within Youngster's ability range. After he has experienced repeated success at one level, you can then progress to a higher, more challenging, level.

If he shows signs of tiredness or frustration, it is best to temporarily discontinue the activity. After he is well rested, he will make more rapid progress and will enjoy the activities a lot more.■

Safety First

Every year more than 60,000 young children are treated in hospital emergency rooms for playground-related injuries that were probably avoidable.

A hard concrete surface, for example, is highly dangerous if a child should fall head first from a ladder or jungle gym. There should be at least six inches of sand, sawdust, or wood chips beneath any equipment from which a child might fall.

An effective way to prevent many injuries is to inspect the playground for any hazards. Also explain safety rules to your child ahead of time.

It is also important for an adult to be nearby whenever preschool children use outdoor equipment. In that way, dangerous play can often be anticipated and prevented. And if an accident should occur, an adult is there to provide immediate needed assistance.

Safety concerns should not, however, result in undue restrictions on outdoor activities. Healthy and safe vigorous outdoor activities are very important for stimulating preschoolers' physical, perceptual, cognitive, and social development.■

CONTINUED FROM PAGE 237

("Your baseball cards are nicely in order. Now see if you can do the same with your puzzle pieces").

• Remember that your tone of voice—the way you say it—will probably have more impact on your child than what you say.

• Remember that it's normal for young children to engage occasionally in undesirable behavior. A few transgressions don't merit a permanent negative label.

• The time you are most likely to say something hurtful to a child is when you are feeling tired, frustrated or under stress. So try to avoid using any labels under these circumstances.

• Become more aware of the labels used by other people—siblings, friends, babysitters—to describe your child. You may need to offset their effect if you think they are harmful.

• It's best to let children develop their own potential without undue pressure from labeling. Children establish their own identities based on their own perceptions of their strengths and weaknesses.

• Above all, maintain a healthy sense of balance and moderation when applying any label to your child.■

www.growingchild.com

Contributing Authors

Phil Bach, O.D., Ph.D.
Miriam Bender, Ph.D.
Joseph Braga, Ed.D.
Laurie Braga, Ph.D.
George Early, Ph.D.
Liam Grimley, Ph.D.
Robert Hannemann, M.D., F.A.A.P.
Sylvia Kottler, M.S.
Bill Peterson, Ph.D.

Growing Child, Inc.
P.O. 620
Lafayette, Indiana 47902
Telephone: 1-800-927-7289
©2005 Growing Child, Inc.

Dear Growing Child:

"Time and time again, you have enlightened me about my daughter and the many stages she has gone through.

"More than once my annoyance and anxiety have disappeared as I read why she developed these 'quirks.'

"Thanks so much!"

Rosalind K.
Madison, AL

Next Month

- *Pretend Play*
- *Listen Closely*
- *Your Child's Self-esteem*

Growing Child®

Your Child's Self-esteem

Will parents' child-rearing practices affect their child's later self-esteem in school? Results of recent research studies of school-aged children appear to shed some light on this important question.

Researchers have generally defined self-esteem as the positive or negative evaluations one makes of oneself. Children with high self-esteem in school, for example, see themselves as accomplishing their own personal goals. Those with low self-esteem perceive a discrepancy between who they are and who they would like to be.

Even though your child is just 3 years old, certain patterns of child-rearing practices in the home appear to be important for the development of later self-esteem in school.

The parents of children with high self-esteem were found, in general, to have the following characteristics:

(1) They listened attentively to what their child had to say.

(2) They praised and encouraged independence.

(3) They were clear and consistent in establishing rules for their child's behavior.

(4) They provided their child with much emotional warmth and affection in the home.

On the other hand, it was found that children who were repeatedly told at home they were "stupid," "irresponsible," or "immature" were more likely to develop a low opinion of themselves and to underestimate their abilities in school. The parents of children with low self-esteem were also more likely to combine permissiveness at home with intermittent severe punishment for misbehavior.

Of course, it is not easy for parents to always exhibit the positive characteristics that will foster high self-esteem in a child. It requires a great deal of patience, perseverance, and self-control. This effort, however, appears to be well worthwhile in promoting a child's psychological well-being.

When children with high self-esteem in school were compared with children with low self-esteem, they were found to be more self-confident, earn better grades, have more friends, and view their relationship with their parents more positively.

The seeds of a child's positive self-esteem apparently are sown in the home during the important preschool years.

The key parental attributes that foster positive self-esteem appear to be encouragement of a young child's ideas and sense of independence, combined with a clear and firm pattern of discipline, provided within a warm and loving home environment.■

Listen Closely

At 40 months children still are developing the ability to make all of the sounds and sound combinations correctly in their speech. At this age we want to encourage an abundance of speech rather than precision.

Before children can express the differences in speech sounds, they have to pay attention to the differences in other kinds of sounds. Therefore, they need to begin by identifying sounds that are the same from those that are different.

Select two grossly different sound-makers such as a whistle and a drum. Tell Youngster, "Listen to these sounds and tell me if they are the same or different." You then make each sound. Reinforce Youngster's correct response, "Yes, you're right—they are different," or "No, they're not the same, they're different."

Make sure later to include two sounds that are the same to test Youngster's ability to recognize sameness.

Next, increase the complexity by asking Youngster to turn his back while you produce the sounds. Now the decision of "same" or "different" will be made exclusively by listening. When the accuracy reaches five out of five trials, you're ready to move on to other sounds, namely speech sounds.

When you start with speech sounds, select those which are

——— CONTINUED ON PAGE 243 ———

Pretend Play

Whether your child is playing alone or with a friend, at home or at her preschool, pretend play—role-playing— has become an important part of her life.

Role-playing serves many functions for your child at 40 months. Perhaps you have overheard her having a tea party, assuming the roles of mommy and her friends. Or as you walked past her bedroom, you may have heard her say: "Vroom ... vroom ... hurry to the fire! Get out the fire hoses."

Although at 40 months Youngster is still basically a self-centered individual, she is becoming increasingly aware of the world around her.

In the months and years to come, your child will pretend to be mommy, daddy, baby, big sister, doctor, nurse, firefighter and police officer—all the people with whom she has come into contact. And whether boy or girl, it makes no difference which role your child assumes at this young age.

According to Jean Piaget,the noted Swiss psychologist, "one of the functions of symbolic play is to satisfy the self by transforming what is real into what is desired." The child remakes her own life as she would like it to be. She relives all her pleasures, resolves all her conflicts, and above all, completes reality by means of make-believe.

Youngster is developing a new concept of herself and a new awareness of the world around her. Symbolic or imaginative play is one of the ways in which she incorporates all that she is learning. She must act out repeatedly what she sees and hears in order to absorb and assimilate these new ideas.

It is good to remember that at this age it is often difficult for

Youngster to distinguish between fantasy and reality. This is one reason why a nightmare may seem so real or why some children suddenly need a light on at night.

Her imaginative play helps her to test the difference between real and make-believe.

In addition, pretend play provides a *positive* way for your 40-month-old to act out her fears and hostilities. By having an opportunity to play out her feelings in fantasy, she will be able to master emotions which could otherwise overwhelm her.

It has been said that play is the work of children. Children learn through play. Many child development experts maintain that never again will imaginative play be as important as at nursery school age.

How do you encourage imaginative play? Primarily through your words of love and encouragement. You can create an atmosphere where your child feels free to "pretend."

You can also provide her with toys she likes to use in her imaginative play such as hats, telephones, dolls and dishes, cars and trucks, nurse and doctor kits. Such toys need not be expensive. As you will notice, your child at 40 months enjoys things that can be used in a *variety of ways*, ways that she will discover for herself.

In addition, we suggest that you read to your child every day. Good children's books stimulate her imagination and expand her ideas. And since your child is not only a keen observer but also a delightful companion at this age, she is ready to travel with you past the confines of her home into the neighborhoods of an ever-widening world.■

Egg Carton Problem

This is a problem-solving game. Get an egg carton. Choose any twelve of these little objects and put one in each compartment.
1. Rubber band.
2. Threaded needle.
3. Bit of cloth.
4. Paper clip.
5. Button.
6. Bit of paper.
7. Piece of string.
8. Pipe cleaner or wire.
9. Cut-off piece of a straw.
10. Stick of chewing gum.
11. White glue.
12. Safety pin.
13. Bottle cap.
14. Cork.
15. Piece of elbow macaroni.
16. Feather.
17. Toothpick.
18. Piece of cardboard with one slot cut in it.
19. Band-aid.

The task is to attach each of these objects—in your mind—to at least one other object.

Tell the child, "Show me which things you think go together, and see if you can tell me why."

Safety note: Do not leave the egg carton unattended. Some of the items can be dangerous if swallowed or used improperly.■

Reading Begins at Home

This article was originally prepared and distributed by the Missouri Department of Education. It is reprinted as a public service through the joint efforts of Field Enterprises Educational Corporation and the American Library Association.

While all of this material may not apply to your child right now, it does include many objectives of *Growing Child*. The ideas presented are important and worth reading.

*   *   *   *

Did you know that 50 percent of intellectual development takes place between birth and 4 years of age?

That means that parents are important teachers. You provide the foundation of your child's learning skills right within your own home.

CONTINUED FROM PAGE 241

different just as you did when you chose sound-makers. Tell Youngster, "Listen to these sounds: 'aaaaa' (pause), 'sssss.' Are they the same or different?" It is preferable to concentrate upon the sounds which the alphabet letters represent ("rrrrr") and not upon the letters' names ("R"). Be sure to reinforce the correct response, "Yes, you are right. They are not the same," or "No, they are not the same, they're different."

Now it's time to introduce sounds that are the same. "Listen. Are these the same or different: 'chchchch' (pause), 'chchchch'?" Again reinforce the correct answer, "Yes, they are the same."

Later in this issue we will describe some activities which can teach a child listening discrimination. (See "Attention-getters" on page 245).■

You can shape the course of your child's educational future by the quality of learning experiences you provide before he or she ever goes to school.

Here are six watchwords designed to help you make the most of your child's early learning experiences:

Listen: Listen to your child. Pay attention to what he or she is saying. Call attention to sounds. Listening and attaching meaning to sounds are essential skills that must be acquired before a child can read or succeed in a classroom environment.

Speak: Talk with your child. Direct conversation to him or her from infancy. Help your child learn to distinguish sounds and imitate them.

Take a walk together. Talk about the things you see and hear. Help the child classify objects as you see them: foods, plants, farm animals, birds, etc.

Sing to your child. This teaches enjoyment of music and rhythm.

Read: Read to your child every day. Make reading seem enjoyable. Then it will be a skill he or she will want to acquire. Let the child choose a favorite book or story to read. When you read stories, stop in the middle and ask your child what will happen next. Talk about the pictures. Have your child point to objects in the pictures.

When your child is old enough, write down words as he or she says them. Let the child know that printed material is really "printed talk."

Take your child to the library. Let him or her see books there. Buy books that "belong" to your child. Provide a place for your child's books at home.

Remember, if the child sees you reading, then reading becomes something useful in his or her mind.

Move: Help your child roll over, crawl, stand, and walk. This develops muscle control. Let your child explore. Provide safe play objects such as boxes of different sizes, blocks, scraps of cloth with different textures, spoons, and pans.

Through these experiences, you can help teach such concepts as wet, dry, soft, hard, inside, outside, under, over, and others such as those of order: first, second, third, and so on.

Parents are important teachers. You provide the foundation of your child's learning skills right within your own home.

Interact: Help your child learn that he or she is a part of a family group. Include your child in planning family activities. Give encouragement and praise when it is merited.

Guard: Control your child's television viewing. Search out better TV programs for children and share them with your child. Talk about the programs. Correct any misconceptions that may have developed from them.■

Prosocial Behavior

 et Jennifer play with your doll while you're playing with the play dough."

"Johnny, don't throw sand."

"Mary, remember you have to wait your turn."

A preschooler's parents are undoubtedly familiar with these exhortations. At one time or another, every youngster gets in trouble and needs to learn how to behave appropriately.

Have you noticed, however, that some preschoolers more often interact negatively with their peers, for example, being bossy or inconsiderate of another's feelings?

By contrast, other preschoolers generally behave in ways that help or benefit the other person, for example, by giving a hug to a child who is crying.

Psychologists use the term "prosocial behavior" for these positive, supportive, helping acts. To have a prosocial orientation means to be a caring person, to experience empathy for others, to wish to interact positively with others.

In recent years many research studies have been conducted on different aspects of prosocial behavior. The questions for which researchers have sought answers should intrigue any preschooler's parents.

At what age does prosocial behavior begin? Is there developmental progression in a child's prosocial reasoning?

How does a child acquire prosocial behaviors—or their opposite: antisocial behaviors? What effects can parents have on their child's development of prosocial behaviors?

It has been observed that even infants will cry at the sound of another baby crying. While this could be merely imitating behavior, it may actually be the first signs of human sharing of

another's feelings.

Certainly by 2 years of age some toddlers will try to comfort another child in distress, for example, by offering to share a teddy bear or a favorite toy.

Infants and young children, however, are by nature egocentric: They see the world only from their own point of view. This does not necessarily mean that they are always selfish or egotistical. It simply means that they are not yet capable of seeing things from another person's perspective. For example, 3 1/2-year-old Paul thinks his Mom would like a toy truck for her birthday because that's what he wants.

One of the major tasks of the early childhood years is to move from an egocentric view of the world to one in which other perspectives are considered.

As a child's egocentrism decreases and perspective-taking abilities develop, there is an increase in prosocial behaviors. And as children become more sensitive to other people's feelings and intentions—usually between 3 and 7 years of age— their concepts of friendship and interpersonal relationships also change.

Gift giving, for example, is a way of establishing and maintaining social interaction. For the egocentric child, a gift may be anything—a pebble, a piece of twine, or something that doesn't even belong to her. The gift is not intended to be permanent. The recipient is expected to give it back as soon as the child considers the social interaction to have ended.

By contrast, for the child who has developed perspective-taking ability, a gift has a more permanent quality. "I know you would feel sad if I asked you to give that back to me."

During the preschool years there is a gradual development— related to the development of perspective-taking—in a child's empathy for another child's pain or distress. Likewise, there is generally an increase in helping behaviors ("What can I do, Mom?") and in cooperative activities to achieve a common goal ("I'll do this while you're working on that.").

In studying cooperative tasks, researchers have found that when 3- and 4-year-olds were asked to divide rewards for a group task, they simply took the largest share for themselves regardless of how much they had contributed to achievement of the task. They were generally more concerned with egocentric consequences rather than with any moral consideration of justice or fairness.

Their reasons for helping another child included such considerations as direct gain to themselves, future reciprocity from the child they helped, or concern for others whom they liked or needed.

By contrast, 6-year-old children were found to be more capable of using concepts of fairness and equality when dividing rewards.

CONTINUED ON PAGE 246

A Healthy Lifestyle

Good habits—like bad habits—are established early in one's life. It's not too soon to teach your child how to develop a healthy lifestyle.

Here are some guidelines:

• Make sure that you and your child have some active physical exercise every day.

• Develop a well-balanced program of nutritional meals. Seek the help of a physician or nutritionist, if necessary, in establishing a sound nutritional program for the family.

• Make mealtimes a pleasant time for the whole family to enjoy being together.

• Choose a time other than mealtime to discuss unpleasant topics such as behavior problems.

• Remember that for 3-year-olds, breakfast is a most important meal. They need a good breakfast for the activities of the rest of the day. Good breakfast foods include cereal, toast, milk, peanut butter, fruits, and yogurt.

Adjust your schedule so that the time for breakfast is not rushed—even if that means getting up earlier in the morning or going to bed earlier the night before.

Recent studies of children's nutritional needs indicate that the current obsession with weight loss is having a detrimental effect on the younger generation. The reason is that a child's metabolism functions differently from that of an adult.

Although adults often need to cut back on their intake of calories, a low-calorie diet doesn't provide 3-year-olds with the nutrition they need for daily exercise and growth.

If you think your child is overweight, it is wise to consult your physician. If the physician agrees that your child has a weight problem, get specific instructions about an appropriate diet program or ask for referral to a professional nutritionist.

The goals for weight loss are very different for a young child than for an adult. An overweight child can often attain normal weight through increased physical exercise combined with avoidance of foods such as fudge or cream-filled cookies. Above all, avoid the "feast-and-famine" routine practiced by many overweight adults.

The best way to prevent weight problems in children is to know what to avoid. Here are some guidelines:

• Avoid letting your child spend too much time in purely inactive pursuits, such as watching TV. Make a daily trip to a nearby park where Youngster can run and jump and enjoy slides and swings.

• Avoid giving candy or pop as treats or rewards. Instead, take your child to the local swimming pool or children's activity center (for example, YWCA or YMCA) as a special reward.

• Avoid too many snacks between meals. If you find your child experiences hunger between lunch and dinner time, make the snack a regular part of the daily routine, rather than providing several little snacks at haphazard times. Be sure the snack provides Youngster with nutritional foods such as raw fruits, vegetables, bread and jam, or unsalted crackers.

• Avoid overindulgence in "fast-food" meals that are high in saturated fat but low in nutritional value. Instead give her the good nutritional meals she needs.

• Avoid overindulgence in soft drinks for Youngster to quench her thirst. Because of her active life she needs to drink lots of liquids. So provide her with milk, fruit juice, and several glasses of water every day.

In order to develop a healthy body, Youngster needs vitamins, minerals, fiber, and proteins. Regular well-balanced nutritional meals, combined with daily physical exercise, are Youngster's best passport to a healthy lifestyle.■

Attention-getters

These attention-getting games help to teach your child listening discrimination. They can also be used to quiet down an overactive child or to calm a fretful one.

1. Whisper Directions. The purpose of this game is to gain your child's attention and help her to learn to discriminate between sounds. It may be necessary to repeat your instructions:

"When I make a quiet (or soft) sound, raise your hand." (Show what raising the hand means.) Examples of quiet sounds: tap pencil on paper, snap fingers, click tongue.

"When I make a loud sound, clap your hands." Examples of loud sounds—drop a block on the floor, shut the door, stomp foot.

2. "What's Making This Sound?" The purpose of this game is to help Youngster become more attentive to the various sounds in her environment. It can also serve as a simple screening device for early identification of any hearing problem.

Ask her to stand in front of you with her back to you so that she cannot see what is making a sound. Examples of sounds to guess: tearing paper, rattling keys, knocking on the table, blowing nose, opening a drawer, whistling.

Once the rules of these games are understood, allow Youngster to play leader and you do the guessing.■

———— CONTINUED FROM PAGE 244 ————

They were also found to be more sensitive than 3- and 4-year-olds to subtle signs of distress such as a change in a facial expression as distinct from a loud cry.

What kind of family environment contributes to the development of prosocial behavior in young children? Researchers have found that parents who explicitly and repeatedly stated their expectations to their child regarding appropriate behavior had toddlers who exhibited more prosocial behavior.

The most successful parents were those who focused on encouraging and rewarding positive prosocial behaviors, rather than on the elimination of undesirable, antisocial behaviors.

Providing a child with justification for prosocial behavior—spelling out the consequences of behavior—was found to be more effective than merely issuing a command. For example, a parent might explain to a child how her behavior might emotionally affect another child, or how the parent might take some corrective measure if the child had physically or emotionally hurt someone else.

Children who had a firm sense of inner security were found to be less withdrawn, more sympathetic to another's distress, and were more likely to be leaders. They were also the ones with whom other children liked to play.

A related research finding was that children who perceived their parents as warm and loving were found to exhibit generous, supportive, and cooperative behaviors. But researchers have found an interesting distinction among these parents.

When parents offer their child warmth and rewards excessively and needlessly they may foster indulgence in their child—the spoiled child syndrome—which restricts the development of prosocial behavior. Parental love is most effective in promoting prosocial behavior when it is provided in response to the child's own expressed need for affection.

In a child's development of prosocial behavior, how the parents behave is more important than what they say. The dictum, "Do as I say, not as I do," carries no weight with children.

When a child observes an adult or peer engaging in prosocial behavior—for example, giving someone a helping hand—the likelihood of the child performing that prosocial act is increased.

The findings from these research studies indicate that children can be taught to be more caring, to experience empathy for someone in distress, and to interact positively with others. It is during the important preschool years that the foundations for prosocial behavior are established.■

www.growingchild.com

Contributing Authors

Phil Bach, O.D., Ph.D.
Miriam Bender, Ph.D.
Joseph Braga, Ed.D.
Laurie Braga, Ph.D.
George Early, Ph.D.
Liam Grimley, Ph.D.
Robert Hannemann, M.D., F.A.A.P.
Sylvia Kottler, M.S.
Bill Peterson, Ph.D.

Growing Child, Inc.
P.O. Box 620
Lafayette, Indiana 47902
Telephone: 1-800-927-7289
©2005 Growing Child, Inc.

Next Month

- *Childhood Fears*
- *Activity Levels*
- *Your Child's Temperament*

Growing Child.

Your Child's Temperament

In describing aspects of child development in *Growing Child*, we have tended to focus on characteristics that are common to all children. This doesn't mean that children are pretty much all alike.

There are important differences in children's basic personality dispositions. These dispositions, known as temperament, affect how a person interprets and reacts to the world around him.

Any parent of two or more children can attest to temperamental differences between their children which are apparent very soon after birth.

Some babies, for example, appear to be born with a happy disposition. They smile a lot and receive many smiles in return. They adjust easily to change and quickly develop good eating and sleeping cycles.

Other infants are easily irritated and hard to manage. They have difficulty in developing regular eating and sleeping cycles. They react negatively to new experiences. They cry more and are more demanding of their parents.

Even though a child's inborn temperament can be affected significantly by his environmental experiences and interpersonal relationships, many temperamental characteristics remain

CONTINUED ON PAGE 248

Childhood Fears

All children experience fear at one time or another. Experiencing fear is a normal part of growing up.

Fear has many positive qualities. Fear of heights, for example, can help a child avoid accidents. Fear of strange animals provides protection from a possibly dangerous bite.

But fear can also have negative qualities. Irrational fear can prevent a child from gaining valuable experiences.

Fortunately, recent studies have greatly increased our understanding of children's fears. These studies indicate that children's fears generally differ from one age to another. Furthermore, at each age level there is a certain range within which fears are considered normal.

The most common fears experienced by 3- and 4-year-olds are fear of the dark, fear of separation from parents, and fear of some animals such as large dogs.

As children mature, they generally outgrow these specific fears. With increasing age, their fears often become more abstract (such as fear of supernatural or imaginary figures) and more future-oriented (such as fear of failing a test).

Three-year-olds who experience childhood fears that are considered within normal limits can generally be helped by their parents to deal effectively with those fears. Here are some specific recommendations for parents:

• Treat your child's fears with respect.

• Listen to what your child wants to tell you without being critical of what he says.

• Give your child reassurance of your love and protection if needed.

• Allow your child to withdraw from the fearful situation for a period of time, if possible.

• Help your child become gradually more accustomed to the fearful situation. (For example, showing him a picture of an animal he fears.)

• Be aware that most childhood fears are normal and are eventually outgrown.

• Seek professional help if you consider your child's fears abnormal.

Here are some questions that are helpful in determining if your child's fears are abnormal:

(1) Has the fear been persistent over an extended period of time?

(2) Is the fear considered inappropriate for the child's age?

(3) Is the fear out of proportion to the circumstances under which it occurs?

If you answered "yes" to these questions, your child may need professional help.■

Order and Structure: Solving His Own Problems

We have had much to say about how important it is for your youngster to learn order and structure.

We want him to get organized and structured *internally*, which is to say that his body should operate smoothly and efficiently. He should be well-coordinated. His eyes and his hands, for example, should work well together.

We also want him to get organized and structured *externally*. By this we mean that the world around him should become an ordered and structured world. The world around him is made up of objects out there in *space* and events which occur in *time*.

It is essential that the young child not only see objects in space; it is just as important that he *perceive* the patterns which these objects form. For example, the coffee table is in *front* of the couch. The lamp is *beside* the chair, and so on. In a given room, each object in that room has its special place. The locations of all the objects form a *pattern*. He should learn where each object is in relation to all other objects in the room.

If a child does not learn to organize basic patterns in space, he may have trouble in reading and writing later in school. He may have trouble telling "b" from "d," for example. This is a problem in organizing patterns in space. The only difference between "b" and "d" is this: "Which side of the circle is the straight line on?" When we see school-aged children who confuse these and similar letters, we often find that their space world is confused.

This is why we think it is important now that Youngster do things which will help him get his space world ordered and structured. For example, we want him to keep his room in order, to help with the laundry and dishes, to do chores around the house. In all these ways he is actively involved in the order and structure of what is happening in your home. In the process he learns about space and the patterns which objects form in space. By helping him to experience space and the objects which fill up space, you are preparing him to be a good reader when he later goes to school.

It is also important that Youngster learn to perceive the patterns which events form in time. He must first learn this at a very basic level. He must learn that some things happen "before," other things happen "now," and still other things happen "after." In separating "before," "now," and "after," he is learning how events in time are ordered and structured.

Take a simple item like his breakfast cereal as an example of learning about time, order, and structure. First he pours the cereal into his bowl. Then he pours the milk. Then he stirs it all together, and finally he eats it. There is a definite time order here. Events must happen in a specific time sequence.

What does time order have to do with later school learning? Think about spelling as one example. In spelling the child must write or say the letters in the correct time order. If the child spells the word "girl" correctly, he must say the letter "g" first, the letter "i" second, and so on.

It is important that Youngster learn about space and time from his own activities. He must learn by doing. Do not try to teach him by means of logic about space and time. He must learn about space and time by his own experiences and explorations. ∎

CONTINUED FROM PAGE 247

stable throughout a child's life.

Recent research studies on children's temperament have important implications for parents of preschool children. Whereas parents have often felt guilt and responsibility for their child's problems, these studies indicate there may be many causes—including the child's own inborn temperament—for these problems. This should put to rest the "blame-the-parent" approach to understanding children's problems.

Parents who are quiet and shy may find an active outgoing child to be a considerable challenge.

On the other hand, parents who are themselves outgoing and friendly may have difficulty in accepting and dealing with their quiet, soft-spoken child.

For these reasons it is often necessary for parents to accommodate their child-rearing expectations to Youngster's own temperament. Awareness of and sensitivity to a child's temperamental characteristics can be most helpful in improving parent-child relationships.

In summary, every child relates to his environment in a different manner—and is subsequently affected differently by the environment—depending on his own temperament. Being sensitive to Youngster's unique temperament can help parents find an appropriate match between their own parental expectations and their child's temperamental characteristics. ∎

Children's Play

uring the early childhood years, play becomes an essential part of a young child's development.

Play can serve many useful purposes. It may stimulate a child's cognitive development, relieve anxiety, encourage social interaction, or simply be a means for exploring the unknown world around us.

Some experts in childhood development have extensively studied children's play. We will discuss some of the categories of play which they have identified.

Solitary Play

This type of play—in which the child plays alone, seemingly unaware of anyone or anything else in his environment—is more commonly practiced by 3-year-olds than by older children. Nevertheless, even older children enjoy having some periods of solitary play when they can enjoy having a good time alone.

In solitary play, children enjoy such activities as solving a simple puzzle, sorting coins, or matching buttons. They begin to become more adept at using scissors and paste. In playing alone with construction toys, they become curious about how things work and why things happen. All of these activities have good educational value.

At the same time, solitary play such as hopping, walking, running, or jumping can help stimulate physical development. As the child spends more time on playground equipment—slides, swings, seesaws, and jungle gyms—his muscles develop and his coordination improves.

Solitary Pretend Play

Another important form of early childhood play is solitary pretend play, sometimes called fantasy play. Pretend play usually involves imaginary roles for the child, as well as imaginary companions.

By 3 years of age, children want to try out many different roles experienced in the real world: father, mother, doctor, nurse, police officer, or fire-fighter.

A child may use pretend play to assume the role of some superhero that is derived either from a television show or simply from fantasy.

Or a child may reenact a previous positive or negative experience—sometimes with a changed outcome to suit his own purpose. For example, if he was frightened by some monster on television, he might later role-play the part of a *kind* monster for the story to have a happy ending.

Preschool children frequently create imaginary companions in their play. At this age, it is perfectly normal to have make-believe friends. Usually by the time a child reaches school-going age, his interests will shift from imaginary to realistic activities.

Imaginary companions serve many useful functions for the young child. They provide comfort and support when needed since they always behave as the child wants. For example, when a young child has to deal with the inner conflict between the need for nurturance and the need for independence, it's possible for him to assume the roles of both baby and babydoll's caregiver. Imaginary companions can also serve as useful scapegoats that can be blamed and corrected as needed (for having soiled pants, for example).

It doesn't help to tell a pre-school child that imaginary companions don't exist. To him they are more than an arena for fantasy. They enable a young child to experience his own developing sense of self. And he does this in the safe environment of imaginary friends over whom he can exercise control.

In this safe world, a young child will often display strong expressions of emotion. This provides both a release of tension and a means to explore a whole new world of feelings.■

Activity Levels

ou have probably been amazed—and at times frustrated—by your 3-year-old's high level of energy.

He dashes across the room just to pick up a piece of paper. He wriggles and giggles while you read him a story.

Just as soon as you take a piece of ribbon from him—because his fidgeting with it bothers you—he finds a piece of tattered string to replace the confiscated ribbon!

Studies of children's activity levels—the amount and frequency of their physical movements—indicate definite age-related patterns. A child's activity level increases from birth until about 3 or 4 years of age.

After that age, there is generally a notable decrease in activity each year.

In other words, 3-year-olds are usually more active than 1-year-olds. But 7-year-olds are likely to have a lower activity level than 4-year-olds.

Within any age group, of course, there is likely to be considerable variation. Some of this variation appears to be

——— CONTINUED ON PAGE 252 ———

Better Discipline through Better Self-control

ave you ever wished you could exercise more control over your own feelings and behavior?

Just about everyone who has ever dealt with young children has exploded occasionally with an emotional outburst that they wished they could control.

Rational Emotive Therapy (RET) is a method developed by Dr. Albert Ellis which parents can use to control their feelings and prevent inappropriate emotional outbursts.

Dr. Ellis says we are mistaken if we think our emotional reactions are *caused* by the behavior of others.

For example, I may think that "I am angry *because* of what my child just *did*." RET is based on the hypothesis that our emotions are caused and controlled by our own inner thinking—even though we may not be conscious of our inner thoughts.

In other words, our own inner language determines how we feel. What *causes* us to experience *anger* is our own *inner thinking* or *belief.*

According to Dr. Ellis, our emotions get out of control when we mistakenly conclude that what we feel was *caused* by an activating event. In reality, what we feel is *caused* by our belief system. An example will help to clarify what we mean.

If I ask myself, "Why did I yell at Johnny just now?" the answer that may immediately come to mind is: "*Because* Johnny came in my kitchen wearing muddy boots."

The relationship between the activating event (A=muddy boots) and the consequence (C=I yelled at Johnny) would seem—at first glance—to be clear! [See box, "Rational Emotive Therapy."]

Our own inner language determines how we feel. What causes us to experience anger is our own inner thinking or belief.

But according to RET, my yelling was brought about by my own irrational inner belief (B="I believe it is AWFUL, ATROCIOUS, UNPARDONABLE for ANYONE at ANY time to walk into MY kitchen with muddy boots").

It was this irrational, unconscious inner statement that caused me to be angry and to yell at Johnny.

If I change my belief to a more moderate and reasonable inner statement (B="It's too bad, but not the worst thing in the world, that Johnny forgot to take off his muddy boots") my emotional reaction would be quite different. A more reasonable inner statement leads to a calmer emotional reaction.

You may have a friend who remains calm, self-controlled and unflappable under great stress or provocation. Even when you both experience the *same* activating event, (A=Spouse comes home late for dinner) your emotional consequences may be very *different*.

According to RET, that is because different people use different inner statements or beliefs.

The person who is easily upset emotionally generally has irrational catastrophic beliefs, (B="It is TERRIBLE, AWFUL") whereas the calm, self-controlled person uses more reasonable and moderate inner statements (B="It's too bad—but it could be worse!").

If we find that our emotional reactions are out of control, we can carefully examine our underlying inner statements and

CONTINUED ON PAGE 251

Rational Emotive Therapy

ational Emotive Therapy (RET) can be represented by an A-B-C-D model:

A=**A**ctivating event (whatever happened to activate an emotional outburst);

B=**B**elief system (our own inner statements or unconscious thinking);

C=**C**onsequence (how we feel—our emotional reaction); and

D=**D**isputing the irrational belief (in order to gain control over our feelings and behavior).

CONTINUED FROM PAGE 250

beliefs. This leads to disputing the inappropriate, irrational belief in order to replace it with a more reasonable inner statement (D=Disputing my irrational thinking).

In order to control how we feel and behave, we must dispute our own self-defeating irrational beliefs and replace them with more reasonable inner statements. (Some examples are shown in the table below.)

We could each probably compile our own list of irrational beliefs. We should also compile a list of the more reasonable inner statements which should replace them.

If we have been making irrational inner statements all of

our lives, it won't be easy to change. But change is possible—with practice and with effort.

Many parents have learned, through RET and other similar

strategies, to change their irrational beliefs into more moderate and reasonable inner statements.

So the next time you get emotionally upset about something, ask yourself: "What irrational belief is *causing* me to be upset?"

In that way you can change your own self-defeating inner belief, which, in turn, will change your emotional reaction.

The more we are in control of our own inner thinking, the more self-control we gain over our feelings and behavior. And the more we can control our own emotional reactions, the more reasonable and better discipline we can provide for our children.■

Irrational Beliefs	Reasonable Inner Statements
It is AWFUL and CATASTROPHIC that MY 3-year-old child is not as advanced in ALL areas as my neighbor's child.	I love my child just as he is, without comparing him to anyone else's child because I believe each child is unique and special.
I ALWAYS have to tell MY child what he is supposed to do. But he NEVER does what I tell him to do.	My 3-year-old is sometimes good and sometimes not so good. I like him just the way he is.
It's MOST important to ME to set the HIGHEST standards for MY child so that he will be FIRST and BEST in EVERYTHING he does.	I want my child to put forth his own best effort. If he does that, I don't mind if he ends up first or last.
It is TERRIBLE when other people don't behave EXACTLY the way I want.	It's too bad when other people don't do things the way I would like, but that's how life is.
I have a right to be MAD when other people NEVER change their ways. Why is it ALWAYS ME that has to suffer?	I'll try to change whatever I can change. I'll try to accept whatever I cannot change—without getting upset if something is impossible to change.
I will NEVER be completely happy until I am ALWAYS loved and approved by EVERYONE at ALL times for EVERYTHING I do.	It's nice to be loved by others and to have their expression of approval at times. But my own self-respect and self-esteem sustain me.■

CONTINUED FROM PAGE 249

genetically based. For example, boys of all ages are generally more active than girls.

Studies of identical twins, when compared with fraternal twins, showed identical twins to be almost identical in their activity levels.

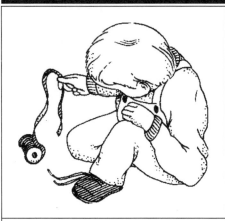

By contrast, for fraternal twins the differences in activity level were similar to those observed in ordinary siblings.

But environmental influences also play a part. For example, it has been observed that some very active children become even more restless whenever adults try to unduly restrict their activity level.

What implications for parenting can be drawn from these studies?

It should be reassuring for parents of any preschool child to know that:

• A fairly high level of activity is normal in children during the preschool years.

• Most preschool children have a short attention span and can't sit still for a prolonged period of time.

• Boys tend to be more active than girls.

• During the preschool years, there are wide variations in what is considered a normal level of activity.

• Expectations for any child should be modulated according

to the child's own characteristics—including activity level—rather than any adult's preconceived ideas.

• Trying to force a restless child to sit still will generally not be effective in settling him down.

• Making minor adjustments in the environment—such as shortening the length of a story being read—will generally produce better results.

• Being sensitive to your child's unique characteristics and making reasonable accommodations to fit his own level of activity will generally be in his best interest.

• If you feel that your child's energy is too much for you, remember there is light at the end of the tunnel: Most children's level of activity decreases throughout the childhood years.

• In the meantime, being patient with your child's activity level is most important during the preschool years, even though at times it may be a great frustration to you.■

Dear Growing Child:

"I've enjoyed receiving **Growing Child** *since my very first copy. I've kept all my copies to help me with my second child.*

"I just wanted to thank you for your wonderful publication. Being a parent is the hardest job I've ever had, and it's a relief to know that my children are quite 'normal.'"

Margaret N.
Anniston, AL

www.growingchild.com

Contributing Authors

Phil Bach, O.D., Ph.D.
Miriam Bender, Ph.D.
Joseph Braga, Ed.D.
Laurie Braga, Ph.D.
George Early, Ph.D.
Liam Grimley, Ph.D.
Robert Hannemann, M.D., F.A.A.P.
Sylvia Kottler, M.S.
Bill Peterson, Ph.D.

Growing Child, Inc.
P.O. Box 620
Lafayette, Indiana 47902
Telephone: 1-800-927-7289
©2005 Growing Child, Inc.

Next Month

■ *The Amazing Brain*
■ *Teaching Time*
■ *Preventable Injuries*

Growing Child®

'She Did That Deliberately'

Do you ever wonder if your child is deliberately trying to upset you emotionally? Many parents have told us about their concern that their child has developed the knack of "driving them bonkers."

Let's consider an example. Dad and 3 1/2-year-old Nancy are learning about her new toy xylophone. Dad shows Nancy how to make different musical sounds and they take turns hitting the notes. They both laugh and smile a lot together.

Then it's time for Dad to go do something else in the house.

After he leaves, Nancy discovers she can use the xylophone mallet to make new and different sounds by hitting some pots and pans within her reach on the floor. She is fascinated with the variety of new noises she can make.

Soon Dad reappears and with great self-control, calmly asks her, please, to make less noise. But, by now, Nancy's fascination with the sounds she can produce is far more compelling than her desire to please her Dad.

The next time Dad appears his face looks angry. In a loud voice he shouts: "Stop making so much noise!"

Dad leaves and for a few moments, Nancy hugs her favorite doll. Then her eye spots another pot she hadn't noticed before. She starts to hit it, very softly at first, then more and more loudly.

This is an experiment that holds her interest. What will the outcome be? Will Dad reappear to

give her his attention again? After all, any attention—even negative attention like scolding—would be better, she knows, than no attention!

Will she locate still another pot—or object—that will make still another new sound?

Like most children her age, she doesn't like waiting too long. So she starts to hit the newest pot more loudly still. These are new and more interesting sounds.

Sure enough, Dad appears at the door again.

We are not told the ending of this story. It could be a sad ending. Or it could be a reasonably happy one. That will depend more on Dad's behavior than Nancy's.

After all, as an adult, Dad has more experience in living. He has had more opportunities to learn how to control his own behavior. And he can read articles and books that help him better understand Nancy's behavior.

Nancy, on the other hand, isn't old enough to study any books about the behavior of adults! She has to learn the hard way, by trial and error.

Through trial and error she will learn about life, including learning about the limits of tolerated behaviors that adults in her life will set.

Nancy is still just a small child, learning new skills every day from her encounters with people and objects. To demand absolutely quiet behavior at this stage of her life would inhibit her desire to learn and to explore.

Inevitably, some of her learning experiments—especially experiments in social relationships—will have the appearance of willful "bad" behavior.

Those are the ones most demanding of a parent's patience, understanding, and love.■

The Magic Bandage

Perhaps by now you have experienced your child's hysterical screaming because of a slight scratch.

At first you think he must be seriously injured. But all you can find is a little scratch that doesn't even need a sterile dressing.

So why all the crying? Probably for two reasons: (1) your child's need for love and attention; and

—— CONTINUED ON PAGE 256 ——

Preventable Injuries

uring the preschool years children generally love to be active. They run, they climb, they throw, they kick a ball. All of these activities help them gain better control of newly developed perceptual-motor skills.

But with a child's increased level of activity comes an increased risk of injury. According to the National Safety Council, accidents are the number one cause of death in children under age 10. The saddest aspect of this information is that many of these accidents are preventable.

One of the ways in which children's accidents can be prevented is by advocating for better local, state, and federal laws. But parental cooperation is essential in order for the laws to be effective.

For example, a federal law now requires the availability of child-proof safety caps on medicine bottles. Parents who are reluctant to use them should be aware that safety caps are credited with an 80 percent drop in the number of accidental deaths due to poisoning in children 1 to 4 years of age.

Likewise, many states now have mandatory safety car seat and seat belt laws. Since these laws have resulted in a great reduction in the number of children's deaths in automobile accidents, it is wise for parents to adhere to these laws.

Now is a good time to talk to your child about safety rules in your home, on the road, and on the playground. Undoubtedly, you will have to repeat these same rules many times during the coming years.

Three-year-olds who ride tricycles should be made espe-cially aware of the important rules of the road which they must observe now and in future years. After all, hospitals in the United States report more than a quarter of a million children's bicycle-related accidents each year, over 1,000 of which result in death. It is believed that many of these accidents could have been avoided by more adequate safety education and better adult supervision.

The issue of preventable injuries has received great atten-tion in recent years. As a result, there has been a 50 percent reduction in the number of children's accidental deaths over a period of two decades. But much more remains to be done to prevent avoidable accidents of children. And the best place to begin to do your part is to provide safety education for your child in your home. ■

Teaching Time

hen some regular event occurs at midday, such as a passing freight train, airplane, or city bus, associate this event with time for lunch. The church bell may signal when it's time for Dad to come home from work. The kitchen timer rings when it's time for bed.

Ordering events in time is an important skill to prepare a child for telling time, learning to read, and doing arithmetic.

Rhyming games also teach order or sequence in time:
1. "Find your nose, then touch your toes."
2. "Put your hands in your lap, then pretend to take a nap."
3. "Jump up high, then reach for the sky."
4. "Spin around, then touch the ground."

5. "Stand up tall, then make yourself small."
6. "Pretend to fall, then roll into a ball."

Movement games can also be used to teach sequencing in time:
1. "Jack-in-the-box"
Say: "Jack in the box." The child squats down. "Jack jumps out of the box." The child jumps up. (Instead of saying "Jack," you can use Youngster's name if you wish.)
2. "Jack-be-nimble"
"Jack be nimble; Jack be quick. Jack jump over the candlestick." When Youngster hears the word "Jump," it is time to jump over a designated object.
3. "Jack-the-jumper"
Place pieces of rubber-backed carpet or pieces of foam rubber in a random fashion on the floor or sidewalk. Have Youngster jump from one to another whenever you say "Jump."
4. "Jack-the-runner"
Have Youngster step into a paper sack and jump from one end of the room to another. A sack race for two children can be fun if there are adequate safety precautions, with the children being far enough apart on a surface that won't hurt them if they fall. ■

The Amazing Brain

In previous issues of *Growing Child* we have devoted considerable attention to the observable aspects of child development. But there are other amazing developments taking place in your child that are not directly observable.

Without question, the most important development that takes place during the early childhood years is the maturation of the central nervous system, which consists of the brain, the spinal cord and nerves.

Although brain development is a highly complex topic, we want to share some information with you that we hope will enhance your parenting experiences.

Let's consider the amazing process that is set in motion in the human brain when Mom tells her 3 1/2-year-old son, Jimmy, to pick up a ball and throw it to her. The sound of Mom's words produces a primary response in Jimmy's *auditory cortex,* a specialized part of the brain.

Although there may be other sounds in the environment which are audible—such as the noise of a passing automobile or a church bell ringing in the distance—Jimmy's brain must learn to block out these extraneous distracting stimuli in order to focus attention on the sounds made by Mom's voice: "Pick up the ball and throw it to me."

Once Jimmy has processed the meaning of the message, signals are sent instantaneously to other parts of the brain.

His brain must initiate a complex series of questions and evaluations, such as: Where is the ball? How will I pick it up? How do I throw a ball? How far will I need to throw it? etc. etc. All of these evaluations can be completed in a few thousandths of a second.

The sight of the ball on the ground produces the strongest brain activity in the *visual cortex* located near the back of the head in the cerebral cortex.

Other visual stimuli—such as the greenness of the grass or the blueness of the sky—must be blocked out in order to focus attention on the ball.

The higher cortical levels of the brain must now formulate a possible plan of action which, in turn, must be instantaneously communicated to other parts of the brain.

The *motor cortex* must become involved to send messages to muscles throughout Jimmy's body that enable him to bend down and pick up the ball.

Jimmy's brain must now calculate a possible trajectory for the ball. If he decides to throw the ball, his brain must control his arm movements.

If his brain judges he can't throw the ball that far, the cortex may suggest another course of action, such as kicking the ball.

All of this activity is, of course, dependent on another important function of the brain, namely, memory, that remarkable mechanism by which the brain organizes, stores, and retrieves information.

Drawing on his memory of previous experiences, Jimmy eventually develops the ability to pick up a ball and throw it to his Mom. It is a truly remarkable achievement which we very often just take for granted.

So, the next time you tell your 3 1/2-year-old child to pick up a ball and throw it to you, you might stop to reflect for a moment on the amazing chain of events in the human brain that your words set in motion.

Child rearing will never be dull as long as parents retain a sense of wonder at the ever-changing manifestations of their child's brain development.

In subsequent issues of *Growing Child*, we will discuss other aspects of the development of your child's amazing brain.■

Family Relationships

Have you noticed how puzzled young children can be when it comes to family relationships? They hear Dad referred to as "John," "Father," "brother," "uncle," "son," "husband." It may be amusing at first but then it becomes plain confusing.

Take the preschool boy who was asked about the other children in the family.

He names "Sally," "Betty," and "Marla." "They're sisters," he explained.

The teacher then asked, "If they're sisters, what are you?"

After contemplating for a time, he replied, "I'm a boy sister."

How can we start to straighten things out?

A family of dolls with grandmother, grandfather, father, mother, big brother, big sister, Youngster, an infant, or however many children there happen to be in your household, may be used as a concrete way to help Youngster sort out the relations of one family member to another.

It will take quite some time to grasp the idea, but once a child understands the family relationship, he can extend it to other family groups such as those of a neighbor or other preschoolers.

Children are fascinated with the notion that each child has a family group.■

More about Play

n last month's issue of *Growing Child*, we discussed some forms of early childhood play in which a child plays alone.

This month we will discuss some categories of play when two or more preschool children are present.

Onlooker Play. In this situation one child is a passive spectator as he watches another child play without participating in the activity. By means of onlooker play, a child may learn new behaviors or may muster up the courage to develop some new skill at a later time.

Onlooker play often enables a shy child, a younger child, or a child who is in unfamiliar surroundings, to adjust more easily to a new situation.

Parallel Play. This type of play may be observed when two or more children play in close proximity but independently of one another. Although playing alongside one another, each child is focused on his or her own activity.

Sometimes a child will alternate from parallel play to onlooker play, and then later imitate the play of the other child in resumed parallel play.

Associative Play. In this form of play, children as young as 3 years of age share materials, while each one pursues his or her own individual goal. Two or more children, for example, may organize an activity around a common theme such as "going to the store." But each child concentrates on his or her own "agenda" or "shopping list."

In associative play, there is a great deal of lending and borrowing—crayons, trucks, stuffed animals—but without any coordinated purpose or other

direct social interaction. The children are more interested in exchanging materials than in performing any specific task.

Cooperative Play. This type of play generally emerges around 4 years of age and continues throughout the school years.

Cooperative play involves organized group activity. The activity may be as simple as collaborating in building a house of blocks or as complex as a structured game such as football, with specific rules which all must obey.

In cooperative play children generally have an opportunity to expand their vocabulary. Facial expressions and vigorous gestures will often accompany their words. Cooperative play also helps children develop better social skills and enlarge their circle of friends.

Social Fantasy Play. Many preschool children enjoy combining cooperative play with pretend play to form what is called social fantasy play.

In this type of play, each child is assigned a specific fantasy role (firefighter, nurse, superhero) in a game with a specific fantasy theme ("search and rescue").

It is interesting to note that research studies indicate that children who engaged frequently in social fantasy play were identified as more popular with their peers and judged by teachers to have better social skills than those who had not participated in this type of play.

Social fantasy play enabled children to assume leadership roles, learn to better manage their own feelings and, through role-playing, be more understanding of others.

As a young child progresses from solitary play to cooperative and social fantasy play, it is apparent that the functions of play are most important elements in his physical, social, emotional, and cognitive development.

In a true sense, a child's play area is his best classroom. Play should indeed be the essential work of every young child.■

——— CONTINUED FROM PAGE 253 ———

(2) his childlike concepts about his own body.

At this age a sense of trust is very important to your child. He needs reassurance that the important people in his life will be there when he needs them. Putting a bandage on his scratch gives him a feeling of importance—not to mention the love and nurturance that accompany it.

Another great "cure" for a minor scratch is to say, "Come here, I'll kiss it to make it better." With that the tears can disappear just as quickly as they appeared.

Another reason some children panic at the sight of a cut is

because of their childlike ideas about their own bodies. A child of this age does not yet understand how healing occurs in the human body. After all, when Teddy Bear's insides fell out of the cut in his tummy, that cut never healed! And when a water balloon was punctured, all the water gushed out! Youngster is thinking that maybe "my cut will never heal" or "I'll lose all my blood."

So a bandage can work wonders not just physically but emotionally as well. Young children need them even when their little scrapes and scratches don't.■

Learning Where the Fences Are

s a reader of *Growing Child*, you are aware that we have encouraged you to give your child as much freedom as possible to explore her environment. We want her to have the freedom to move, touch, smell, hear, talk; to do all those exciting things which put her in direct contact with the great big world around her.

But there is another side to this coin. Your child also needs structure. And only you, as a parent, can supply the "structured freedom" she needs.

What does "structured freedom" mean? A concrete example may help. At this age it is important that your preschooler do a lot of scribbling to promote eye-hand coordination. She should have many crayons, pieces of chalk, magic markers, or pencils. She should have much freedom to just scribble. A lot of scribbling at this age will help your preschooler develop the kind of eye-hand coordination she will need for later years in school.

At the same time Youngster needs to learn that scribbling can take place only in approved places such as on paper or on a chalkboard. You may decide to paint one wall of her room with green chalkboard paint. Then she can be given the freedom to scribble on that wall. But there are other places in your house where scribbling is *not* permitted. She may not scribble on the living room walls, for example. In this way you provide what we call "structured freedom."

This means that your child has freedom (for example, to scribble in certain specified places) but that you set *boundaries* on her freedom. On the one hand your child must be free to explore her world. On the other hand she must learn that her freedom is not absolute. It is restricted by the constraints which you impose.

Someone has described the process of growing up as learning where the "fences" are. "Fences" represent the restrictions upon our freedom. When we are very young, the fences enclose a very small area. As we grow older, the fences are moved back, so to speak, until they enclose larger and larger areas.

Two things are important here: (1) First, within the fences your child must experience freedom. She is free to do her own thing. (2) Second, there are fences, and she must learn where they are. She must learn what is permitted and what is not permitted. It is up to you to teach her.

In learning about the fences, your growing child really learns that you love her. If there are no fences, then a child learns that she can do whatever she pleases. This causes her frustration. She *wants* to know where the fences are. Otherwise she will probably hurt herself in some way. So, we ask that you provide loving fences.

As adults we still have fences. We still have to cope with restrictions upon our freedom. Every stoplight is a restriction. It limits our freedom to do just as we please. So, it is important for preschoolers to begin learning about the world of *freedom* and *fences* since these are an important part of all of our lives.■

Geometry

eometry at this age? Yes, Youngster is ready for some basic training with geometric forms.

1. For a cylinder, you can use an empty juice can.
2. For a sphere, use a rubber ball.
3. For a rectangle, use a cookie box.
4. For a cone, use a pointed party hat.
5. For a cube, use a wooden block.

In order to make the forms longer-lasting and to provide uniformity (reducing the irrelevant features such as printing or pictures) paint all objects alike. If possible, have all of them essentially the same size.

Introduce the shapes. Children love big names so don't be afraid to use the names for the shapes— "rectangle," "cylinder," etc. Avoid calling the object by name—"hat," "can," or "box," since you are teaching geometric shapes.

If the child says, "This isn't a sphere, it's a ball," you should answer, "Yes, it's a ball. And a ball is a sphere."

When the child is familiar with two or three of the objects, put them into a large box. Ask Youngster to feel around inside the box with two hands and identify the objects one by one.

As she names each, she can bring it out in order to look and check her accuracy. This is an exciting challenge for a 3 1/2-year-old.

Once all of the forms are familiar, add other objects which have the same geometric shapes. Allow her to see you add the new objects—a different size ball, a smaller box, a bigger cylinder, etc.

Ask Youngster to again reach in, feel, and identify each geometric shape. You will be amazed with the associations; the similarity between the shapes of the geometric solids will be perceived.

Allow plenty of time for discovery—that the lipstick is a cylinder, the compact a rectangle, etc.■

Learning by Doing

It's a good idea at this age for Youngster to engage in activities that will help to improve eye-hand coordination. By describing what you are doing together, and then by asking Youngster about what you have just done, you can also help stimulate his language development.

Here are some fun activities that both you and Youngster will enjoy doing together:

1. **Cutting with scissors.** Begin by demonstrating the use of scissors—"open," "shut," and the proper fingers to use. (Make sure to use small scissors, with safe rounded ends.)

Allow Youngster to snip and cut up newspapers or colored construction paper without worrying about the straightness of his lines.

After he has developed finger dexterity with the scissors you can introduce some simple purposeful cutting tasks.

For example, on a piece of paper draw a thick line—a broad felt-tipped pen makes a good trace without requiring highly developed cutting skills.

The language experience can be extended by making the line a fun story.

For example, if you draw a barn, some cows, and a line connecting them, Youngster will cut along the road from the barn to the cows in the pasture.

You can create many other similar stories. So can Youngster. For example, rolling a rock down a hill to the lake will change the direction of the line to be cut from horizontal to diagonal.

2. **Playing with clay.** Here is an excellent opportunity to teach different descriptive words.

As you work with the clay, talk about the kinds of things you can create—"long and skinny snakes," "short and fat sausages," "thin and straight spaghetti."

After you've finished your creations, talk about how they're different from each other ("My snake is longer than yours."), and how they're alike ("Your sausage is just as long as mine.").

Youngster is now learning by doing. And you can both enjoy every minute of the fun!■

www.growingchild.com

Contributing Authors

Phil Bach, O.D., Ph.D.
Miriam Bender, Ph.D.
Joseph Braga Ed.D.
Laurie Braga, Ph.D.
George Early, Ph.D.
Liam Grimley, Ph.D.
Robert Hannemann, M.D., F.A.A.P.
Sylvia Kottler, M.S.
Bill Peterson, Ph.D.

Growing Child, Inc.
P.O.Box 620
Lafayette, Indiana 47902-0620
Telephone: 1-800-927-7289
©2005 Growing Child, Inc.

Next Month

- *Learning to Cope with Disequilibrium*
- *Elbow Injuries, Sprains and Fractures*

Growing Child.

Learning to Cope with Disequilibrium

At about this age Youngster may exhibit behaviors related to general emotional disequilibrium—like being on a seesaw of opposite feelings.

For example, when playing with a friend, she may alternate between being friendly and hostile.

Likewise, at one moment she may be a bossy "Miss-know-it-all," yet the next moment show signs of insecurity and anxiety.

There are a number of reasons for the inconsistencies in Youngster's behavior at this age. For one thing, she is confused by the variety of opposite emotions she is now experiencing, such as joy and sadness, love and hatred, contentment and anger.

She is also confused by the variety of reactions to her own behaviors.

For example, if she throws a temper tantrum, one person may choose to ignore her behavior, while another may scream back at her.

Even with the same person, the reaction to Youngster's behavior may be quite different, depending on the particular

Your child continues to need a great deal of emotional support, warmth, and understanding as she learns to cope with feelings of insecurity in her life.

circumstances.

Another source of uncertainty and disequilibrium is her size. At 43 months she often feels powerless, surrounded by all-knowing "giants" in the adult world around her. She is aware that she is getting bigger every year but is nevertheless sometimes impatient with the rate of her own physical growth.

Not being able always to distinguish between fantasy and reality is another source of insecurity. To a child of this age the clouds, for example, appear to have their own independent existence with the freedom to travel wherever they wish across the sky.

Likewise, wind and fire appear to have the powers of living beings. The wind can knock you down when it blows and the fire will burn you if you don't treat it with respect.

There are many ways in which you can help Youngster cope with her feelings of

disequilibrium:

(1) The first step toward understanding and helping her is to be aware of her insecurities and anxieties—such as the ones we have identified above.

(2) Provide her, as much as possible, with *consistency* in rules of behavior and a *routine schedule* which foster a sense of security and trust.

(3) Provide her with an educationally rich environment—with the type of games and toys we have previously recommended.

Educational activities not only enable her to develop new skills but also help to enhance her self-esteem.

(4) Become a good listener to enable her to express her innermost feelings.

(5) Avoid criticizing her, even when her thoughts are irrational and immature.

(6) Attend not only to the words spoken but also to her nonverbal communication such as tone of voice or facial expressions by which she also reveals her innermost self.

At 43 months your child continues to need a great deal of emotional support, warmth, and understanding as she learns to cope with feelings of disequilibrium and insecurity in her life.

Parents, more than anyone else, can help a child to cope with disequilibrium and develop a sense of trust and security. This is the solid foundation on which a child can later build more positive self-esteem. ■

Early Mathematics Learning

At what age do children begin to grasp the basic concepts of mathematics? In recent studies at the University of Chicago, researchers have found that children as young as three years of age have the ability to recognize numbers as well as add and subtract.

The researchers found that these mathematical abilities develop at about the same age in children from widely different socioeconomic groups.

They also found that mathematical abilities can be greatly enhanced with the help of adults, including parents, and that students bring more mathematical understanding to the classroom as kindergartners than many teachers have probably realized.

In the past, mathematical ability has often been measured by requiring a child to make an audio-visual match between what they heard ("three") and what they saw (● ● ●).

What the researchers found was that children under 3 years of age were unable to make the audio-visual connection between the sound they heard and the corresponding number of objects.

But when the researchers used a visual-visual match to test mathematical ability, they made some interesting discoveries. Even infants looked longer at two sets of objects which contained the same number than at those which contained a different number of objects.

The researchers found that children usually developed the ability to perform non-verbal calculation between ages two and a half and three.

To test that ability, using a visual-visual match, they hid a set of objects under a box and then, while the child watched, they added or subtracted objects from the set before hiding it again under the box.

Each time the child was asked to form a set of objects, which corresponded to the number hidden under the box.

By the time they were three years old, most of the children in the study were able to select the correct number of objects, indicating that by that age they understood the basic elements of addition and subtraction.

In contrast to this visual-visual match, when three-year-olds were asked to perform an audio-visual match, they made only the same number of matches as they would have made had they been guessing.

Four-year-olds, however, performed significantly better on both the visual-visual and audio-visual tasks, indicating that this is an important stage for a child's development of basic verbal and nonverbal mathematical concepts.

Parents can easily put into practice the knowledge gained

Mathematical abilities can be greatly enhanced with the help of adults, including parents. Students bring more mathematical understanding to the classroom as kindergartners than many teachers have probably realized.

from such research studies. In everyday life—around the house, in the grocery store, or while riding in the car—there are numerous opportunities to reinforce a child's visual-visual learning (pairing socks, for example, while doing laundry) and audio-visual learning ("We don't need three boxes of cereal. Let's put one box back because we only need two").

In this way a child will not only develop mathematical ability but will also improve verbal comprehension essential for solving mathematical word problems.∎

Dealing with Mistakes

Do you sometimes worry about the mistakes you may make inadvertently as a parent?

Do you fret about possible harmful effects your mistakes might have on your child?

Have you lost the ability to relax as a parent?

These questions need to be addressed because they are of concern to so many parents.

Some of the anxiety parents experience is undoubtedly due to being bombarded with modern media information—sometimes contradictory—about

child development. So we need to consider each of these questions in turn.

First, do you sometimes worry about the mistakes you may make inadvertently as a parent?

Actually, everyone—even the most renowned child development expert—makes mistakes at one time or another. It's part of being human. So there is no need to be consumed by guilt if you make a mistake from time to time.

Do you fret about possible

CONTINUED ON PAGE 261

Fun Learning Games

Fun learning games can be used to teach a variety of skills. Here are two games that can help Youngster improve observation skills, perceive relationships and develop language. Both of these games can be played again and again in more complex forms over the next several years.

"I Spy"

Purpose: The purpose of this game is to get Youngster to identify objects from your description of their characteristics.

Materials: Select materials for which Youngster already knows the name: plate, knife, ring, cotton ball, toothpick, etc.

Procedure: Once you know that Youngster is familiar with each of these items, tell her: "I'm going to say, 'I spy something,' and then I'll describe an object on the table. I want you to find the object and tell me its name." Examples: "I spy something round and hard." (Plate)

"I spy something round that you can wear on your finger." (Ring)

"I spy something short and sharp." (Toothpick)

As Youngster's vocabulary expands the descriptions can become more complex and/or more abstract. For example: "I spy something oval made of brown leather." (Football)

"Which Ones Go Together?"

Purpose: The purpose of this game is not only to teach language but also to help Youngster identify relationships and associations.

Materials: Select pairs of household items that have something in common but which also have basic differences: apple and orange, glass and cup, brush and comb, fork and spoon, pen and pencil, glove and mitten, etc.

Procedure: Arrange six or more of these pairs of items in haphazard order on the table. Select one item at a time (for example, the apple) and say:

"Find the one that is similar to this one."

When Youngster makes the correct selection, you can ask, "In what way are those two items (apple and orange) alike?" Youngster may reply: "You can eat them both." Then you can ask, "In what way are they different?" Youngster may reply, "Their taste is different."

If Youngster has difficulty with either of these two games, you can give her the answer ("It's the plate because it is round and hard" or "The fork and the spoon are alike because you eat with both of them.").

You can return later in the game to ask the item she missed to check if learning has occurred.

When Youngster has become familiar with the rules of these games, you can allow her to play the role of the adult, choosing the items for "I Spy" and selecting the pairs of items for "Which Ones Go Together." She will have fun seeing if you can answer her questions.■

CONTINUED FROM PAGE 260

harmful effects your mistakes might have later on your child?

Fortunately most child development experts tell us that a young child is a highly resilient creature.

This means that your mistakes generally will not harm your child provided you are being reasonable and are genuinely trying to help him.

So the important question to ask is: "When I made that mistake, was I genuinely trying to help my child or did I do it just for my own convenience?"

As long as parents continue to strive to do what they think is best for their child, their love—even with some mistakes—will eventually triumph over all else.

Have you lost the ability to relax as a parent?

If so, step back from what you are doing. Give yourself a break so that you can enjoy raising your child.

By doing yourself this favor, you are also doing your child a favor. Your child needs a relaxed and happy environment in which to grow and develop.

So, if you answered "yes" to the questions at the beginning of this article, we have a threefold message for you:

(1) Realize and accept that you will make mistakes.

(2) Focus your attention on doing what is good for your child rather than on guilt for what you may have done wrong.

(3) Give yourself and your child the gift of a relaxed home environment.■

Your Child's Brain Development

In last month's issue of *Growing Child* we indicated that the most important development taking place in your child throughout the preschool years is the maturation of the central nervous system, including the brain. During these important years, the brain is developing faster than any other part of the body.

By age 3, the average child's brain has already attained about 75 percent of its adult weight. By age 5, it will have reached about 90 percent of its adult weight. By comparison, the weight of your child's body as a whole, at age 5, will have attained only about 30 percent of its eventual adult value.

Of course, weight gain, by itself, is only a crude measure of a child's remarkable brain development. More important are some other aspects of brain development that are taking place throughout the preschool years which we will discuss shortly.

Compared with other species, the human brain is more immature at birth and develops more slowly. It is therefore more susceptible to the effects of the environment—both positive and negative—during the early childhood years.

There is a continuing reciprocal interaction between a child's developing brain and the child's environmental experiences. The neurological changes that take place in a child's brain influence the way she responds to and interacts with her environment.

Likewise, the stimulation she receives from good environmental experiences can produce more growth of brain cells. This leads to better brain functioning which ultimately influences a child's cognitive, affective, and social development. That, of course, is one of the reasons why, in *Growing Child*, we stress the importance of good learning experiences and good nutrition during the early childhood years.

The human brain has many different parts. The *cerebellum* is the part of the brain concerned with maintaining bodily equilibrium (balance) and the smooth functioning of the muscles.

The *cerebral cortex* is the grayish layer of nerve cells that constitutes the largest and most important part of the brain. Memory and intelligence functions take place here. It also contains the centers for seeing, hearing, taste, and smell.

Everything that we come to know about the world around us—through seeing, hearing, or remembering, for example—is learned by means of long thin nerve cells in the brain called *neurons*, which specialize in communication. There are between 10 and 20 billion neurons in a mature brain, many of which have interconnections with one another—almost like a gigantic telephone switchboard. Neurons are so densely packed in some parts of the brain that one cubic inch may contain more than 100 million of them.

The neurons of most nerves are covered with a fatty substance called *myelin*. The process by which the neurons become covered by myelin is called *myelinization*. Rapid myelinization begins at about 18 months and continues until about 4 years of age. Myelinization greatly increases the speed and efficiency with which neural impulses are transmitted.

The neural fibers that connect the cerebellum and the cerebral cortex usually complete myelinization around 4 years of age. It is these fibers which are responsible for control of fine motor movements, such as those involved in writing and drawing.

Once myelinization is completed, a child's fine motor skills will generally improve. But much practice will be needed to develop all the muscles that are needed in later school years for more sophisticated tasks like handwriting.

That is why we have been recommending in *Growing Child* that you give your preschool child lots of drawing materials: crayons, paints, pencils, markers and, of course, plenty of scratch paper. Now is not the time to worry about neatness or precision in work. Just let your child enjoy making those great big scribbles.

Having some basic information about brain development can help parents to have a better understanding of the learning experiences which are most appropriate for their child's own developmental level.

This information should also help parents to understand why we do not advocate rushing a child's development. We think that such efforts—trying, for example, to produce "Young Mr. or Ms. Super Brain"—are generally misguided. We believe it is best to let a child's learning keep pace with her brain development. It has been found that children learn more efficiently and more easily when their learning experiences are appropriately matched to their developmental level.

Knowledge about brain development also makes parents aware that some learning tasks—such as those involving highly developed attentional skills—must wait until later years. That is because some forms of myelinization, namely, those involving consciousness and attention, will not be completed until a child reaches puberty.

In presenting information about brain development, it should be emphasized that it is not necessary to become an expert in neurology in order to

CONTINUED ON PAGE 263

Elbow Injuries, Sprains and Fractures

Parents of preschool children are likely, at one time or another, to have to deal with emergency injuries. Having some advance knowledge about the kinds of injuries that can happen will help prepare you to deal more effectively with an emergency situation.

We will discuss three types of injuries that commonly occur in young children: elbow injuries, sprains and fractures.

Elbow Injuries

Even though Youngster may enjoy being swung in a circle by his hands or being lifted up by his wrists, these practices may easily cause "pulled elbow." It can also occur if a child falls on his outstretched arms, or if he suddenly jerks his arm while being held by the hand. This injury is also known as "nursemaid's elbow."

This is a fairly common injury in children under 4 years of age.

CONTINUED FROM PAGE 262

be a good parent. It is possible to be an excellent parent without even knowing, for example, that breathing involves the complex coordination of over 90 different muscles!

At the same time, we want our *Growing Child* parents to have knowledge about important facets of child development. What has been happening and what will continue to happen in your child's brain is, without doubt, the most important and the most fascinating aspect of development during these preschool years.

Next month we will discuss another intriguing aspect of the development of the brain, namely, its organization, during these years, into left-brain and right-brain functions.■

It occurs when the arm is over-stretched allowing soft tissue to slip into the elbow joint and remain trapped there.

It will cause a child considerable pain if he tries to straighten his arm. This injury should be treated by a doctor who may have an X-ray taken to be sure no bone is broken.

On your way to the doctor's office it is best not to give your child any pain medication, food or drink, unless your doctor has given prior approval for your doing so.

If no fracture is suspected, the doctor will gently use a relocation movement to release the trapped tissue which, in turn, allows the joint to return to its normal position. The doctor may recommend the use of a sling for a few days while the tissue is healing.

Once a child has had this injury, care should be taken not to repeat the type of action that caused it because the same injury may occur more easily a second time. Therefore, when lifting your child, it is best to lift him under the armpits or grip him by the waist, rather than pulling him up by his wrists.

Sprains

A sprain is an injury that causes ligaments, which hold bones together, to be torn or stretched excessively. Although sprains are not too common in young children,they occur most frequently in the ankle, knee, and wrist.

It is sometimes difficult to tell the difference between a sprain and a broken bone. In both cases, there is likely to be tenderness to any touch, rapid swelling and pain, especially with any movement of the injured area. If in any doubt, it is wise to consult your doctor who can have an X-ray taken, if necessary, to diagnose the injury.

Immediate first aid for a sprain

includes the following:

1. Prevent movement of the injured area. Generally this calls for rest. The doctor may also recommend the use of crutches or a cast to prevent any stress on the injured area.

2. Elevate the injured joint (for example, with a pillow) so that less swelling will occur.

3. For the first few hours after the injury, an ice bag or cold compress may be applied several times (for 10 to 15 minutes) to help prevent swelling.

4. The injured area may need an elastic bandage, but this should be removed if it increases the swelling.

Minor sprains will generally take about one or two weeks to heal. If healing doesn't take place within this time period, or if there is recurrence of the swelling, consult your child's doctor.

Fractures

A fracture is any break in a bone. It always requires the attention of a physician.

It's not always easy to tell when a bone is fractured. Usually there is swelling in the area, accompanied by pain. Being able to move a bone, however, doesn't rule out a fracture.

Whenever there is any doubt, it is wise to consult a physician. After examining the injury, the doctor will generally have an X-ray taken to determine the nature of the problem.

A type of fracture that is common in young children—whose bones are still quite flexible—is known as a "greenstick" fracture. It is one in which the bone bends like fresh green wood and breaks only on one side.

The clavicle or collarbone is one which is sometimes fractured in a young child. This usually occurs when a child falls directly

CONTINUED ON PAGE 264

CONTINUED FROM PAGE 263

on his shoulder. It is generally very painful, particularly if the child tries to raise his arm on the side with the fracture.

Fractures of bones in the arms and legs are also common in young children. They are most likely to occur when a child falls or jumps from a height, or tries to break a fall with outstretched arms.

Sometimes a fracture may be accompanied by a sprain, making it more difficult to identify. An X-ray will usually be needed to diagnose the type of injury.

Different types of fractures have different names. For example, a "compound" fracture is one in which the bone penetrates through the skin, whereas in the case of a "closed" fracture, the skin remains intact.

A fracture is classified as "displaced" when the broken ends are out of alignment, and "nondisplaced" when both broken ends are still in their proper positions.

The type of immediate first aid for fractures that can be provided in the home will depend upon the bone that is broken.

If you suspect that a leg or the spine has been fractured, do not move the child. Wait until the ambulance arrives so that paramedics can supervise the transportation.

Until then, avoid any movement of the child. Have someone stay with him at all times, if possible, to comfort him.

If a long bone is fractured—in the arm, for example—it should be splinted with firm material like a board to prevent unnecessary movement.

If the fracture is in the collarbone or elbow, the arm may be supported in a sling made with soft material such as a scarf or towel. This will help decrease movement of the injured area.

The following general treatment methods apply to all types of fractures:

(1) The bones must be properly aligned so that healing can take place.

(2) Until healing is completed, the broken bone must be provided support, usually with a fiberglass or plaster cast.

(3) Normal functioning must then be restored to muscles, joints and tendons, with the use, if necessary, of physical therapy.

While a bone is healing, the doctor may order periodic X-rays to make sure that proper healing is taking place. Fortunately for young children, their bones are more flexible and heal more rapidly than those of adults.

We hope your preschool child will never suffer an elbow injury, sprain, or fracture. Nevertheless, it's best to be prepared and know what to do if any of these injuries should occur.■

Dear Growing Child:

"I am a parent and a teacher in an infant special education program. I have studied child development for years and subscribe to the professional journals. Yet each month I learn something new or am reminded of a valid point from your newsletter.

"Thank you for information that goes beyond the obvious."

Jayne L.
Carmel Valley, CA

www.growingchild.com

Contributing Authors

Phil Bach, O.D., Ph.D.
Miriam Bender, Ph.D.
Joseph Braga, Ph.D.
Laurie Braga, Ph.D.
George Early, Ph.D.
Liam Grimley, Ph.D.
Robert Hannemann, M.D., F.A.A.P.
Sylvia Kottler, M.S.
Bill Peterson, Ph.D.

Growing Child, Inc.
P.O. Box 620
Lafayette, IN 47902-0620
Telephone: 1-800-927-7289
©2005 Growing Child, Inc.

Next Month

■ *Two Types of Discipline*
■ *Left-brain, Right-brain*
■ *Sex Education Begins in the Home*

Growing Child.

Two Types of Discipline

arents frequently ask, "When do I start disciplining?" or "How should I discipline?" You start disciplining a child as soon as he can understand *what* you are doing and can learn *why* you are doing it. This occurs usually at about 18 months, although some children may be nearer 2 years of age before discipline can become effective.

Let's discuss two types of discipline. One type of discipline involves changing behavior that is undesirable. Just be sure that the behavior is bad enough to justify disciplining. An example would be if your child ran into a busy street. Since being hit by a car can have serious consequences, this kind of behavior has to be stopped.

How parents discipline a child for undesirable behavior may vary a great deal. Some children have very sensitive feelings and respond to a simple "no-no." For others a loss of some privilege may be more appropriate. Remember, however, the punishment should fit the crime. So, don't use your most forceful methods for minor misbehaviors such as sibling rivalry or not sharing toys. Save it for the really serious problems. Otherwise it won't work when you really need it.

A second type of discipline is a little more difficult to teach. It involves training your child to control behavior in order to reach a certain goal. That goal might be mastery of a skill, success in sports, arts, or a craft. The attainment of any of these goals

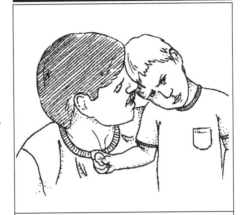

requires discipline. Sometimes a very talented child may not have the discipline to train for the thing he desires. At the same time, a less talented child may reach a desired goal because he has learned how to discipline himself.

Self-discipline becomes even more important when a child becomes a young adult. It is the

disciplined tee-ager who can get good grades in school, and can successfully resist the attractions of drugs, skipping school, and other forms of juvenile delinquency.

How do you teach this second form of discipline? It is best to start as early as with the first type. Encourage your child not to give up on a task just because it is hard or long. Show him that practice and hard work pay off with increased rewards.

These rewards need to be very tangible at first, such as praise, a favorite treat, or extra allowance. Later the satisfaction of "doing well" will be its own reward.

So, remember both types of discipline. The first type keeps your child out of trouble. The second type teaches him how to live successfully. Both are very important. Both require your active involvement as a parent.■

Dental Health

any people tend to ignore young children's teeth, because they are "baby teeth" and will fall out anyway. But decay in baby teeth is a signal that the child is susceptible to continual decay.

There is increasing evidence that fluoride in the water supply has been an effective means of strengthening teeth and reducing cavities.

Unfortunately not all water supplies have sufficient fluoride. Your dentist or local public health officer can tell you about yours.

Fluoridated water and its substitute, fluoride treatments, are not the only answer to prevention. (1) Regular tooth brushing, (2) a healthy diet with a minimum of sweets and soda pop, and (3) regular dental checkups will offer growing children the best chance to have excellent dental health.■

Poisons

During the early childhood years, children are generally very active and inquisitive. These are positive qualities which we value in a preschool child. But being active and inquisitive, without having the wisdom that comes with age, can result in accidents. Some of these accidents may involve poisons.

It is important for parents of any preschool child to be aware of the first basic steps to be taken in case of a child's accidental poisoning. The need for immediate action is usually very urgent.

Step 1. It is best to provide immediate treatment in your home, as long as you are certain the treatment is medically appropriate for the type of poisoning involved.

We will elaborate later on what immediate treatments can be provided for four different types of poisoning. If you are unsure about what to do, call a specialist immediately. (See Steps 2 and 3 below.)

Step 2. As soon as you have provided any appropriate immediate treatment in your home, call the nearest regional poison control center for advice on what to do. Keep this telephone number readily available in case of an emergency.

If the number is not listed in your telephone directory, contact your nearest hospital to find out whom you should call if a poisoning should occur in your home.

Step 3. After you have provided whatever immediate treatment was appropriate or advised, take your child to the hospital's emergency room or to your own doctor. If possible, bring with you any evidence—such as a suspected medicine or household product—that will help the doctor determine the nature of the poisoning. Even a child's vomit can be analyzed to provide an essential clue for diagnosis. So don't be squeamish about bringing it to the doctor.

The type of immediate treatment, in Step 1 above, that you can provide in your home, will depend on the nature of the poisoning. We will therefore discuss four different types of poisoning that can occur.

Swallowed Poisons

These are likely to be of two kinds: (1) swallowed medicines, and (2) swallowed household chemicals, such as oven cleaner.

In the case of swallowed medicines, don't give your child anything to eat or drink without seeking professional advice from the poison center or from your doctor.

If you are aware of the type of medicine swallowed, report this immediately to whomever you call.

In the case of swallowed chemicals, such as household products, give your child water or milk to drink, unless he has difficulty swallowing, is experiencing convulsions, or is already unconscious.

For some swallowed poisons, inducement of vomiting may be the most appropriate treatment. For other poisons, such as toilet bowl cleaner, vomiting will only increase the damage. Therefore don't try to induce vomiting without having professional advice.

Whenever you contact the regional poison control center, you may be told to use one of the following:

(1) Activated charcoal which will be used to bind a poison; or

(2) Epsom salts which will act as a laxative.

It is important to have these remedies readily available in your home in case of an emergency. Do not use any of these remedies

Keep the telephone number of the nearest regional poison control center readily available in case of an emergency.

without first seeking professional advice.

One of the most difficult situations to deal with is when a parent suspects—but isn't sure—that their child has swallowed some type of poison.

Some of the signs of swallowed poison include sudden severe sore throat, shortness of breath, excessive drooling, uncharacteristic drowsiness, or convulsions.

If in doubt, take your child to your doctor or to the hospital.

Inhaled Poisons

If your child has inhaled poisonous fumes, bring him into fresh air immediately.

If his breathing has stopped, give mouth-to-mouth resuscitation. Then call the poison center, hospital, or doctor for further advice.

Make sure to thoroughly ventilate the area in which there were poisonous fumes.

Eye Poisons

If some chemical poison has entered your child's eye, place him immediately in a position where you can pour lukewarm water—but never hot water—into the eye.

Since you may need to continue to do this for about 15 minutes, it will help if another person is available to hold him still in this position. Then call the poison center, hospital, or doctor for advice, giving as much information as possible about the type of poison that entered the eye.

CONTINUED ON PAGE 267

CONTINUED FROM PAGE 266

Skin Poisons

If some chemical poison happens to spill on your child's skin, the appropriate immediate actions are:

(1) Remove all clothing from the affected area without tearing any skin.

(2) Rinse the poisoned area for several minutes with lukewarm water. Then call the poison center, hospital, or doctor.

Preventive Approaches

Any consideration of the problem of poisoning in young children should include discussion of preventive approaches.

In previous issues of *Growing Child* we have indicated the importance of childproofing your home, especially during the preschool years.

The following recommendations will serve as a reminder to help prevent poisoning in young children:

1. Keep all dangerous chemicals, such as household or gardening products, out of reach of young children.

2. Even everyday personal products, such as nail polish, perfume, aftershave lotion, or shampoo, should be kept out of their reach.

3. Also keep all medicines out of their reach.

4. Use medicine containers that have childproof caps.

5. Make sure that all household products and medicines are kept in their original labeled containers. (If you don't do so, your babysitter, for example, could innocently cause a serious poisoning accident.)

6. Don't keep any poisonous plants in your home. Ask your doctor or poison control center about a list of poisonous plants.

7. Don't allow your child to experimentally taste unknown plants, (such as wild mushrooms), or other potentially poisonous objects.■

Games of Discovery– Problem-solving

t this age Youngster is capable of solving some simple perceptual problems in her mind without having to use a hands-on, trial-and-error approach.

Here are some problem-solving games of discovery that will help her to develop her ability to solve a problem mentally.

1. Grid Game.

Purpose: To improve visual attention and spatial perception.

Materials: A variety of items such as plastic combs, toy cars, blocks, pieces of cloth in three or four different colors, plus a cardboard grid (as shown below). Make sure each item is available in each of the colors you choose.

Method: Place the items in a pattern on the grid.

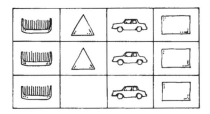

Now, hold up the blue triangle and ask, "Where does this triangle go?" Allow her plenty of time to explore the materials and consider the problem in her mind. Since there is only one slot, Youngster will surely have a success.

Next, restructure the grid so there is a new arrangement and a different order of items As Youngster meets the challenge, increase the number of vacant spaces by omitting more than one item. Also you can have her make the selection of what's missing from a pool of objects.

Variations: (a) Use cardboard shapes instead of objects. The shapes may be any designs you choose to trace. (b) Vary the colors of the shapes you use.

2. Spool Game

Purpose: To improve observation skills and short-term memory.

Materials: Three spools of thread in different colors, a shoestring, and a cardboard tube.

Method: Pass the string through one of the spools until the spool is in the middle. Then loop the string over and through the spool once more in order to hold it in place. Repeat the procedure with the other two spools, spacing them about 1 1/2 inches on either side of the center spool. Now pull one end of the string through the cardboard tube just far enough to bring the front spool forward but not quite inside the tube.

Example:

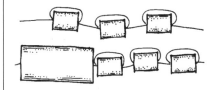

Tell Youngster, "Watch while I pull these spools inside the tube!" As soon as the spools are concealed inside the tube, ask, "If I continue pulling the string, which color spool do you think will come out first?" After the response, allow Youngster to pull the string in order to check for accuracy.

Next, take the other end of the string and pull the spools inside the tube again. Now ask the second question: "Which spool do you think will come out first if you pull this end (the opposite end) of the string?" Again allow her to check for accuracy by pulling the string.

This game enables Youngster to solve a problem mentally, even though she cannot see the object with her eyes or touch it with her hands. The development of this ability sets the stage for later mental development.■

Left-brain, Right-brain

One of the most intriguing aspects of the development of the central nervous system is the phenomenon known as *brain lateralization.* This refers to the specialization of functions in the left and right sides of the brain.

The "highest" brain center, the *cerebrum,* is composed of two halves which are called *brain hemispheres.* These hemispheres are connected by a band of neural fibers called the *corpus callosum.*

Myelinization (the process by which the neurons become covered by myelin) of the corpus callosum is fairly advanced by 4 years of age though it will continue to develop into the adolescent years. This development greatly speeds up the transmission of information from one part of the brain to another. There is also a noticeable improvement in coordination between the visual and motor systems.

This improvement, however, takes place gradually and children should not be rushed into activities for which they are not yet ready. For example, children under age 6 are not always capable of the sustained and systematic visual focusing required for reading. At age 4, they may correctly guess a word simply by identifying its first letter, without having the capability to scan the entire word.

Contrary to a common misconception from the popular media, no normal person is totally a left-brain or right-brain thinker. For a person to function normally, both sides of the brain must work in conjunction with one another.

Oddly enough, it is the left side of the brain that generally receives sensory input from, and

controls, the right side of the body. Likewise, the right side of the brain receives information from, and controls, the left side of the body.

In most people, the left side of the brain is specially equipped for processing language (including speech), for processing sequential information (such as remembering a phone number), and for logical analysis (such as verbal reasoning). Scientists and mathematicians use their left-brains a great deal.

The right side of the brain, on the other hand, specializes in processing spatial information (such as determining an object's shape), processing simultaneous information (putting objects into categories, for example), interpreting the world through meanings and emotions, and developing visual, artistic and musical skills. Hence writers, artists, and musicians use their right-brains a great deal.

A simple way to test for brain lateralization is to give a child a plastic or wooden cube which she is unable to see inside a paper bag. If she uses her right hand—involving left-brain functioning—to feel and explore the cube in the bag, she will be able to count quickly the corners of the cube. (This task

requires counting the corners in sequence.)

If, on the other hand, she uses her left hand to explore—involving right-brain functioning—she will more easily determine its overall shape. (This task is more integrative and spatial in nature.)

A similar auditory test of brain lateralization is to use headphones to feed information to each ear separately. If the information is fed only into the right ear, the left-brain will function more effectively and with fewer errors in processing sequential or linear information (such as recalling a string of numbers). But if information is fed only into the left ear, the right-brain will more quickly process information which has some unifying pattern (such as a musical melody).

Generally speaking, brain lateralization is not noticed in a child's everyday play. That is because most preschool children use both sides of the body when playing with an object. This means that both sides of the brain may be involved simultaneously in processing different aspects of the same event.

Brain lateralization is seen most dramatically in people who suffer damage, such as a stroke, for example, in the left side of the brain. This may result in loss of language and impaired functioning of the right side of the body.

If the brain damage occurs in a young child it is possible that the child will learn to speak normally again. This is because the central nervous system, including the brain, continues to grow and develop during the childhood years. As a result there is plasticity, or flexibility, in how the brain reacts to early damage which might be caused,

——— **CONTINUED ON PAGE 269** ———

CONTINUED FROM PAGE 268

for example, by a closed head injury, a tumor, malnutrition, or disadvantaged environment.

If the brain damage occurs in someone who is past adolescence, the loss of language is more likely to be permanent. This is because the process of language specialization is generally completed by then.

Another manifestation of brain lateralization is the emergence of "handedness" during the early childhood years. This phenomenon is evident, of course, in more ways than the preferred use of the left hand or right hand.

Handedness may also be seen in the development by most people of a preferred foot for kicking a ball, a preferred eye for looking through a telescope, and a preferred ear for listening on the telephone.

During the preschool years, children should be allowed to experiment with using both sides of their bodies. We recommend that parents should let their child's own behavior determine which eye, ear, hand, or foot assumes dominance.

Lateral preference or dominance will generally not become stable until about the time children begin school. Even then the dominance will not always be uniformly on one side or the other. A left-handed child, for example, may prefer to kick with the right foot or use the right eye routinely when looking through a telescope.

One of the most important implications of our knowledge of brain lateralization is the recognition that each child has a unique learning style. Since no two brains function exactly alike, no two children learn in exactly the same way.

Parents who develop some awareness of the marvelous workings of the brain can appreciate all the more the uniqueness of their own child's amazing brain.■

Sex Education Begins in the Home

A milestone is Youngster's newly acquired interest in the facts of life. From now on you can expect questions, anytime and anywhere. Our best advice is to answer the questions simply but truthfully. Good sex education begins in the home.

Don't be deceived into thinking that children at this age want the whole story of sex and conception. They don't. But they do want simple answers to their questions.

When they ask, "Where does a baby come from?" tell them it grows in a special place inside the mommy. Then you should expect further questions like, "How does the baby get inside?" or "How does it get outside of the mommy?"

Children have a natural curiosity about where babies come from. Reassurance from you—"A seed was in mommy all of the time"—will usually suffice as an answer at this age.

As for how baby gets out, a conventional answer (such as, "When the baby is old enough to be born, a special opening for just this purpose is readied for baby to come out,") will be accepted. The role of dad does not usually arise for a few more months.

Our concern is that the children's curiosity at this time is satisfied without burdening them with information beyond their understanding.■

Parenting Can Be More Fun

Some parents really enjoy the job of parenting. They bring as much vitality and creative energy to parenting as they bring to other things in life they enjoy doing.

Here are some ways to make parenting more enjoyable:

1. Read books, newsletters, or magazine articles that keep you well informed about parenting issues. The better informed you are, the more confident you will be. Self-confidence is a key to success and enjoyment.

2. Search for new and innovative ways to deal with recurring problems in the family. Discontinue old methods that you know from experience have been unsuccessful in the past.

3. When you find a good solution, write it down. That will help you to remember your success. Your success will generate more success.

4. Share your parenting experi-ences—good and bad—with other parents whose friendship you value. Knowing you are not the only parent who has problems can be a very consoling experi-ence.

5. Actively promote fun and humor in your family. For example, display on the refrigerator door a humorous cartoon or funny saying for all the family to enjoy.

6. Keep a journal. Briefly note funny incidents that occur in your home. Learn to laugh at yourself. Whenever you are feeling down, read your entries from last year to regain your sense of humor.

7. Take pictures and/or videos of some fun activities you share as a family. The longer you keep those records, the more they will be enjoyed and appreciated.

Nobody ever said that parenting would be easy. But nobody ever said it couldn't be fun and enjoyable. So have some fun and enjoy your experiences.■

"I'm Beautiful"

 There's your child, wearing a purple hat with embroidered yellow rabbits, a red striped shirt, too-short dungarees that she refuses to part with, green socks, and patent leather Mary Janes. Around her neck hang rhinestone necklaces. Smiling sweetly, she retrieves a large, white plastic pocketbook from under the table. Here is Eleanor, ready to go to the supermarket. She thinks, "I'm beautiful."

Do children just have bad taste? No, they have a child's impression of adult taste.

Adults too feel more beautiful with the help of cosmetics, more powerful in boots and a broad belt, more adorable in frills, more courageous under a hat. Of course, we can put it all together better than a child. Out of the bits and pieces that so strangely bedeck a 4-year-old "lady," we can make an outfit, a "look" that becomes us.

Perhaps there would be less conflict over clothes between our children and ourselves if we could, in all good humor, observe that we dress less for the sake of exterior appearance than for our own interior feelings. And children—with a little help—should be able to do the same.

It's not too hard to discover from your child what it is he likes about a certain shirt or socks. Just ask him. What is surprising is that it is most likely not the whole garment, but only a certain feature of it that appeals to him. It could be just the alligator appliqué on a shirt rather than its color. Perhaps it is zippers that make him feel special, or pockets, mitten clips, or hoods. It may be that it looks like something worn by some-one he admires. Or maybe it's how things fit that expresses how he feels about himself: stretch pants, leotards, and skinny shirts that cling to his body, and show it off. Or the cloth itself: velvety or furry fabrics that make him feel cuddly and huggable.

As you discover what separate features of clothes are important to your child, you may find it easier to satisfy both you and your child. Rhinestones, only in a hairclip. Turtleneck shirts, but not that expensive turtleneck sweater. Dark corduroys instead of black ones. Appliqué's, but ones you buy yourself to sew on shirts. Or a windbreaker you like better.

You may also discover how your child sees himself by working with the bits and pieces to which he is so attached.■

www.growingchild.com

Contributing Authors

Phil Bach, O.D., Ph.D.
Miriam Bender, Ph.D.
Joseph Braga, Ed.D.
Laurie Braga, Ph.D.
George Early, Ph.D.
Liam Grimley, Ph.D.
Robert Hannemann, M.D., F.A.A.P.
Sylvia Kottler, M.S.
Bill Peterson, Ph.D.

Growing Child, Inc.
P.O. Box 620
Lafayette, Indiana 47902
Telephone: 1-800-927-7289
©2005 Growing Child, Inc.

Next Month

- *Exploring New Roles*
- *When and How to Discuss Sexual Topics*
- *Handling Anger*

Growing Child.

Exploring New Roles

By now your child has probably begun to play cooperatively with other children. But as she strives to build her own self-image, she often wants other people to do things her way.

She is now reaching for more independence. She develops strong likes for some foods, for some people, for some toys or playthings. Then just as suddenly, she shifts. The "best friend" of yesterday is suddenly ignored. The dress, pants, or shirt she adored yesterday are now abandoned in favor of something she may have just seen on another child.

She is usually intense in her likes and dislikes. She seems to immerse herself completely in an activity, sometimes to the exclusion of all else. She may role-play just as intensely—even rejecting her own name because of the role-of-the-moment she is playing. ("My name isn't Jane. I'm Princess Zelda!")

Why does she seem so unpredictable, so changeable? Simply put, she is exploring herself. It is almost as though she "tries on" different characters or personalities to find the one that is really "self," really "me."

While she tries out new "selves," she continues to need the security of a stable environment. Thus, she may react strongly and negatively to a family move from one place to another, to some change in her daily routine, to rearrangement of furniture, or to the introduction of a new food.

Routine and familiar surroundings are her anchor. As a ship at anchor remains secure even when a change of wind direction results in a change of position, so she needs the predictability of routine and home surroundings as her anchor while she explores herself and her relationships with others.

So, provide her with the security she needs. But allow her to explore new roles and new dimensions of her personality. Remember, she is learning. She is developing her imagination. While finding out what it is like to be someone or something else, she is usually behaving appropriately *for the role* she is playing. If you can be flexible, understanding, and reasonably accepting of her "tryouts," you will be amused, amazed, and sometimes even enchanted by her behavior.∎

Childhood Friendships

During the first 3 years of life, a young child forms secure attachments with parents and other family members. Once a child reaches 3 years, however, attachments to other children outside the family become an important part of social development. But first Youngster has to learn how to interact appropriately with other children.

Although children at this age can develop genuine friendships, these encounters are quite different from friendships among older children or adults. For example, two 3-year-olds may be laughing together at one moment and struggling with one another for the same toy the next moment.

Just as suddenly, they may revert to some form of cooperative play, such as pulling their two trucks across the floor together.

Adults can do a number of things to foster friendly cooperative play among children of this age:

1. Provide the children with toys that are developmentally appropriate for their ages. Any child will quickly lose interest if a task is either too easy or too difficult.

2. Have a sufficient number of toys so that each child has at least one toy with which to play. Having only one toy to be shared by several children will most likely result in a squabble.

3. Make sure that toys are in good condition. Trying to pull a truck which has a wheel missing can be a highly frustrating experience for a young child.

It is generally through play that childhood friendships are formed. Although such friendships during the preschool years are often short-lived, their importance in the overall social development of the child should not be underestimated.∎

Organizing Time

Young children organize time on the basis of important events which are repeated.

Some events like a birthday or a holiday occur only once a year. Grocery shopping occurs weekly while eating takes place three or four times daily.

The regularity of these events helps children acquire an internal clock about when things will happen.

At this age Youngster is ready to participate in some planning for future events. Such planning will teach two related time concepts: (1) The past, present and future are separated by time; and (2) there is a need sometimes to delay gratification of one's expectations and desires.

Some children have difficulty organizing events in time. Activities to promote good time organization at the preschool level can be incorporated into daily events such as dressing, using songs and rhymes, or helping with a daily chore. Let's examine some examples of each.

Routine activities of daily living, such as dressing or bathing, involve the sequencing of events in time.

Children who dress themselves may occasionally put shoes on before socks. Or they omit underpants because they have not followed the correct sequential order. Discovery of an omission or error is a learning experience.

Equally valuable is the planning, in advance, of what clothes to put on and in what order.

For example, you tell your child to select what she would like to wear tomorrow. She then places these items in a row on the bed: what comes first, what comes next, what follows this, etc.

Songs that have a theme which is repeated have always been

popular with young children.

"The Farmer In The Dell" is an example. The story unfolds in a sequence, while there is a constant, the farmer, who makes decisions about whom "to take."

Rhymes and rhythms have the same role—to teach about events in time. The Dr. Seuss books, for example, often don't make a lot of sense to a young child. But she likes the sounds and the beat which occur in patterns through time.■

Organizing in Space

Youngster also needs to learn about organization in space. Here's one easy activity that incorporates learning by helping with a daily chore.

Every day the table has to be prepared for eating. Involving your child in making place mats may help to contribute to the aesthetic aspects of dining as well as teach the regularity of mealtime.

How to make place mats? Select construction paper (12" x 18") which is absorbent and comes in many colors. (Substitutes are desk blotters, posters, or shelf-lining paper.)

Procedure: Have Youngster trace a place setting on the construction paper.

It is a challenge to select the proper place for napkin, fork, plate, knife, spoon. Trace each one on the paper.

This activity is also a language-learning experience. You can comment about placements such as the glass is *above* the knife, the fork is on the *left* of the plate, the spoon is *next* tomthe knife.

We don't expect Youngster to use these terms correctly at this age, but exposure to the words

will be helpful in learning them.

A direct experience such as the one we have just described helps develop association between the words and characteristics of space such as *above, left, next,* etc.

Why is this important? Later on when Youngster approaches school age, she will need to be able to discriminate "ball and stick" letters of the alphabet (p, q, d, b).

The difference between these letters is their position in space—sticks which go *above* or *below* the line, or balls which are to the *left* or *right* of the stick.

Youngster needs to learn by using her hands, so that these directions and the words used to describe them will later be translated into operational skills in reading, writing, and arithmetic.■

Handling Anger

ow do you handle your anger? Everyone is born with the capacity to feel anger. Our culture may try to tell us that nice people don't display their anger.

Consequently we may work hard to conceal our feelings. But we can't conceal the body changes that occur: Blood pressure rises, heartbeat increases, blood vessels expand. The result may be a massive explosion of energy!

How we handle such an explosion is often related to how we were raised by our parents. Some families practice physical punishment. They hit, beat, slap, kick, or use even more abusive attacks.

Other families tend toward verbal punishment. They use name-calling, sarcasm, yelling. Still other families suppress and repress their anger. The anger is still there, however, in the form of headaches, asthma attacks, itching, insomnia.

What is the best way to deal with one's anger? Here are some suggestions:

(1) Acknowledge that your anger exists. It is a human characteristic. It's all right to be angry with Youngster. And Youngster can be angry sometimes with you.

(2) Agree that it is not acceptable behavior to injure someone as a result of anger. Anger is an emotion. Aggression is not an emotion. It is an action.

(3) Talk about the anger. It's okay to admit how angry you are. Tell Youngster, "I'm angry when I see those crayon marks on the wall. I have to clean up that mess." Or, "I know it makes you angry when I have to do this" as you deprive the child of a treat.

(4) Emphasize your own feelings rather than attacking your child. To do this, use statements which begin with "I feel."

It is not acceptable behavior to injure someone as a result of anger.

Say "I feel upset when ..." instead of employing words which attack and hurt, such as "You always ..." "You never ..." "You are a ..."

(5) Avoid anger-producing situations. Sometimes we ask questions we know will produce the opposite of our wishes, such as, "Do you want to go to bed?" We could anticipate that the answer would be "No!" So, to avoid getting angry with your child's negativism, use a statement ("It's time to go to bed") instead of a question.

(6) Seek strategies cooperatively. Encourage Youngster to generate ideas to solve a problem. If Youngster is involved in developing the solution to a problem, the solution will more likely be successful.∎

Was It Really Stealing?

o a young child, all things seem to be available in marvelous abundance, there for the taking. If you need money, she sees you go to the bank. The newspaper appears to be delivered to your door every day without paying. At the grocery store, you walk up and down all those aisles, filling the cart with whatever you choose from the enormous assortment offered.

Money as a medium of exchange is not something your child understands yet. At this age she's still learning what is and isn't hers, what she can touch and what she can't, what she can take without asking, and what she has to ask about first. That's a lot to learn.

Even if she has a pretty good idea about the way things work in her own family, there's still the rest of the world—with all its rules and exceptions—to find out about. She's just beginning to learn what morality is, what conscience is, who she is.

At this age when a child takes something that is not hers, it's not really stealing as it would be if she were an adult.

What if your almost-4-year-old picks a plastic-framed pair of sunglasses off the rack at the supermarket without your knowing it? What do you say to this child, smiling at you on the way home, quite proud of the way she looks in her new sunglasses?

Explain to her that you'll both have to go back to the store first to pay for them.

Tell her that's the way it works: Everything in the store costs money. Before you can take something home, you have to pay for it.

Take her to the checkout counter. Let her hold the money and the sunglasses, and let her pay for them like a regular customer. Now the sunglasses are really her very own.

If someone were to tell her that she *stole* those glasses, she would feel that she has done something very *bad* without being old enough to understand what that means. She will feel that she is a *bad* person, although she can't understand why.

So, without ignoring these behaviors, try to deal with your child with the love and understanding she needs.∎

When and How to Discuss Sexual Topics

henever parents ask when and how they might best discuss sexual topics with their child, they are frequently advised to tell him only what he asks about. This kind of response is encouraged so that the parent will not relay information to the child that he is neither interested in nor ready to absorb. When restricting their responses in this way, however, parents tend to miss opportunities for easy, open discussion on sexual topics with their child.

In actuality, sex can be discussed as openly and naturally as other topics the child initiates. For example, a 3-year-old child sees a watermelon sitting on the kitchen counter and asks his mother what it is. She might assume that since the child has not asked what a watermelon is used for, what the watermelon looks like inside, or if there are any seeds in the watermelon, that he is neither interested in this information nor ready to absorb it. And she would respond merely with the answer, "It's a watermelon."

What is more likely is that she will respond to her child's question about the watermelon by telling him its name, and then discussing its outside color and texture. If he shows interest, she will cut it open to show him the inside color and texture. She will tell him that it is sweet and allow him to taste it. She will show him the seeds and explain to him that the seeds may be planted.

A parent may give a child who has asked about a watermelon any part or all of this information without concern that she is telling him too much about the watermelon. She can determine the extent of information she imparts by assessing the child's interest and comprehension level.

The same criteria could be used for discussing sexual topics with a child. If a 3-year-old girl notices her brother's penis and asks her mother what it is, the mother need not assume that since the child has not asked for more detailed information about it, that she only wants to know the name for the penis. This can be a natural opportunity to permit the child to learn something about sexuality, just as the inquiry about the watermelon was a natural opportunity to facilitate the child's learning about food and plants.

The mother, therefore, using the child's interest and comprehension level as her guide, can at this time tell her child the name for the penis. She can tell her daughter that although women and girls do not have a penis, they have a clitoris and a vagina. If the child is interested in this information, the mother can show her where her clitoris and vagina are.

If the mother has noticed her daughter touching her genitals from time to time, she can explain that touching the clitoris is pleasurable for the girl and touching the penis is pleasurable for the boy, like scratching one's back can feel good.

Parents who will discuss sexual topics openly with their young child will find that the task of teaching about sex is greatly facilitated. Sometimes the parent who has not openly talked about sexual topics from the time the child is very young may find it extremely awkward to begin to relate sexual information to an older child. For example, it is more difficult to teach a 10-year-old girl about menstruation when she is unsure of where her vagina is than it is to show a 3-year-old where her vagina is.

Parents may find that their child has already obtained the "facts" from other sources. Generally, children who are left to absorb information about sex from sources outside of the family also absorb a great deal of erroneous information. The parent then finds it necessary to try to erase some of these incorrect ideas as well as teach the correct ones.■

Making Music

ost young children enjoy a simple sing-along. The more impromptu and spontaneous it is, the more they seem to enjoy it. Here are some suggestions to get you started:

1. Finger Games. "Put Your Finger In The Air" (Woody Guthrie).

**Put your finger in the air,
In the air.
Put your finger in the air,
In the air.
Put your finger in the air,
And just leave it there.
Put your finger in the air;
In the air.**

Variations: Put your thumb, index finger, middle finger, ring finger, pinky, in the air.

2. Circle Game—an activity designed to reinforce the family constellation. (Rhythm—"Johnny has one friend.")

The children pretend to be Johnny's brothers and sisters and join him in the center of the circle as everyone sings:

**Johnny has one brother,
One brother, one brother.
Johnny has one brother,
Johnny has one.
Johnny has one sister,
One sister, one sister.
Johnny has one sister,
Johnny has one.**

Change the song to correspond to each child's particular brother or sister.■

More Fun Activities

In previous issues of *Growing Child,* we have identified some fun activities with simple materials you probably have around your home. These activities can become excellent learning experiences, especially if you interact with Youngster as much as possible in each activity.

Activity #1: Making a necklace

Purpose: To develop fine motor skills and better eye-hand coordination.

Materials: A button, a shoelace, and some pieces of pasta.

Procedure: Tie a knot in one end of the shoelace. Then thread the shoelace through the button.

Next thread the shoelace through various pieces of pasta until you have made a necklace of the length you desire.

Tie a big knot in the other end of the shoelace. Then join the two ends of the shoelace to form the necklace.

Variation: Paint the pasta different colors before stringing it on the shoelace.

Reminder:

1. Involve Youngster as much as possible in the activity. If necessary, first demonstrate what to do; then have Youngster repeat your action, if he can.

2. Try not to get angry if Youngster makes a mess or doesn't cooperate as fully as you would like. Remember, this is meant to be a fun-filled learning experience.

3. Throughout the activity, talk about what you and Youngster are doing. (For example, "You're putting the shoelace through a hole in the button.")

In this way, Youngster not only learns new words, but also relates what is *said* to what is *done*.

Activity #2: Making a print

Purpose: To develop eye-hand coordination and to stimulate your child's creative interests.

Materials: A raw potato, a knife, two tempera paint colors, and a sheet of paper.

Procedure: Cut the raw potato in half with a knife. On each of the two flat surfaces, cut out a different shape (for example, a square, a star, or a triangle).

Then with one of the paints, paint the remainder of the flat surface that was not cut out.

Now hand the potato half to Youngster to "print" the pattern on paper.

Youngster will not yet have the skill needed to use a cutting knife, so you should do all the cutting. But he will enjoy "printing" a design, especially if you exclaim, "Look, you've just made a beautiful star!"

Activity #3: Making a mask

Purpose: To develop role-playing ability.

Materials: A paper sack, scissors, and some markers.

Procedure: Place a large paper sack loosely over Youngster's head.

Determine where his eyes and mouth are. Remove the bag and cut out holes for the eyes and mouth with the scissors.

When he puts the paper bag over his head again, be sure to have him stand in front of a mirror so that he can enjoy his own role-playing.

Variations: It is possible to add a lot of features (for example, nose and ears), with the help of some magic markers.

Also cotton may be used to add hair, eyebrows, moustache, or beard. Youngster may even want a cape (for example, a towel) around his shoulders to add to the fun.

Reminder: This is an excellent opportunity to invite Youngster to *talk* about who he is, what he is doing and why he is doing it. (You may be amazed how inventive and creative young children can be when they use their imaginations!)

Safety note: Be sure Youngster uses only a sack made of paper, not a plastic bag. A young child could suffocate if he puts a plastic bag over his head.

Activity #4: Making a musical instrument

Purpose: To improve auditory discrimination and stimulate interest in musical sounds.

Materials: A block of wood, hammer, nails, and rubber bands.

Procedure: Hammer two nails in a piece of wood. Place a rubber band around the nails.

Then hammer two more nails parallel to the first two but farther apart. Place a rubber band around these two nails.

Continue hammering a few

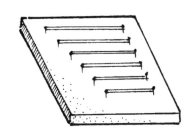

more pairs of nails, increasing the distance between them each time.

You may now invite Youngster to "play" his new musical instrument by gently plucking the rubber bands. Soon he will notice that particular sounds are related to the length of the rubber bands. ■

A Child is a Person– Not a Pet!

It is important for your child to feel respected by adults. Unfortunately, some adults talk about a child who is present as though she were an inanimate object (saying, for example, "Mrs. Jones, what is your daughter's favorite toy?" instead of asking the child directly, "Mary Jo, what is your favorite toy?").

Bring your child into a conversation by saying: "Yes, Mrs. Adams, this is our daughter Mary Jo. Mary Jo, this is Mrs. Adams."

Now you are teaching good manners to your child—how to meet strangers and how to acknowledge introductions.

If you have role-played "going to visit," "meeting grown-ups," or some similar game with your daughter, she will be prepared to answer the introduction with a simple "Hello," or even with a more formal "How do you do, Mrs. Adams."

Now she is no longer a non-person, a pet, attached to the situation by your hand as though on a leash! After all, by now she is capable of speaking for herself.

Mrs. Adams' next words may be, "My, but she is big! How old is she now?" You can continue to make Mary Jo a part of the conversation by saying, "Mary Jo, tell Mrs. Adams how old you are."

If you know your child is shy with strangers, don't put her on the spot. Instead include her by saying, "Mary Jo, show how old you are on your fingers."

Continue to bring Mary Jo into the conversation. Remember—no one wants to feel like a non-person.

No matter what Mrs. Adams says, you can make sure that Mary Jo knows that you know she is a person, not a pet.■

Shoes

What kind of shoes are best for your child? Shoes are meant to protect the foot. The type of shoe is not as important as the fit. An inexpensive shoe that fits is better for a child than wearing a more expensive shoe that he has outgrown.

To check for a good fit, make sure there is about 1/4 to 1/2 inch (thumb width) between the big toe and the end of the shoe. Another check is to "pick up" a little leather between your fingers when you pinch them together over the widest part of the shoe.

Some children need "corrective" shoes which should be prescribed only by your doctor. Such shoes are used to correct marked "toeing in" (pigeon toe), "toeing out," and "flat feet." The correction is usually done by putting a wedge on the outer or inner sole and/or heel. Sometimes an arch support is also needed. These corrections force the foot to take a more normal position. Because of this force they are sometimes prescribed in a high-top shoe. This type of shoe provides more support. It is also more difficult for the child to remove.■

www.growingchild.com

Contributing Authors

Phil Bach, O.D., Ph.D.
Miriam Bender, Ph.D.
Joseph Braga, Ed.D.
Laurie Braga, Ph.D.
George Early, Ph.D.
Liam Grimley, Ph.D.
Robert Hannemann, M.D., F.A.A.P.
Sylvia Kottler, M.S.
Bill Peterson, Ph.D.

Growing Child, Inc.
P.O. Box 620
Lafayette, Indiana 47902
Telephone: 1-800-927-7289
©2005 Growing Child, Inc.

Dear Growing Child:

"I truly enjoy Growing Child and read it soon after its arrival ... usually more than once. Your newsletter has given me a stable base that I can easily expand upon with my two preschoolers.

"Thanks for a great newsletter!"

Teresa P.
Colfax, IL

Next Month

- *Is Your Child Right-handed or Left-handed?*
- *Gender Differences*

Growing Child®

Praise and Criticism

There are two ways to praise a child for something she has done. Let's consider the wrong way first. You might say, as you watch her finish her latest painting, "Oh, what a lovely picture. It looks just like a sunset. You are a great artist."

When you say her painting is "a lovely picture," the praise fails to match what the child has actually done. She has been playing around with paint, experimenting with how it works. You say it is "a sunset." She knows it isn't. So your praise has a false ring. It's phony. She gets the message that her picture has to *be* something for you to like it, that practicing with paint isn't worthy of praise. And she knows she isn't a "great artist."

A better approach might be to say, "I like the way the colors drip together. You really used a lot of paint this time. And I could see you enjoyed doing it."

The second and better way to praise states the obvious: She has used a lot of paint, and you appreciate that; you like "the way the colors drip together." What gives her pleasure gives you pleasure too. Her experimenting with color is an admired skill. She did it well.

Praising her this way helps her to judge her work appropriately, to feel that what she actually does is valued by people who count.

Likewise, there are also two ways to criticize a child for something she has done. Let's again consider the wrong way first. You might say, as her glass of milk spills onto the floor, "Look what you've done. You are so clumsy."

When you tell a child *what* she is—"a clumsy person"—you judge her. She learns from this that she is clumsy, and always will be. That's the way things

will always go with her.

You can use a better approach by saying, "You put your glass too close to the edge of the table. Now you can help me clean up the floor."

When you tell her exactly what she has done, ("You put your glass too close to the edge of the table."), she can judge her action as it really is. She can avoid spilling her milk like that next time. She has annoyed you. But you have also given her a way to deal with spilled milk ("You can help me clean up the floor.").

If parents can avoid praise and criticism that judges the child herself, and instead use praise and criticism that judges the child's action, the child will learn better to evaluate her own behavior, pursue what she is good at, work on what she finds difficult, and like herself just the way she is.■

I See Something

There are times—waiting in the doctor's office, sitting on a bus—that can be boring. Here's a game to play anywhere, whenever time drags. It teaches your child to get information by asking good questions.

Say: "I see something." (It has to be something you can both see.)

Then give a clue: "It's on the table," is pretty easy. "It's red and square," may be pretty tough. "It's made of leather," is more difficult.

If one clue isn't enough, add another: "It's red and square and soft." "It's red and square and soft and I'm leaning against it."

Children just starting this game have no good strategy for getting the answer: They look around and guess wildly. "Is it my shoe?" "Is it the box?" So get your child to pick something ("I see ...") Listen to his first clue. Then ask questions of him that will help reveal your strategies: "Is it up high or down low?" That tells a person where to

look. "What color is it?" "Is it smaller than my shoe?" Those questions help narrow the choice.

At first a child's questions will be very concrete: "Is it this book?" "Is it that shoe?" As your child listens to your more abstract questions ("Is it made of wood?") he will eventually begin to think more abstractly. But that won't happen without more cognitive development. You are giving him the kind of practice he needs to stimulate this development.■

Gender Differences

When a baby is born, the question most frequently asked is, "Is it a boy or a girl?"

Although this distinction of gender is based on purely physical characteristics, a number of sex-typed expectations for a girl or boy immediately come into play in terms of presumed personality characteristics, abilities, interests, and behaviors, including manner of dress.

What does it mean to a preschool child to be a boy or a girl?

The answer is a complex one because (1) a child's understanding of gender differences is different from that of an adult; (2) that understanding changes and develops during the preschool years; and (3) our society's gender-role stereotypes and expectations are also changing.

In this article we will deal with the child's own developmental understanding of gender differences. Next month we will discuss gender-role concepts and stereotypes.

Child development experts consider that children develop the concept of gender in three steps: (1) gender identity, (2) gender stability, and (3) gender constancy.

By 3 years of age, most children have acquired *gender identity*. This means they are capable of using correct gender labels in classifying themselves and others as male or female (for example, "I'm a boy." or "Mom is a girl."). Correct labeling, however, does not imply clear understanding of the gender concept.

Three-year-old children, generally, don't base the male-female distinction on anatomical genital differences, as adults would do. They are more likely to base male-female differentiation on secondary characteristics

Three-year-olds have probably been taught by now that in our culture girls play with dolls and boys play with trucks.

such as a person's clothes, jewelry, or length of hair.

They have also probably been taught by now that in our culture girls play with dolls and boys play with trucks. But at this stage they have the impression that, by playing with trucks, a girl can be a boy if she wants. Or a boy who plays with dolls can grow up to be a Mommy if he wishes.

The development of a child's understanding of gender is, of course, related to the child's level of cognitive development.

For example, at this age a child has not yet developed what psychologist Jean Piaget has called the concept of *conservation*: namely, that an object, or amount of liquid, for example, will remain the same regardless of the height of the container in which it is poured.

As a child's cognitive abilities become more highly developed, his understanding of gender changes. By about age 4, a child has developed at least a partial understanding of the permanence of gender, namely, *gender stability*.

This means he understands that gender will not change over time: Boys will grow up to be men and girls will grow up to be women.

But a 4-year-old's understanding of gender is still imperfect and, at times, contradictory. Studies have found that children of this age are likely to assert, for example, that if a man wears a dress, he has become a woman.

While these findings may seem strange to some parents who have a mature adult's understanding of gender differences, they are not too surprising in light of the child's level of cognitive development.

It is not until sometime between 4 and 7 years of age—generally at about 5 or 6 years of age—that children develop the concept of *gender constancy*: namely, the understanding that gender will remain the same not only over time but also across different situations.

It is interesting to note that gender constancy coincides with children's grasp of the conservation of mass, weight, number, and quantity.

Gender constancy may therefore be considered as "conservation of gender" across time and situations.

Once children understand the constancy of their own gender, they quickly develop rigid rules regarding appropriate and inappropriate gender-role behaviors.

Next month we will discuss the development of children's gender-role concepts and stereotypes and will be telling you more about the findings of recent research studies.

This is an important area of child development that has only recently received the attention it deserves from researchers and scholars.■

Is Your Child Right-handed or Left-handed

What is handedness and why is it important? A child usually has a dominant *eye* (the eye the child uses in aiming or sighting), a dominant *hand* (the hand the child uses in eating, grasping, throwing, etc.), and a dominant *foot* (the foot she kicks with, for example).

Some children have a clearly dominant *side* when the dominant eye, hand, and foot are all on the same side. Other children have crossed-dominance if, for example, a child is right-handed and left-footed.

It is important to distinguish between crossed-dominance and mixed-handedness. Mixed-handedness means the child uses *either* hand in writing, eating, throwing, etc. In other words, she does not have a dominant or preferred hand.

From research studies we may draw the following general conclusions:

1. Crossed-dominance does not seem to be a factor in reading problems.

2. Mixed-handedness after age 7, on the other hand, seems to be related to reading problems.

It is important for your child to develop a dominant or preferred hand. Don't worry about whether her dominant hand is on the same side as her dominant eye or dominant foot.

Your almost-4-year-old has probably not yet developed a dominant hand. If she is mixed-handed now, this is perfectly normal. Mixed-handedness is not abnormal until about age 7.

The key to proper hand dominance is: *The child himself should make the decision.* This means that you do not decide whether she should be left-handed or right-handed.

It is quite possible that there are biological factors involved in being either left- or right-handed. It is best for the child to discover for herself her own unique handedness. So, don't try to make her either right- or left-handed.

There are things you can do *now* to help her develop a dominant hand *later.* Here are some recommendations to promote an appropriate dominant hand in your child.

1. Be aware of the fact that your child lives in a right-handed world. If you are right-handed, your tendency may be to place objects in her right hand.

2. Present objects in front of the middle of her body. If she drops a toy, for example, and you pick it up, give it back to her by placing it before her exactly in her middle.

As she reaches for it, she may begin to show a preference for her right or left hand.

3. Have her use *each* hand in performing many different tasks. For example, have her scribble first with one hand, then with the other.

4. Observe carefully which hand she begins to prefer. You may even want to keep a record of how many times she uses her right hand and her left hand in a given task.

With careful observations you may get some clues about her hand preference.

5. Talk to her about her handedness. "Which hand feels better to you?" Questions like this will also help her become more aware of differences between the two sides of her body. ■

Twelve Alternatives to Lashing Out at Your Child

The next time everyday pressures build up to the point where you feel like lashing out— STOP! And try any of these simple alternatives.

You'll feel better ... and so will your child.

1. Take a deep breath. And another. Then remember *you* are the adult ...

2. Close your eyes and imagine you're hearing what your child is about to hear.

3. Press your lips together and count to 10. Or better yet, to 20.

4. Put your child in a time-out chair. (Remember the rule: one time-out minute for each year of age.)

5. Put yourself in a time-out chair. Think about why you are angry: Is it your child, or is your child simply a convenient target for your anger?

6. Phone a friend.

7. If someone can watch the children, go outside and take a walk.

8. Take a hot bath or splash cold water on your face.

9. Hug a pillow.

10. Turn on some music. Maybe even sing along.

11. Pick up a pencil and write down as many helpful words as you can think of. Save the list.

12. Write for prevention information: National Committee for Prevention of Child Abuse, Box 2866L, Chicago, IL 60690. ■

Reprinted with permission: National Committee for Prevention of Child Abuse

An Obstacle Course

An obstacle course can provide Youngster with many hours of fun. It can also provide a great learning experience.

In an obstacle course Youngster will be challenged to move in a variety of postures and styles—"through," "across," "into," "between," "on top of," "under," "next to," etc.

Shown below are some materials that can be used to create an obstacle course:

When your child has mastered the course, make a new one with his help. Change the position of the equipment or change the pattern of movement.

This fun obstacle course serves many useful purposes:

1) It helps a child expand his repertoire of motor patterns.

2) It provides the necessary motor experiences to acquire knowledge of the dimensions of space: up/down, left/right, front/back, over/under, across, between, around, etc.

3) It also helps him learn the vocabulary for these dimensions of space.

4) It offers an opportunity to match vocabulary with perceptual-motor experience as he associates the experience in space with the words. He also internalizes the association so that the words are available for use when similar events occur later.

5) It allows him to be creative in the design of the course. Using or reusing materials already available allows for change and innovation.■

Fun and Learning in the Kitchen

Some of the happiest, most pleasant hours you spend with your child may well be in the kitchen.

The taste, touch, sights, sounds, and smells of good food appeal to all your youngster's senses. And the results of this activity provide almost instant gratification and feelings of success.

The kitchen is a place where your child can perform *real* work. When she is preparing food, she is not *pretending* to do something—she is actually *doing* it.

When she is finished, she will have something tangible and tasty to show for her efforts—something that will give her the very real sense of achievement she needs. Your child now loves to feel important and show how smart she is.

There's a lot more to cooking than an enjoyable afternoon with Mommy or Daddy. Cooking is an ideal way to learn by experience. It involves the entire child—muscles and senses, intellect and emotion, personal growth and social interaction.

Although at 46 months your youngster is still too young to grasp abstract mathematical concepts, cooking provides a concrete foundation for these concepts which will be understood later on.

Cooking involves simple fractions and measures. It also involves such concepts as "in," "out," "smooth," "lumpy," "hard," "soft," "hot," and "cold."

It involves structure and order. That is why it is important to read recipe directions aloud to your child. By doing this, she learns to follow a sequence. And, of course, cooking also builds vocabulary.

Step by step, she acts upon what you tell her and observes the change that takes place. Let her do as much as she can handle. As she mixes, mashes, measures, and stirs, she is learning new skills, using her muscles, and improving her eye-hand coordination.

Working in the kitchen also stimulates your child's curiosity about the world in which she lives. From her observations in the kitchen, she learns that applesauce did not start out in a can, or that bread did not originate in a supermarket.

All the time she is working in the kitchen, she is questioning. "Why is this apple red?" "Who made the bowl?" "Where does a carrot come from?" "Why do we get hungry?" Through endless questions (not always easy to answer), your child tries to understand her world.

Some of the things you make with your child will be related to seasons and holidays. This will be a good opportunity to explain the significance of a particular feast or special food.

At other times, you may want to draw upon a favorite nursery rhyme or story as you prepare a certain food.

There is bread to bake like "The Little Red Hen," or porridge to make as in "Goldilocks and the Three Bears." Vegetable soup sounds a lot more interesting after reading the story of "Stone Soup." And every child is delighted by the rhymes and pictures of Maurice Sendak's "Chicken Soup With Rice."

It's not surprising that cooking often tempts a child to try new food. While your youngster can help with almost anything you cook, here are a few particularly safe and suitable ideas for "almost-4." They require little or no cooking skills.

Peanut Butter Candy
1 cup peanut butter
1 cup honey
1 package powdered milk
Mix together well. Let your youngster shape into small balls. Refrigerate and eat later.

Butter
1/2 pint heavy cream
salt
large jar
Shake heavy cream in a large jar until it becomes thick. Pour out excess liquid. Add salt. Spread on bread or crackers.

Turkey Hand Cookies
Heat to boiling—1/2 cup molasses.
Add:
1/4 cup sugar
3 tablespoons butter
2 cups flour
1/2 teaspoon each of baking soda, salt, nutmeg, cinnamon, powdered cloves, and ginger.

Mix well. Roll out. Then trace your child's hand for turkey shapes. Place raisins for eyes.

Bake about 8 minutes at 375° on greased cookie sheet. Let cool.

Let Youngster decorate the cookie with frosting. Use toothpicks for legs and gum drops for feet. (Any favorite cookie dough may be substituted.)

Something for the Birds
Hang this on a tree for the birds to eat.
1/2 cup lard
1 cup peanut butter
bird seed
pine cones
Mix the lard and peanut butter and spread it on the pine cones. Then roll the pine cones in the bird seed mixture. Finally, hang the cones outdoors on a tree. Watch the birds come to eat it.

These are just a few suggestions. You can develop many more recipes of your own. Even your youngster may suggest adding a favorite ingredient—such as chopped nuts—to your cookie recipe.■

Avoiding Mealtime Hassles

Is there a way to avoid hassles while encouraging your child to make real decisions? Parents often want to give their child freedom to choose, but become upset when he chooses something different from what they wanted.

At mealtime, for example, a conversation such as this might take place:

Parent: Charles, do you want some carrots?

Child: No!

Parent: Well, then would you like some string beans?

Child: No!

Parent: Well, you *have* to *eat* something!

In such a case, parents set themselves up for failure. To avoid such hassles, learn to think about what answer(s) you want *before* you ask the question. Then phrase your question so that you will get the answer(s) you wanted, while, at the same time, giving your child a real choice to make.

Ask, "Would you rather have carrots or green beans tonight?"

There is no "yes" or "no" answer. He may not be enthusiastic about carrots. But he may clearly prefer carrots to green beans. In which case he will answer "Carrots."

How can you avoid mealtime hassles with a finicky eater who does well with routine foods but doesn't want to try any new food? This time try a different approach with the new dish. Make up a fancy name for it such as "Friday Freebie" or "Holiday Huddle."

Serve it with a flourish, giving Mary a small portion, saying, "There's a little serving for you. When you want more, you can have it!"■

Surprise Surprise!

By now your child has developed a strong imagination. As a part of growing up, he likes to explore different roles. As far as possible, play the game with him. Use *your* imagination.

Is he a cowboy? Then the kitchen is the chuck wagon. Is he an astronaut? Then offer space food. A pony? Offer the feedbag.

A king, queen, prince, or princess? A formal dish for his/her majesty!

At almost 4 years of age, a child's information and imagination is still very concrete. His behaviors will reflect the role with which he is experimenting. So go along with your "stranger."

Explore with him. Help him learn new behaviors appropriate for the role. Take some photographs or make a video recording of your budding young actor. And relax—have fun! In later years you will enjoy the memories of these imagination experiences.■

www.growingchild.com

Contributing Authors

Phil Bach, O.D., Ph.D.
Miriam Bender, Ph.D.
Joseph Braga, Ed.D.
Laurie Braga, Ph.D.
George Early, Ph.D.
Liam Grimley, Ph.D.
Robert Hannemann, M.D., F.A.A.P.
Sylvia Kottler, M.S.
Bill Peterson, Ph.D.

Growing Child, Inc.
P.O. Box 620
Lafayette, Indiana 47902
Telephone: 1-800-927-7289
©2005 Growing Child, Inc.

Dear Growing Child:

"Thank you so much for your words of guidance and reassurance each month. You really have become a good friend!

"You've given me practical advice, fun ideas, and, more importantly, the confidence to believe that my baby and I are doing just fine.

"With your help, my baby has become a wonderful toddler, and I look forward to our future with you at our side."

Judy Z.
Rochester Hill, MI

Next Month

- ***10 Ways to Help Build Your Child's Self-esteem***
- ***Gender-Role Concepts and Stereotypes***

Growing Child®

10 Ways to Help Build Your Child's Self-esteem

The term "self-esteem" refers to people's evaluation of their own worth as human beings. Persons with high self-esteem think well of themselves. Those with low self-esteem have feelings of inferiority about themselves and about their own abilities.

Did you know that self-esteem is something that is learned, not something we are born with? Young children develop a sense of their own self-worth—good or bad—mainly from interacting with their parents and other significant adults in their lives.

Parents who give their child positive messages ("I like what you just did") create feelings of positive self-esteem. Those who give mainly negative messages ("You're a dummy") create feelings of inferiority in their child.

The early childhood years are a particularly important time for building high self-esteem in your child. Research studies indicate that children who have acquired high self-esteem by the time they enter school earn better grades, are more popular with their peers, and need less disciplining at home and in school.

Here are ten ways in which parents can help build high self-esteem in their child:

1) **Plan specific activities for positive parent-child interactions.** These activities will usually be ones that both parent and child enjoy such as a trip to the playground or an indoor game ("Let's try to put these puzzle pieces together again"). Working together in the kitchen (for example, preparing food with a simple recipe) or helping your child get dressed are also opportunities to let her know she is a special person.

2) **Capitalize on opportunities for spontaneous interaction.** These interactions build on interests displayed by your child ("I like that picture you are drawing. How can I help?") A good educational TV program, such as *Sesame Street* or *Mister Rogers' Neighborhood,* can facilitate spontaneous parent-child discussion.

By contrast, parents who routinely spend their evenings watching TV while ignoring their child's pleas for attention and interaction are letting her know (unintentionally, perhaps, but nonetheless unmistakably) that the TV set is more important than she is.

3) **Try to pay attention to what your child wants to tell you—not just to what you want to hear or what you want to say to her.** Your attention will be perceived by your smile, eye contact, a pat on the back, or nodding of your head.

Your interest in what she says will be demonstrated by your willingness to listen. Such nonverbal messages help to make your child feel important and valued.

4) **Ask your child to elaborate on what she tells you.** ("Tell me more about that," or "Then what did you do?") Such questions let her know that what she wants to tell you is important to you.

Make sure to be patient by waiting for her response to your questions, even if she has difficulty finding the words she wants to use.

5) **Don't be judgmental about what your child has just told you.** Children who are constantly being judged, criticized, or corrected because of what they tell their parents will eventually decide it's smarter for them not to communicate. If you are horrified by something your child has just told you, try to wait until a later time to make your comments.

This will give you time to think about what you want to say rather than reacting impulsively. You will then be able to discuss the matter with your child in an atmosphere that is less emotionally charged. And your child will more likely listen to your words without feeling threatened or humiliated.

6) **Become more aware of** *what* **you say to your child,** *when* **you say it, and** *how* **you say it.** Imagine your words and actions are being recorded. In that way you will see and hear yourself as your child sees and

CONTINUED ON PAGE 284

CONTINUED FROM PAGE 283

hears you. If you catch yourself saying or doing things you wish you hadn't said or done, being aware of your own behavior will help you avoid such inappropriate interactions in the future.

7) Show affection for your child not just in actions but also in words. Open expressions of affection help a child to develop feelings of self-worth. Some parents unfortunately are shy or reluctant to tell their child openly that they love her and care about her.

8) Pay attention to and reward your child's good behavior. Positive recognition for good behavior ("I like the way you put away your toys.") will reinforce the occurrence of more good behavior. By contrast, parents can create feelings of inferiority in their child if they routinely take good behavior for granted and only give attention to what a child does wrong ("Look at the mess you just made.").

9) Give your child some real age-appropriate responsibilities which you know she can do. Such responsibilities (helping to dust or to mop the floor, for example) give a child feelings of autonomy and importance. Just be sure the responsibilities and expected outcomes are appropriate for your child's age and stage of development.

10) Make a deliberate decision to help build your child's self-esteem. To build your child's self-esteem it is important not only to be aware of how to do this, but also to make a deliberate decision to implement these strategies. Select one of the above recommendations that you think will most help build your child's self-esteem. Practice it until it becomes second nature. Then try another technique that will help you become a more effective parent.

Efforts parents make to help build their child's self-esteem will provide enormous long-term benefits. These efforts will also increase their own joys of parenting.∎

Physical Development

reat changes have been taking place in Youngster's motor development. These changes are not always obvious because they have been taking place gradually over a period of several months.

It is a good idea, therefore, to review some of the motor skills Youngster has mastered by now.

Gross motor skills involve the use of the large muscles of the body, including the arms and legs. These large muscles mature earlier than the smaller muscles needed for fine motor skills which we will discuss later.

By now Youngster has developed the large muscle control needed to walk in a straight line. He can also run with greater ease. He enjoys jumping over small objects and avoids obstacles. He can hop and gallop and then bring himself to a sudden stop.

His muscles are now strong enough to enable him to balance on one foot or climb playground equipment. He enjoys jumping or dancing to music even though his timing is sometimes off. And, of course, he loves to pedal his tricycle.

Coordination of the smaller muscles needed for fine motor skills is usually dependent on the development and coordination of the large muscles of the body. As large muscle skills improve, the development of new fine motor skills becomes possible.

Let's review some of the fine motor skills Youngster has developed by now.

Youngster is now capable of dressing and undressing, provided some adult is nearby to provide encouragement and assistance if needed. In general, he can fasten and unfasten zippers, handle Velcro™ fasteners, and unbutton the front of his clothing.

He is also better able to feed himself with fewer spills. He can pour from a small pitcher and can stir the contents of his glass. Although he can spread butter or jam on his bread, his muscles are not yet strong enough to cut a piece of bread or meat.

He has also developed better control when drawing with crayons, paints, or pencils. He can now work jigsaw puzzles with five or more pieces.

He enjoys being creative with assembly toys that have snap-on pieces. And, of course, he still enjoys building a variety of structures with blocks.

As Youngster's motor development improves with these educational experiences, so too his brain development is stimulated by his new motor abilities. His self-concept and self-esteem are also affected as he gains new mastery over the world around him.

In reviewing these developmental abilities, it should be obvious how important it is, during the preschool years, to provide Youngster with good development experiences, such as the ones we have described in *Growing Child* over the past several months.∎

Nosebleeds

Bleeding from the nose happens to every child. It is usually caused by one of the "four I's": Injury, infection, irritation, or inheritance.

Injury may be caused by a fall or a blow from a playmate. It may also be caused by the child himself who picks or rubs too vigorously or puts an object into the nostril. Objects in the nose are frequently overlooked but should be suspected when the child has repeated mild bleeding, drainage, or a bad odor from one nostril. Injury can also occur from breathing dry air which causes the sensitive nasal lining to shrink, crack, and then break one of the small surface blood vessels.

Infection usually takes the form of a cold which inflames the lining of the nose, resulting in an increase of blood circulating through it. Then a very minor injury will cause bleeding. Another infection which can cause a nosebleed is impetigo. This is a skin infection which starts under the nose and gradually works its way up into the nostril, causing the nosebleed.

Irritation to the lining of the nose may be caused by dust, mold, or pollen. It causes the same type of inflammation as a cold. It can lead to a bloody nose, particularly if the child sneezes or blows his nose too hard.

Inheritance plays a part in some nosebleeds, particularly those caused by nasal blood vessels located near the surface. Nasal allergy and certain types of blood clotting diseases are also inherited and frequently are first suspected when bleeding from the nose occurs.

Nosebleeds can usually be handled by the "three P's": prevention, pressure, and posture.

Prevention of accident-induced bleeding is almost impossible. Self-inflicted, dry air, and irritant types of problems, however, are preventable. Daytime nosepicking and rubbing can be stopped by gentle reminders and nail clipping. Nighttime nosebleeds usually occur during sleep and can be prevented by covering the hands with light-weight mittens. Dryness in the air can be counteracted by the use of a humidifier. If one is not available, a pan of water near the heat vents or radiators will help. Irritation from dust and mold can be prevented by more stringent household cleaning.

Pressure on the nose by holding it between the thumb and first finger will stop most nosebleeds since the bleeding most often occurs from the front of the nose. Pressure must be held for at least five minutes.

Posture is very important when treating a nosebleed. The child should be in an upright or semi-reclining position. This decreases pressure in the nasal blood vessels and prevents blood from running back into the throat.

If the bleeding is not stopped by the pressure method in five to 10 minutes, or if it occurs repeatedly, particularly from both nostrils, your doctor should be consulted.∎

Sounds Ears Catch

This is a good age at which to help develop your child's sensitivity to sounds. Even adults are sometimes not attentive to the sounds around them. Often we may become so accustomed to a sound (for example, the distant sound of trucks on the highway) that we no longer attend to it. So you and your child can have some fun listening to and identifying the sounds in your environment.

To start, both of you sit down and close your eyes. Ask, "What do you hear?" He may not identify anything at first. If you say, "I hear a bird," he'll probably say he hears birds for the next 10 minutes. That's okay. He's learning to identify bird songs from the myriad sounds around him.

When you hear the sound of a truck going by, you can heighten interest by asking: "Was that a truck, or a motorcycle, or a car?" Listen for the next one and see if he can tell the difference.

You can also help your child identify familiar sounds around your home. First, get him to cover or close his eyes. Now switch on a machine—a mixer, or vacuum cleaner. See if he can correctly identify each sound.

Here are other sounds to produce: boil water in a kettle, turn on a water tap, flush the toilet, click a light switch, close a door, open a drawer, drop a spoon.

If he identifies all these sounds correctly, you can provide a greater challenge by rapping your knuckles on the door, the window, the wall, the floor. Put something—a pencil, a ball, beans, a stuffed toy—in a box and shake it. See if he can recognize the sounds of each object.

When you have a chance to go for a walk in the country, be sure to take time to listen to sounds: the barking of a dog, the mooing of a cow, or the cooing of a dove. These activities make a walk much more enjoyable. They also help your child to be more alert and attentive to the different sounds in his environment.∎

Gender-Role Concepts and Stereotypes

Are boys naturally more aggressive and achievement-oriented than girls? Are girls more emotionally sensitive and nurturing than boys?

It is not always easy to determine which gender-role behaviors are biologically predetermined and which ones are most influenced by environment.

Apart from the obvious genital differences, there are other physical differences between males and females—such as the proportion of muscle to body fat—which are indeed biologically determined.

Researchers have noted that as early as 2 years of age, boys are more active and aggressive than girls. They prefer to play with trucks and blocks whereas girls prefer softer toys and dolls.

While these preferences may be related to the purely physical differences between boys and girls, it is obvious that environment also influences the development of gender-role concepts and stereotypes.

Every newborn baby, for example, experiences immediately some environmental gender-role stereotyping in terms of name, dress, and toys.

Research studies indicate that a complex combination of nature and nurture influences are involved in the development of children's gender-role concepts. Here are some of the findings:

• By about 3 years of age, children (both girls and boys) already associate some occupational items more with males (tools and cars, for example) and others with females (food, stoves, vacuum cleaners).

• By age 5 they even identify some personality traits as masculine (strength, independence, aggression) or feminine

(gentleness, nurturance, soft-heartedness).

• It is interesting to note that cross-cultural studies in over 30 countries have found these same gender-role stereotypes in virtually all cultures.

• But the perceived differences were less between male and female gender-role stereotypes in more highly developed nations than in less well-developed ones.

• Likewise, lower socioeconomic class groups were more likely to enforce traditional gender-role stereotyping (for example, "Boys don't cry") than higher socioeconomic class groups.

It is obvious that gender-role stereotypes in our society—particularly with regard to occupations—are undergoing change. More women are becoming construction workers or engineers, for example, while more men are entering professions, such as nursing, which were once considered for females only.

How children develop their gender-role concepts depends not only on their biological characteristics, but on many important influences in their environment, such as family, peers, television, and children's books.

During the preschool years,

parents have a very important influence on their child's gender-role development. Research studies have found that:

• Parents often have different expectations for boys and girls. Generally, they expect their sons to be assertive and competent, but expect their daughters to be more gentle, warm, and caring.

• Fathers are more likely to engage in rough-and-tumble play with their sons than with their daughters.

• Fathers also become more concerned if a son plays with dolls than if a daughter engages in what is considered to be cross-sex behavior (the "tomboy" girl).

• Mothers, on the other hand, are more likely to treat sons and daughters alike.

• Mothers are also more often responsible for the physical care and emotional nurturance of both sons and daughters.

Child development experts claim it is not in the best interest of young children to limit them to gender-typed toys (for example, dolls only for girls and trucks only for boys). Rather it seems best to encourage a wide spectrum of behaviors and feelings during the preschool years.

Girls can thus be encouraged to be more assertive and self-confident (by being given toys such as cars and trucks to play with) while boys can be encouraged to be more nurturant and caring (by being given dolls and other nurturant toys to care for).

Peers also have an important influence on the development of gender-role concepts. As early as 3 years of age, children show a preference for same-sex playmates.

By the time children reach school age, they play almost exclusively with same-sex peers. These peers sometimes impose

CONTINUED ON PAGE 287

CONTINUED FROM PAGE 286

more rigid gender-typed rules of behavior than parents do.

Those who engage in cross-sex activities (such as a boy playing with a doll) are generally either left to play alone or are sometimes ridiculed by their same-sex peers.

Television has become another important influence in the lives of young children.

With some notable exceptions, television programs generally adhere to gender-role stereotypes (the role of the business executive is played by a male, for example, while the role of secretary is played by a female).

Lastly, children's books have an important influence on the development of gender-role concepts.

In recent years, educators and publishers have become more aware of and sensitive to the hidden messages in children's books (such as pictures that repeatedly portray doctors as male and nurses as female), as well as the not-so-hidden messages (such as when the content of a story is blatantly sex-biased).

The development of gender-role concepts in preschool children is therefore quite complex.

When children later enter school and eventually reach adolescence, it becomes even more complex, especially as gender-role stereotypes in society change.

Each new generation challenges the wisdom of doing things "the old way." And new ideas about gender-role stereotypes—some considered unthinkable just a short time ago—gain ever broader acceptance in our society.

Parents who themselves are comfortable with their own gender-role identity and who are sensitive to changes in our society are generally the best role models for the development of healthy gender-role concepts in their children.■

Nonverbal Communication

 oung children usually understand more than they are able to communicate through spoken language. We only have to observe their use of nonverbal language—hand gestures, body movements, facial expressions, eye contact, voice intonations—to realize that these cues can be both subtle and explicit. They convey important information about what children are experiencing and thinking.

For example, as Molly is drawing a picture, her mother interrupts by asking, "What's that?" It's an innocent question that was meant to encourage Molly to talk about her drawing.

Instead, without saying a word, Molly tears up her drawing, throws it into the wastebasket, and runs out of the room. Her actions speak louder than any words she might have uttered that she is upset.

This example illustrates the importance of nonverbal communication. Social psychologists claim that in a typical conversation, only about 35 percent of the social meaning is transmitted by actual words whereas about 65 percent is transmitted by nonverbal channels.

Vocal cues, for example, provide remarkable amounts of information. Even if we didn't understand the words spoken, we would know that a person who is angry uses a higher pitch voice, louder volume, and a faster rate of speech.

On the contrary, someone who is sad uses a lower pitch, less volume, and a slower rate of speech.

Children are remarkably perceptive of nonverbal messages. Even before any words are spoken by an adult, a young child has already formed some impressions based on nonverbal messages. These messages could include the person's height, weight, skin color, and manner of dress.

Once the adult begins to speak, the child usually attends not only to the words, but also to the gestures and the emotional tone of the voice.

Because the vocabulary of young children is not as highly developed as that of adults, it is likely that young children rely more heavily on nonverbal cues than adults.

The poet Oliver Goldsmith once described in these immortal words how the children in the classroom learned to detect the village schoolmaster's mood:

"Well had the boding tremblers learned to trace,
The day's disasters in his morning face."

Sometimes the relationship between verbal and nonverbal communication can be complex. Nonverbal communication can generally serve one of three different functions.

(1) It can simply *augment* verbal communication. For example, the person who laughs loudly and says, "That's very funny."

(2) At other times nonverbal communication *contradicts* verbal communication as in the case of the angry parent who shouts loudly, "I am NOT angry!"

(3) Nonverbal communication can *replace* verbal communication as when one person gives a friendly smile or a hug to another without saying a single word.

Researchers in the education of young children have recently stressed the importance of nonverbal behaviors in human interactions.

It is hoped that this increased awareness will help parents to gain insights into their own behavior and become more sensitive to their child's nonverbal communication.■

The Role of Parents in a Young Child's Learning

In *Growing Child* we have repeatedly stressed the importance of positive parent-child interactions during the preschool years. Recent research studies not only support this viewpoint but also indicate its relationship with a child's later success in school.

In a study of the interactions of fathers with their children, it was found that the most competent fathers of preschool children (1) regularly set aside a special time to be with the child; (2) become involved in the child's play and generally demonstrate an interest in his activities; and (3) listen to the child, talk with him, and respond to any questions he may ask.

If the child attends a preschool program, it was found that his father can help his schooling by communicating regularly with the preschool teachers, by demonstrating genuine interest in the child's progress and development, and by participating actively in the program's organized functions.

A longitudinal study of the behaviors of mothers during a child's preschool years indicated a relationship between these behaviors and the child's later academic success in sixth grade.

During the preschool years the following maternal behaviors were found to be the best predictors of a child's sixth grade academic success: (1) a warm and loving mother-child relationship; (2) effective two-way communication; (3) positive and realistic expectations for achievement; and (4) use of rule-based, rather than authority-based, discipline in the home.

In another study which investigated successful preschool programs, it was found that the most important factor for success was the active involvement of parents in their child's learning and education.

It is clear, therefore, that parents—both fathers and mothers—play an important role in the development of young children's attitudes toward learning. These research findings should provide reassurance for most of our *Growing Child* readers. After all, the purpose of this publication is to help parents better understand the important developmental changes that take place in their child during the first few years of life.

Based on this knowledge, we have consistently suggested activities to enable parents to become more actively involved in their child's learning.

We believe that such parent involvement in learning will enhance a child's present development and later success in school.

It's nice to know that this viewpoint has been repeatedly supported by recent research studies.■

www.growingchild.com

Contributing Authors

Phil Bach, O.D., Ph.D.
Miriam Bender, Ph.D.
Joseph Braga, Ed.D.
Laurie Braga, Ph.D.
George Early, Ph.D.
Liam Grimley, Ph.D.
Robert Hannemann, M.D., F.A.A.P.
Sylvia Kottler, M.S.
Bill Peterson, Ph.D.

Growing Child, Inc.
P.O. Box 620
Lafayette, Indiana 47902
Telephone: 1-800-927-7289
©2005 Growing Child, Inc.

Next Month

- *Learning about Numbers*
- *Growing into Bigger Thoughts*
- *Genital Touching*

Growing Child®

Four Years Old

t 4 years of age, your child is entering an exciting new period of development. With her newly acquired visual-motor coordination skills, she is now better able to take care of herself: getting dressed and undressed, brushing her teeth, or feeding herself at mealtimes. She can also participate more actively in arts and crafts activities.

Although she is very proud of her new ability to imitate grown-up behavior, her motor skills are likely to be more highly developed than her sense of good judgment. As a result, she may sometimes attempt to do more than she can safely accomplish.

For example, she may give you a shock by proudly proclaiming that she is now old enough to cross the street without having to hold your hand. Hence frequent reminders about safety are needed at this age.

She may also want to reach out to other children. She has become more outward-oriented emotionally, sometimes displaying a sense of self-confidence which verges on cockiness. In trying to impress her peers, she may sometimes brag or become a "show-off."

Within a matter of moments, however, her self-confidence may suddenly disappear. She may exhibit whining behavior and may want to be held and cuddled to relieve her feelings of insecurity.

When playing with other children, she may also exhibit a confused notion of "property rights."

For example, while she is

At 4 years of age, a child's sense of what is "good" or "bad" is based mainly on what some important authority figure (usually a parent) has told her.

playing with a toy, she still believes that "possession" and "ownership" are synonymous. If another child stops playing with a truck, Youngster believes it became *"hers"* just as soon as *she* started to play with it.

On the other hand, she will defend vigorously her right to retrieve a toy which she herself had earlier abandoned.

In other words, she will test the limits of behavior in many different ways as she seeks to unravel the rules which apply to her behavior.

Her sense of morality in general is just beginning to be formed. Although she shows some ability to consider the

implications of her actions, she has as yet only a rudimentary awareness of the difference between "good" and "bad."

At 4 years of age, her sense of what is "good" or "bad" is based mainly on what some important authority figure (usually a parent) has told her, or else on the punishment she might associate with some transgression.

In other words, her sense of morality is still externally-based rather than being guided by an internalized conscience.

In dealing with her misbehaviors, it is important for parents to distinguish between the behavior itself and the child: Identify an undesirable behavior as "bad," but never tell a child she is a "bad girl."

It is also normal for a child at this age to show interest in basic sexual information. "What's my navel for?" "Where are my genitals?" "Where do babies come from?"

Parents may sometimes be surprised by the open and frank manner in which young children will ask such questions. It is best to answer them in an equally open and frank manner, giving the information in words the young child will understand.

She likes to be read to, talked to, told stories, and to be informed about things she wants to know. She is constantly learning new concepts: numbers, the alphabet, the time of day, days of the week, the seasons. To satisfy her curiosity, she is constantly asking "what," "why," and "how" questions. All of this is part of a 4-year-old's eagerness to learn about life. ■

Developmental Milestones–4 Years

Gross Motor Skills
- Touches toes without bending knees.
- Stands on one foot for about 8 seconds at a time.
- Hops forward about three steps on each foot.
- Walks skillfully on a narrow straight line.
- Enjoys playing with a ball.
- Runs on toes.
- Climbs, slides, swings on playground equipment.

Fine Motor Skills
- Threads a shoelace through beads.
- Builds a tower of 10 or more blocks.
- Holds and uses a crayon with good control.
- Copies an "O" (circle), a "+" (plus), and a "V."
- Draws a house.

Language
- Enjoys listening to stories and simple jokes.
- Speaks intelligibly—exhibits only a few sound substitutions.
- Gives name, address, and age when asked.
- Counts by rote up to 20.
- Knows several nursery rhymes.
- Asks questions—"why," "what," "how," "when."

Social/Emotional Behavior
- Eats with fork and spoon.
- Dresses and undresses except for laces, back buttons, some zippers, and snaps.
- Enjoys companionship of other children.
- Understands the concept of "taking turns." ■

These milestones are guidelines only. All children do not develop at the same rate, nor do they spend the same amount of time at each stage of their development. Usually a child is ahead in some areas, behind in others, and "typical" in still other areas. The concept of the "typical" child describes the general characteristics of children at a given age.

Genital Touching

ll children crawl, play with their toes, scribble, sing silly songs. Parents find these activities normal. Genital-touching is an equally normal behavior for young children. All children, male and female, engage in self-stimulation at some time or another.

In the natural course of exploring the body, children discover that touching genitals creates a pleasurable sensation. They may use their hands or rub their genitals against a favorite teddy bear or blanket. The effect is the same: They experience pleasure. Of course, they want to repeat the experience. They may be using self-stimulation as a way of going to sleep or soothing themselves when feeling tense.

How should a parent react to a child's genital-touching? Calmly and purposefully. Let your child know in a matter-of-fact way that you know what he/she is doing. Then, try to ignore it as much as possible, with the following two exceptions.

First, if a child tends to touch his/her genitals in public—such as at preschool, at the library, or at the store—make the child aware that this activity is not appropriate in public. To fail to make this clear would expose the child to possible contempt and derision by other people. Deal with the subject in a casual, matter-of-fact fashion as you would a commonplace rule of etiquette such as saying "excuse me" after a burp or learning to chew with the mouth closed.

Second, there is some cause for concern if a child engages in excessive self-stimulation. Self-stimulation would be considered excessive if it interferes with normal everyday life, or if the child would rather do it than take part in other pleasurable activities. In such cases it is good to look for a possible underlying cause for excessive self-stimulation.

Children who touch their genitals excessively may have been too often left to their own devices. They may have learned to depend upon themselves for most of their mental and physical stimulation.

They may be engaging in genital-touching simply to comfort themselves if they feel hurt or neglected. Or they may be trying to convey anger or frustration through an act they know can shock and distress others. In any case, genital-touching is a behavior that is learned.

The vital thing to remember is this: Self-stimulation will not likely cause psychological harm. On the other hand, fear, guilt, or anxiety induced by excessive parental reaction may hurt a child. Even if a severe reprimand causes the child to stop touching genitals, the child will find other outlets for tensions.

More likely, the child will continue the stimulation in secret, but with added guilt feelings. In either case, the negative feelings the child will develop about himself and his body may seriously impair his future sense of self-worth.

Dealing with genital-touching can be a great challenge for some parents: allowing children the right to their own privacy, letting them live their own lives, yet providing loving guidance when needed. ■

Growing into Bigger Thoughts

Some months ago, we talked about the way that ideas and understandings are formed. A child's understanding of the world around her is not based on adult logic, which contains a lot of worldly wisdom mixed in with the basic ability to reason.

For instance, if adults see something rising into the air, be it a kite, an airplane, or a balloon, we know from experience that something external is pushing or pulling on the object to make it rise. But such logic escapes the young preschooler, because of her limited experience. She is more apt to devise explanations that fit with her narrower point of view.

If an object moves without visible force or human guidance, she may endow the object with a mind and will of its own and say confidently that the object moved because it wanted to. This fits with her knowledge of her own will and that of other people. She knows that movement can result simply from a desire to move.

A person's explanation of a happening will stay the same until something comes along to challenge the explanation—something that makes the explanation fail to work anymore. Then the explanation must be changed, either a little or a lot, until it again covers all the experienced happenings, new and old.

In month 13 we noted that when Toddler learned to put blocks through holes into a container, she formed the idea that small objects fit through the holes. But then along came an object that was too big to fit through any hole. Then she had to change her idea to a slightly different one: that only objects up to a certain size fit through the hole.

Later when she fit objects into holes of different shapes, she had to modify her idea again: An object has to be smaller than the hole, and of the same shape as the hole, if it is going to fit through the hole.

You can graphically demonstrate the process of idea development in your child by carefully controlling a set of experiences and then challenging her newly formed idea at the appropriate time.

One way to encourage your youngster to look for alternative explanations is to call attention, occasionally, to apparent inconsistencies or contradictions in her world. This could be in the form of a question, like, "Why don't animals wear clothes?"

What appears to be a contradiction is really not, as you explain that an animal's fur or hair gives warmth and protection in the same way that clothes would.

Or maybe she will ask the question, "How can airplanes fly?" You could ask, "Do they flap their wings like birds do?" This will dramatize an inconsistency that can easily be recognized by your child, or will be recognized the first time she sees an airplane fly.

After she has pondered that problem a little, you can help her with the idea that a bird's wing pushes on the air to make it go. An airplane has those noisy engines to push on the air so it doesn't have to flap its wings.

She will fall silent to digest this piece of information. When she is ready for more, she will come back to you with another question. Detailed explanations aren't necessary or even desirable.

When you see a cat, you can say, "Cats don't like to go in the water. How do you think they keep themselves clean?" If she doesn't have an answer, you can ask her to watch the cat. Pretty soon the cat will show her how it keeps itself clean. If she thinks that all things must be scrubbed in the tub, she will find that, with some animals at least, nature has another way.

For her understanding to grow, she must feed on a rich diversity of experiences in the world around her. The common, familiar things let her strengthen her older ideas. The surprises and mysteries in the world help her form the all-important new ones.■

A Snapshot Note

When preschoolers are allowed to use a simple camera, you can expect a certain strangeness in the snapshots taken. Their point of view is different from yours; so is their eye level. The best camera for children as young as 4 years is an inexpensive one-time-use camera.

Their pictures give you a window into their world. Corners of ceilings and their own two feet appeal to 4-year-olds. They love to aim up into the treetops. They're pleased and proud of a picture of a rock, a sidewalk crack, the dog's tail. They take pictures of people from behind. They photograph faces from very close up.

Older children can take their own "Tricky Pictures" to see if they can fool the younger kids. They are very clever at it. Textures interest them: rug, fur, basket, stone, concrete, wood, grass, sand, bark, burlap. And they will almost certainly enjoy objects taken from odd perspectives: a flag pole straight up, a kettle straight down.■

Color Matching

arents of preschoolers may find themselves bombarded with mail-order advertising for "Teach Your Child" kits.

One of the more popular ones, "How To Use The Telephone," is not particularly unique but it has been used effectively with the mentally retarded who do not recognize letter and number symbols.

We'd like to share our version of the color-coded telephone system which should be fun to create and use.

Materials:

1. One cardboard disc that fits over your telephone and has ten different circles or squares, depending on whether your telephone is rotary or push button.

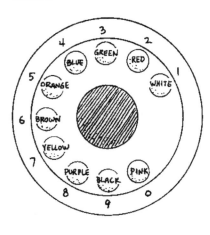

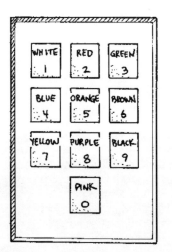

2. A scrapbook which will be the color-coded phone directory.

3. Photographs of the people whose phone numbers will be color-coded in the directory.

Decide what color you want to code each number. (It is unimportant that your child know the color names. Only color recognition is needed for this task.)

Color in the circles or squares, and your telephone is ready.

Now for the directory. Say you want your child to be familiar with important numbers such as Grandma's, Dad's or Mom's work phone, the doctor, or a close friend.

Paste a photograph, one to a page, and beneath each picture draw the appropriate seven colors.

For example, if the number is 468-3296, the colors on the page will look like this:

It will take a bit of practice for him to learn to start at the left and work toward the right. Young children frequently don't have a consistent sense of direction.

If you observe that this is a problem, give a starting cue such as an arrow or a star and explain, "We start at the arrow."

You may want to print the name of the person in capital letters next to the picture. This can become a subtle way of learning letters and words.

The child, without any special help from you, will eventually associate a picture of the person with the printed name and eventually recognize the name even when the picture is removed.■

Logical Thinking

ere are some games to develop your child's logical thinking. Approach each game with a flexible and open mind. Let your child set the pace. Don't rush her. Let her think things through for herself.

The "What Are You Not" Game

Ask your child what she is *not*. This may sound nonsensical to an adult. But to a 4-year-old the question is taken very seriously. You may have to prompt her a little, perhaps by naming something or someone you are not. (I'm not a horse.") Take turns saying what you are not.

The point you are stressing is that in logical thinking, what a thing is *not* is as important as what it *is*. This game helps a child to sort things into two sets—what something is, and what it is not.

Tell Me What This Isn't

Hold up something like a teddy bear or a toy truck and ask what it isn't. Your child must think of other things, perhaps some not even in sight. Take turns. Let your child choose something to hold up. Occasionally make an error and call the object what it *is*. Does your child correct you? If so, she really has learned the idea you are trying to teach.

Let's Put Our Toys Away

A sorting game can be a helpful way of getting a child to put toys away after playing. You will need several boxes for storing toys rather than a single "hold-all" chest.

Say: "Let's put all the *soft* toys in this box, and all the *hard* toys in that one." For instance—Soft set: teddy bear, paper hats, paperback picture books, rag dolls.

CONTINUED ON PAGE 293

Learning About Numbers

Perhaps you have had the experience, when one of two identical cookies broke into many pieces, that your child chose the damaged cookie because "there's more." Or perhaps you have set the table and thought you miscounted when there appeared to be too many water glasses for the number of place settings.

In exploring objects in space, it is important that your child perceive that distance between objects and difference in size does not in fact change the number of objects.

How do we help a young child accept the fact that the cookie is still the same, that nothing has been added in spite of the abundance of crumbs?

And how do we help him to resist the deception of his senses that the number of objects remains unchanged even though they have been moved about in space and placed in new positions?

You help by permitting him to actively engage in exploratory experiences, answer questions about his experiences, and support his answers with simple reasoning. Some examples:

1. The Tea party
Materials: Cookies, juice, glasses, a table runner or strip of masking tape (designed to partition the table in half).

Have your child place a cookie on the table runner, one cookie for each guest. Next, have the juice glass placed in a one-to-one match with the cookie, one glass for each cookie, on the outside of the table runner or line.

Ask him to count with you the number of cookies and the number of glasses in order to establish that there are "the same" number of cookies as glasses.

Before allowing everyone to "dig in," you ask him and "his guests" to watch as you move the cookies and extend their length to about double the length of the glasses.

Next ask, "Is the number of cookies the same as the number of glasses?"

Allow plenty of time for discussion and replacement of the cookies into their initial positions. Observe how he's deceived by his perceptions.

Hopefully with a variety of experiences, he will begin to volunteer increasingly more logical answers.

2. Match-ups
Materials: Pairs of shoes of different sizes and pairs of socks of comparable sizes, a runner or line down the center of the table.

Check out with your child what family members would be likely to wear each size pair of shoes and socks.

Next, ask him to grade the shoes, placing them in order, small to large.

Have him match the socks, small to large, with the corresponding pair of shoes.

Now, the challenge: Tell him to watch as you gather all the socks and put them in a pile.

Ask, "Is the number of socks the same as the number of shoes?" The answer will probably be "no."

The reason will certainly be illogical, something like, "There are lots more shoes. See how much more room they take" as he gestures the length of the line or runner.

Don't correct such a response in spite of the fact that it is based upon perception rather than reason. Simply ask him to restore the position of the socks to their shoes.

Repeated experiences again will be more convincing to him than anything you try to explain.■

CONTINUED FROM PAGE 292

Hard set: toy cars, trucks, planes, music box, marbles, blocks.

A variation of this game is to have your child sort the toys into two boxes. But this time she must not tell you how she has done it (soft ones/hard ones or red ones/non-red ones.) You must guess!

Remember—games are meant to be fun. They are usually most successful when they arise spontaneously out of an ongoing activity. So be creative in turning what might be a chore into a fun game that can help your child learn logical thinking skills.■

Long and Short

ctivities of seriation—the opportunity to explore and develop concepts of order (size, length, color hue, texture)—are great challenges for your child. Scholars say that such activities are essential for a child's integration of perceptions, language, and thought. Here are some suggested activities to learn about length.

Materials:

(1) 1" dowel rod which has been sawed into lengths ranging from 6" to 30" in 6" increments.

(2) 3/4" square sticks which have been sawed into lengths from 3" to 15" in 3" increments.

Here's what the dowels will look like:

Here's what the square sticks will look like:

Ask your child to sort the sticks from the dowels. (Don't hesitate to call them dowels—young children love new words.) Next engage her in the grading process: "Find the longest dowel; find the shortest dowel."

Now you are ready to consider comparative lengths of all of the dowels.

Start out by asking for the "longest dowel," then the "next (second) longest dowel," etc. Later you can work in reverse order: "Find the shortest dowel" and "next shortest dowel." Since this is a learning experience,

allow your child plenty of time to compare the different dowels.

If she is having too much difficulty, you can offer a prompt by placing two dowels next to one another and then asking: "Which one is longer? Which one is shorter?"

Some children confuse size and length. If asked to identify the 15" stick, such children label it the "largest" or "biggest" rather than the "longest." They may have had insufficient experience with seriating objects. Or the adults in their lives may have used imprecise language when dealing with these concepts.

Learning about length is purposeful as well as fun. As soon as your child understands the concept of relative length, elaborate upon its applications in the environment.

On a walk outdoors compare automobiles to determine which is "longer" and which is "shorter." Discuss the lengths of legs, arms, fingers. Encourage her to speculate about lengths of objects she can't see, explaining why one object is longer or shorter than another. ■

www.growingchild.com
Contributing Authors

Phil Bach, O.D., Ph.D.
Miriam Bender, Ph.D.
Joseph Braga, Ed.D.
Laurie Braga, Ph.D.
George Early, Ph.D.
Liam Grimley, Ph.D.
Robert Hannemann, M.D., F.A.A.P.
Sylvia Kottler, M.S.
Bill Peterson, Ph.D.

Growing Child, Inc.
P.O. Box 620
Lafayette, Indiana 47902
Telephone: 1-800-927-7289
©2005 Growing Child, Inc.

Next Month

- *How Young Children Think*
- *The Importance of Play*

Index

To place an order: fill out this form and send it via mail, shop on line at www.growingchild.com or call us at 800-927-7289.

Growing Child Book + E-mail Bonus

Receive Growing Child in book form, plus Growing Parent and special messages by e-mail. Each Growing Child book contains 24 monthly issues.

	Cost	Quantity	Total
Book 1 • Birth to 24 months (Plus 1 year free e-mail bonus)	$14.95	_____	$ _____
Book 2 • 25 months to 48 months (Plus 1 year free e-mail bonus)	$14.95	_____	$ _____
Book 3 • 49 months to 72 months (Plus 1 year free e-mail bonus)	$14.95	_____	$ _____

With E-mail Bonus You Receive:

- One-year free e-mail subscription to *Growing Child* for each child in your family under 6 years of age.
- *Growing Parent*, a monthly e-mail newsletter to help you better understand yourself and cope with the reality of living, sent via e-mail at the beginning of each month.
- *Monthly Activity Calendar* to enjoy with your children.
- *Grandma Says*, a series of special messages via e-mail that include parenting tips, words of encouragement or helpful comments, plus recall notices and health alert messages.

E-mail bonus may be transferred to a friend or relative.

Purchase all three books for the same family and the e-mail subscription will extend until last child is 72 months old.

Guarantee

- Book and e-mails are free of commercial bias with our no-advertisement policy.
- E-mail and postal mail addresses are used only to administer subscription accounts and are not disclosed to other individual or organizations.

Growing Up Books from Kindergarten to Grade 12

Growing Up is a series of newsletters for parents of children in Kindergarten through Grade 12, organized into five books. **Special note to teachers:** *Growing Up* newsletter may be copied and shared with your parents.

	Cost	Quantity	Total
Kindergarten	$5.95	_____	$ _____
Grades 1-3	$9.95	_____	$ _____
Grades 4-6	$9.95	_____	$ _____
Grades 7-9	$9.95	_____	$ _____
Grades 10-12	$9.95	_____	$ _____

Blocks

Every box contains 64 blocks, each 1-3/4" square. The set has 248 alphabet letters, 64 numbers (0-9) as well as 64 different pictures of birds and animals.

	Cost	Quantity	Total
Blocks	$99	_____	$ _____
Optional Name Plate	$ 5	_____	$ _____

Each line may have up to 20 letters (including spaces) and you can use up to 3 lines.

_____

_____

_____

See Blocks at www.Growingchild.com/blocks

Check Out

Shipping

Books: Add $2.50 for shipping per order regardless of the number of books ordered. USA only.
Blocks: Add $10.00 for shipping for each set of blocks ordered. USA only.
For foreign rates call 800-927-7289.

Total Cost

Total cost of books ordered.	$_____
Shipping charge for books (see above).	$_____
Total cost of blocks ordered.	$_____
Shipping charge for blocks (see above).	$_____
Total:	_____

❑ Check   ❑ Visa   ❑ MasterCard   ❑ Discover   ❑ American Express

Card Number: _____ Expiration Date: _____

Signature: _____

Name: _____ Phone: _____

Address: _____

City State Zip: _____

E-Mail: to confirm order and fulfillment of e-mail subscription. _____

You may contact us via-e-mail at service@GrowingChild.com or telephone 800-927-7289

Gift Information:

Name of person to receive gift: _____

Address of person to receive gift: _____

City, State, Zip of person to receive gift: _____

The name you wish to have on the gift card, as the giver: _____

service@GrowingChild.com
800-927-7289
PO Box 620
Lafayette IN 47902-0620